Fine WoodWorking *on* Woodworking Machines

Fine WoodWorking on Woodworking Machines

40 articles selected by the editors of *Fine Woodworking* magazine

The Taunton Press

Cover photo by John Lively

Taunton
BOOKS & VIDEOS

for fellow enthusiasts

©1985 by The Taunton Press, Inc.
All rights reserved.

First printing: 1985
Second printing: 1986
Third printing: 1989
Fourth printing: 1990
Fifth printing: 1995
International Standard Book Number: 0-918804-31-0
Library of Congress Catalog Card Number: 84-052102
Printed in the United States of America

A FINE WOODWORKING Book

FINE WOODWORKING® is a trademark of The Taunton Press, Inc.,
registered in the U.S. Patent and Trademark Office.

The Taunton Press, Inc.
63 South Main Street
Box 5506
Newtown, CT 06470-5506

Contents

Introduction

The Indian woodcarver, demonstrating his traditional craft outside the museum, fires up a chainsaw and begins to pull his ideas out of the log. The crowd is fascinated by the shapes emerging from sawdust and noise. But when the artist pauses, one onlooker scolds him: "Your grandfather never carved with a machine like that!" "No," the carver replies, "but if he'd had one he sure would have."

Most woodworkers, at some time during their shop lives, must come to terms with the machine. Some decide that true craft values reside in handwork alone. Some shift the grueling side of working with wood onto their machinery, reserving hand tools for personal expression in sensitive details. And some devise electrical ways of doing every kind of shop operation.

This book is for all those woodworkers who welcome at least some machinery in their shops. In 40 articles reprinted from the first nine years of *Fine Woodworking* magazine, authors who are also craftsmen explain which machines they use and why, and how they choose the ones to buy. They also tell how to get the most out of the machines you have, and how to keep your woodshop machinery running well and true. A companion volume, to be published later in 1985, will be about how woodworkers can build their own shop machines.

John Kelsey, editor

Mechanical Advantage

About woodworking machines, and a visit to Rockwell and Powermatic

by John Lively

"It's a shame," he said, "that they don't make machinery like they used to." But there wasn't much sorrow in his voice, for Bob Johnson is one of the few men in the country who can claim to be a Victorian millwright. He and his wife, Mary Ellen, make their living selling exotic woods and restoring vintage machinery for such clients as the Smithsonian Institution. For the last 20 years the Johnsons' special passion has been putting together their own collection of classical machines, which are housed in several timber-frame buildings on their wooded farm in Rossville, Ga. To complete the grand scheme, they are building a railroad into the neighboring woods to fetch timber to feed a steam-powered sawmill. "This is our museum," he said as he pulled open the huge door, "but we have to work in here too. Once we've restored one of these old machines, we use it as hard and as often as we would a new one."

As my eyes got used to the dim light, I made out a hulking presence just beyond the doorway, but it took me a moment to recognize the thing—a leviathan jointer. Its beds were 30 in. wide and 8 ft. long, and its cutterhead so massive that three Babbitt bearings held the shaft on its axis. Built by Oliver Machinery Co. in 1905, this monster could joint an entire tabletop or door face in a single pass, or straighten structural timbers of any size. Yet its pinstriped base and thoughtful proportions made it appear lighter and friendlier than you'd expect a ton of cast iron to look.

"Everything's a mess right now," Johnson lamented, pointing to a dismantled steam engine in the next room. "I traded a 180-year-old engine for that one, and until I get it going, I'll have to run my overhead line shafts with this awful electric motor." He threw a wall switch and the whole place came to life. It was like being inside a giant wind-up toy, with big wheels turning little ones and leather drive belts slapping from one end of the shop to the other. "Look at this," he beckoned, while prodding a wide belt from its idler onto the drive pulley of his bandsaw, made in 1886 by Connell & Dengler and standing a full 8 ft. tall. It ran with a ghostly silence, without the slightest whisper of mechanical noise or vibration—just a gentle whoosh as its wheels fanned the air.

Johnson killed the power. All the wheels coasted to a stop, while I continued to stare at this marvelous bandsaw. With its spiral-spoked wheels, its gracefully curved main frame, fluted column and contoured base, it looked more like sculpture than like a machine for cutting wood. There could be no doubt that its makers were as much concerned with the aesthetics of its form as with the smoothness of its operation.

Just behind the bandsaw squatted the ugly member of the family, an 1895 American No. 1 variety saw. It looked gawky, a grim triumph of function over form, but with a businesslike quality you had to admire, an unabashed utilitarian aspect.

Johnson spoke affectionately about the machines, explaining that 19th-century millwrights often blended practicality

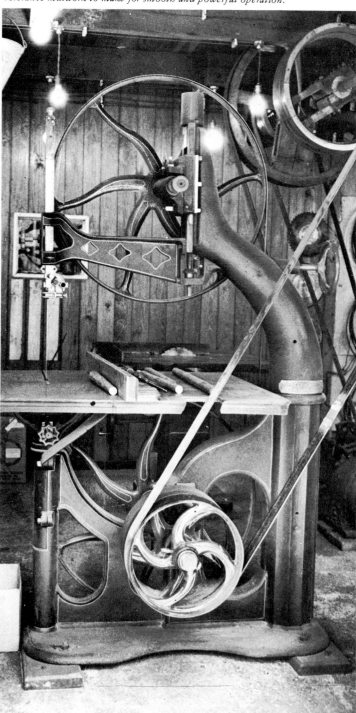

This bandsaw epitomizes 19th-century woodworking-machine design and manufacture. Made in 1886 by Connell & Dengler, its graceful form and imposing stature combine with rugged mass and close-tolerance millwork to make for smooth and powerful operation.

and fair shapes into a harmony unequaled since. Their foundrymen, he told me, were generous with cast iron, believing that a heavy machine was a good one. You won't find any fabricated steel bases on this old machinery, or any pot-metal castings or any die-stamped parts. They are all grey iron and alloy steel, with working parts precisely turned or milled and mating surfaces hand-scraped and often honed.

We walked out of the shop into the bright spring sunshine. In the yard, beneath the dogwoods and lying among the weeds, was a myriad of rusting machine parts—cogged wheels, flywheels, bushings, connecting rods and boilers, which when put back together again would become the logging train and the sawmill at the end of the line. Trying to imagine Johnson's finished fantasy, the fully operational mill and shop, the brightly painted steam engine puffing off into the North Georgia hills, pulling its train of log cars behind, I had to wonder how far we've really come from those halcyon days of big and beautiful machines. Has modern metallurgy and industrial technology made them obsolete? Has OSHA banned them from the marketplace? Or have they just become economic impossibilities, impractical in a world of mass production and costly transportation?

The truth is, such machines are obsolete. Bandsaw wheels must be enclosed, so it doesn't matter much how they look. Cast iron is expensive stuff that must be used sparingly now if a profit is to be made; cast parts are heavy, increasing the cost of transportation and handling. So today's manufacturers of trade tools use cast iron only where they must, and fabricate the remaining parts from weldments of sheet steel or die stampings. Ornament has been lost almost altogether, replaced by design notions of clean, functional shapes.

The old mechanical wonders have given way to lighter, sleeker machines, and 19th-century millwrights have been supplanted by industrial engineers and behemoth corporations, whose assembly lines turn out more machinery for more woodworkers than were ever dreamt of in the 19th century. And what every woodworker wants to know is how much quality has been sacrificed along the way. Did the good machines go out with the old ones?

Shop machinery hasn't lost its ability to do hard work. Indeed, without it most contemporary woodshops couldn't exist, and the phrase "amateur woodworker" would be a contradiction in terms. Regardless of the romantic attachment we have for our jack planes, spokeshaves and chisels, despite our skill in using these tools, the heavy gut-work in our shops gets done by the machines. Our table saws, jointers and thickness planers leave us free to hand-cut dovetails, smooth-plane tabletops and experiment with various finishes for our chests and cabinets. When we're rushed to get that job out the door, the machines do everything but prepare the surfaces for finishing, and sometimes they do even that.

Even so, woodworking machinery has frequently been an embarrassment to those who consider themselves true craftsmen. The very nature of machine production has been conceived to be at odds with the spirit of craftwork, and some heavy philosophizing has been aimed at making the craftsman rest easy with his machines. Gustav Stickley, whose writings early in this century popularized the Arts and Crafts Movement in America, argued persuasively that every woodworker should make full use of machinery, for it alone could relieve him of mindless toil, giving him the leisure to perfect his designs and to add those finer decorative touches that only the hand can create. Yet, Stickley believed that machine work should be limited to preparing materials for use—for sawing, planing, boring, mortising and sanding. He warned against using machines to achieve ornamental effects, as this made impossible the craftsman's only real means of self-expression, and rendered his works sterile and anonymous. Stickley's injunctions are still valid. The best of contemporary woodworking combines the sensitive and skilled use of hand tools with the intelligent and efficient use of machinery.

Such an ideal situation depends, of course, on machines behaving like good servants, and not like cantankerous flunkies. It's a satisfying experience to operate properly working, well-tuned equipment, while a malfunctioning machine is often worse than no machine at all. The bandsaw that vibrates to excess and takes a ragged cut, the cumbersome table-saw fence that's warped and won't align, the jointer whose tables droop and cut concave edges, and the thickness planer that is forever jamming up and sniping boards are just a few of the problems that bedevil woodworkers every day. Machine down-time is costly in terms of production lost and repair expense, and the frayed nerves of the woodworker are an inevitable part of the bad bargain.

*   *   *

The term "trade tools" refers to medium-priced woodworking machines that are commonly used by tradesmen— carpenters, cabinetmakers and patternmakers—and in school shops. They are also designed to hold up under production-line operations in furniture factories and millworks, though often you will find heavier, more expensive machines in these situations. In the broad spectrum of machinery on the market, from the hobby-craft tools for the weekend handyman to the extra heavy-duty machine tools designed for industrial applications, trade tools occupy the middle ground in quality, performance and cost. For the average woodworker, whether a professional or a serious amateur, trade tools are the best bet.

Although there are quite a few smaller manufacturers of trade tools—Vega, General, Boice-Crane, Davis & Wells and Poitras—Rockwell (now Delta) and Powermatic are the largest in North America. Since these two are the Chevrolet and Ford of the woodworking-machinery industry, we decided to visit them to get some general impressions about their manufacturing processes, and also to ask some specific questions about their machine quality and customer service. The people at Rockwell said they would arrange for me to tour one of their plants and to interview several executives. The people at Powermatic suggested that I spend five days at one of their workshops on machinery maintenance. I accepted both offers, expecting that the experiences would be entirely different. And so they were.

The majority of Rockwell's woodworking tools are made at their factory in Tupelo, Miss. This is where the venerable Unisaw is made, along with their complete line of radial saws, the 14-in. bandsaw, the several models of shapers, the 4-in., 6-in. and 8-in. jointers, the 6-in./12-in. belt/disc sander and the 24-in. scroll saw. All of their other woodworking ma

EDITOR'S NOTE: Pentair Inc., which bought Rockwell's hand power tool division (now called Porter Cable) in 1981, also purchased Rockwell's stationary power tool division in 1984, renaming it Delta Intl. (Rockwell originally bought Delta in 1945; the tools will eventually bear the Delta name again.)

chines are manufactured at their plant in Bellefontaine, Ohio.

My visit to the Tupelo factory began in Bill Ramsey's office. He's plant manager and is directly responsible to Rockwell Power Tool management. Also there were Lou Brickner, marketing manager for woodworking machines, and Bernie Cox, product manager for Rockwell's Power Tool Division. "How do you know how many machines you need to make in a given month?" I asked. Ramsey explained that this is a complex calculation; output varies and is based on marketing data compiled in the home office, taking into consideration orders from distributors, sales promotions and the availability of certain parts and raw materials. "What about the person who buys one of your Unisaws and finds it's got a bad bearing or warped extension wing?" I asked. "Can he expect to get the faults corrected or the defective parts replaced?" Ramsey replied that all new machines are guaranteed against defects and that Rockwell's service system is advanced and efficient. "All the parts in all the distribution centers throughout the country are carried on a computer file," Ramsey said. "If one distributor doesn't have a particular part, he can call the home office and learn the location of the nearest service center that has it in stock, and can order it for his customer."

I listened to this with keen interest, and then recounted how several years ago I had bought a Rockwell lathe duplicator and had discovered upon opening the box that what should have been an angle-iron tool rest was just an unformed flat bar. I had taken it back to the dealer and asked for a replacement part. The dealer told me to go to an iron yard and buy a length of the stuff because ordering parts from Rockwell was like trying to get sympathy from the IRS. He said it would take months to get the piece, if I got it at all. Ramsey gave me a hard, sober look and there was a moment of quiet. "Well," he said, "That was several years ago, and mistakes do happen, and sometimes communications with distributors are not as good as they should be." He went on to say that the Rockwell people are quite aware of the fact that product quality suffered during the 1970s, but now they've made a renewed commitment to quality control.

I told Ramsey that a number of woodworkers have written to us saying that the old Delta machines were well built and reliable but that since Rockwell has been manufacturing the Delta line, there's been a decline in quality, that some parts have become tinnier and flimsier. "There's some truth to that," he replied, "but we're now reversing that trend." He offered an example. The platen for the Delta belt/disc sander was originally a cast part. Then someone decided to cut costs by making the part from a die-stamped piece of sheet metal. But they then discovered that during prolonged use the sheet-metal platen would deform from the heat of heavy sanding. So now they've gone back to using the cast-iron platen. Lou Brickner cited another example: The Unisaw rip fence, which used to be made from stamped steel, is now a hefty, ribbed-aluminum extrusion, two extrusions actually, one nested inside the other. By loosening a couple of lock screws, the lower half of the fence can be brought into contact with the table surface, a handy feature for ripping veneers and other thin materials.

I had one more question: "Suppose a customer needs a part badly or has just bought a defective machine and wants it corrected. Suppose the distributor he bought it from won't or can't get the part or fix the machine within a reasonable time. What recourse does the customer have? Is dealing with Rock-

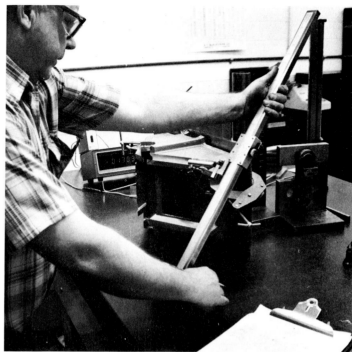

A quality-control engineer uses mechanical and electronic gauges to see whether the milled dovetailed ways in this base for a Rockwell 8-in. jointer fall within the prescribed tolerances. The engineers select bases off the line at random during the day. A test failure stops the run until the error is corrected. Rejected parts are re-machined or scrapped.

well really a bureaucratic hassle?" Ramsey smiled. "Of course not. I've got letters right here in my desk from customers I've dealt with directly. I spent several hours on the phone just the other day trying to run down a part for a fellow, only to find out that he'd been using the wrong part number all along." He said that most customer-service problems are communication problems. In the first place a customer should get good service from his distributor; but if he can't he should write or call the nearest Rockwell service branch. If that fails to produce results, he can call or write the home office (Power Tool Division, Delta International, 400 Lexington Ave., Pittsburgh, Pa. 15208) or the plant in Tupelo (PO Box 1508, Tupelo, Miss. 38801). "We're serious about customer service," he said, "and will do whatever we have to, within reason, to see that problems get ironed out. The president of the Power Tool Division sits on our service committee. That's how serious we are about it."

I spent the balance of the day touring the plant, and saw how the most important shop tools are manufactured. The plant doesn't have an in-house foundry, so cast parts are jobbed out and must be inspected on arrival. Some castings, I was told, are annealed—heated to 1400°F for 30 minutes—to relieve stress. This makes the iron easier to mill and to grind, and also makes for more stable, warp-free cast parts.

Such stability is particularly important for jointers. Their tables must be perfectly flat and parallel to one another, or they won't cut a true edge on a board. If built imprecisely, they're useless. For this reason, and because jointers are made almost wholly from grey iron castings, I was especially interested in seeing how Rockwell made theirs. The 8-in. jointer begins as several castings—a trapezoidal base, infeed and outfeed tables, a fence and a number of smaller castings that make up the fence-support assembly. Dovetailed ways are

Above, at the end of a long assembly line, these workers in Rockwell's Tupelo, Miss., plant make the final checks on 14-in. bandsaws. One adjusts the blade-guide system, while the other sets the 45° positive stop on the tilting table. From here the machines go to be packaged and to await shipping.

machined into the sloping sides of the base and into corresponding inclines on the tables. The ways allow both tables to travel up and down (chiefly to adjust the depth of cut) and still remain parallel to one another. Cutting these ways precisely is so important that the operation gets checked several times during the day by a quality-control engineer, who selects a base at random and takes it to his lab. There, he clamps the base to a surface plate, and using a vernier height gauge and other measuring devices, he finds out whether the component falls within the prescribed tolerances. If it doesn't, all the pieces in the run—since the last test—are checked. If the defective components cannot be corrected by re-milling, they're scrapped.

When the base, with the cutterhead installed, and the two tables meet at a sub-assembly station, they are wedded, the gibs installed and the tables aligned and locked into place. Now the entire machine is mounted on a jig and passed several times beneath an overhead grinding wheel, which surfaces both tables at once, ensuring parallel alignment end to end. This is a sensitive operation, and the person doing it must be careful, as excessive head pressure on the grinding wheel can burn and discolor the iron or produce an uneven surface. Such errors can be eliminated by further grinding, but too much of this will yield thin table surfaces, and the jointer beds will end up as expensive pieces of scrap iron.

All the machines I saw being built were fairly old designs; most of them haven't been altered in 30 years. I asked Brickner if Rockwell was planning new machines to compete with trade tools made by such overseas companies as Makita and Injecta/Inca. He answered that in 1981 Rockwell would introduce a medium-priced thickness planer, made in Brazil, to be sold under the name Rockwell/Invicta. (This line will now carry the name Delta.) Then I asked whether Rockwell plans to

bring out anything else in the way of new machinery. His answer was a cagey "yes and no." Yes, they do have several things in the development stage presently; no, they don't intend to redesign any of their basic Delta machines. He said there wasn't any point in tampering with successful products that had been industry standards for so many years.

Before I left, I made a point of asking Brickner what he though about Powermatic machinery. "They make good stuff," he admitted without hesitation. Then he added, "It's good to have good competitors."

* * *

Along with 22 others, mostly salesmen who'd been sent to Powermatic's plant in McMinnville, Tenn., by their bosses to learn about operating and maintaining woodworking machinery, I sat in a large classroom sipping coffee and waiting for the instructor to arrive. About 14 times each year, Powermatic holds these five-day workshops. The fall and winter sessions are attended by dealer salesmen and servicemen, while the six summer sessions are conducted for university industrial-arts students and teachers, who usually earn college credit for their participation.

Around 8:30 A.M. Jim Ramsey, Powermatic's product manager (no relation to Rockwell's Ramsey), walked into the room. After giving a brief history of the company, he got to the real reason we were listening. Most service problems, he told us, could be avoided if the machine operator understood his equipment thoroughly, and knew how to adjust it and how to keep it in tune. "I can't be emphatic enough," he said, clutching the podium. "You'd be surprised at how many people start turning knobs and screws without having the slightest idea what they're doing."

Before beginning the lesson on jointers, Ramsey talked at some length about the advantages of having an in-house pattern shop and foundry. Powermatic is licensed, he said, to use the Meehanite process, a patented technology for making a high-grade, close-grained grey iron that is superior for use in machinery castings. The process ensures that the molecular constitution of the cast iron is consistent from day to day and from year to year, a condition that makes milling and grinding more efficient and that contributes to product uniformity. "We can control," Ramsey added, "the aging time for our castings." He explained that the traditional method of letting cast parts sit for months uncovered in the open air is still the best means of relieving internal stresses created by the casting process. Aging gives these stresses time to resolve themselves before the part is milled and ground. "By having our own foundry," he said, "we don't have to machine green castings, and consequently we wind up with fewer warped saw tables and jointer fences."

But regardless of aging and other means of relieving stress, he continued, some castings do warp after they leave the plant. Jointer fences, he said, are the worst offenders. He walked to the rear of the classroom, where all the machines were set up for demonstration, and pointed to the fence on the 6-in. jointer. "Now, no one will want to believe this, and I've had a hard time convincing a lot of smart people, but cast iron *will* bend; you can straighten a warped fence. (See "On jointer maintenance," page 6, to learn how.)

Over lunch I got a chance to ask Ramsey about Powermatic's customer service. The upshot of it all was that their machinery should hold up for decades of hard use, given the usual amount of maintenance and care; bearings might need eventual replacement, but the basic cast parts should last indefinitely. They are guaranteed to be free of defects, or they'll be replaced. "We train our distributors to be able to tell whether a machine is really defective or whether it only needs adjustment or re-alignment; these guys will go into someone's shop, inspect the tool and try to fix it there." It's a rare thing, he said, when a machine has to be returned to the factory for repair or regrinding. "Since we've been conducting these workshops," he concluded, "we've minimized customer service problems." However, a customer who can't get satisfaction from his local dealer should write Customer Service, Powermatic Houdaille, McMinnville, Tenn. 37110.

The afternoon session on motors and electrical controls was conducted by Roy Baker. Though his chief function is customer service, he's intimately acquainted with the machines themselves, and serves along with Jim Ramsey as the other instructor in the maintenance workshops. After class he took me on a two-hour tour of the plant. Baker and I walked up and down the labyrinthine aisles, and I was a little surprised at how similar the whole operation was to Rockwell's, with the exception that Powermatic doesn't make a line of radial-arm saws, whose manufacture takes up considerable space in Rockwell's Tupelo plant. At one station along the way I reached down into a parts box and picked up a handwheel for a Model 66 table saw. "This is a pretty nice casting," I said, "but why go to all the trouble to cast such a good handwheel and then make the little center locking knob out of a plastic that can crack when the setscrews are tightened?" I once owned a Model 66 table saw and had cracked both its locking knobs while trying to tighten their setscrews. "Geez," Baker answered, "we've got to save money somewhere." (Two months later, I was told in a phone conversation with Jim

On jointer maintenance

"The most common complaint about jointers," says Jim Ramsey, chief instructor at Powermatic's machinery workshops, "is that the tables droop, or that jointed edges aren't true." To correct these problems several checks are required. First see how the operator is jointing his stock. If he concentrates his feed pressure on the infeed table, he'll probably wind up with a concave edge (a spring joint). Proper jointing calls for applying feed pressure over the infeed table only long enough to establish a straight edge about 18 in. long at the front of the board; then the feed pressure should be shifted to the outfeed table and be concentrated over the stock about 6 in. beyond the cutterhead.

Drooping tables can result from insufficient pressure on the gibs, the flat, steel bars that fit in the dovetailed ways between the bearing surfaces of the tables and the base. Their job is to compensate for wear. Ramsey demonstrated by loosening all the gib screws on the in-

feed table of the jointer in the classroom. Then he laid a straightedge across both tables, and as he had predicted, the infeed table was close to $\frac{1}{16}$ in. lower on its outboard end than at the cutterhead. As he tightened the gib screws, the table was gradually raised and finally made uniform contact with the straightedge along its full length. The gib screws must be tight enough to hold the tables parallel, but no tighter.

Another thing to check for is the proper alignment of the countersinks in the gibs with the tapped holes along the ways in the base (see drawing, lower left). The cone-head screws must fit into these countersinks or the beds can't be properly snugged up in their ways and the tables will sag. If a gib has to be re-aligned, loosen all the screws, position the gib (you'll need a flashlight to peer into the hole), and then lock the handle down. Next tighten the gib screws firmly and back off each a quarter turn. Finally tighten the jam nuts. Now the two tables should be perfectly parallel.

Ramsey maintains that the way you change and set the knives is critical to a jointer's performance. Never remove all the knives at once and then re-install them or replace them with a new set. Rather, remove a single knife and then replace it with a fresh one (or with the same one resharpened) and then set it. Taking out the knives all at once and replacing them one at a time can subject the cutterhead to harmful stresses and cause it to distort. If you must replace all the knives at one time, you should gradually torque the chipbreaker bolts down, going from one knife to the next, keeping the pressure equal all around the cutterhead. When tightening chip-

breaker bolts, begin in the middle and work out to the ends. Otherwise the knife can creep up or down as you apply more pressure, and you'll have an awful time trying to keep the knife at its proper height during installation.

If a jointer fence is twisted or warped or not perpendicular to the surface of the tables, your jointed edge will not be a consistent 90° to the face of the board, and you'll find you're gluing up big barrels instead of tabletops. So check the right-angularity of the fence often, and should you discover that the fence is perpendicular to the table at one point and not at another, you probably have a twisted fence. If you hold a straightedge lengthwise along the fence and detect any deviation, your fence is bowed. Ramsey says you can correct both of these problems.

If the fence is bowed, detach it from the fence-support assembly, and set it (crown up) astride two blocks on the floor. Slowly apply weight to it, usually by standing on it in the middle. At a critical point, you will feel the metal give slightly, which signals that it has returned to its original shape. It will not bend beyond this point, but will break if further pressure is applied. And, Ramsey says, it will not warp a second time, as all the wicked stresses have been exorcised by bending it again. If the fence is twisted, clamp one end in a woodworking vise and tighten a pipe clamp or bar clamp on the other end. Using the leverage from the bar, slowly apply gradually increasing pressure in the required direction. When you feel the metal give, stop. Don't try to muscle out the warp with a quick jerk, or you will break the fence.　　—J.L.

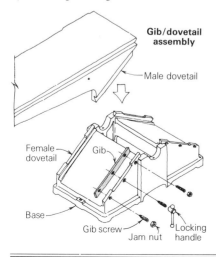

Gib/dovetail assembly

Male dovetail

Female dovetail

Gib

Base

Gib screw

Jam nut

Locking handle

To reduce the chance of warping and to help relieve internal stresses, castings are seasoned. These jointer tables (above) in Powermatic's "boneyard" will lie rusting in the open air from three to six months. At left, Jim Ramsey, Powermatic's product manager and instructor for the company's oft-held maintenance workshops, tells how jointer tables will droop if the gib screws aren't properly snugged up. Loose gib screws, along with gunk and build-up along the ways are, according to Ramsey, the chief causes of sagging jointer tables.

Ramsey that Powermatic's engineers had redesigned this part. The new knobs will be cast from solid, not ribbed, plastic and will have threaded brass inserts to hold the setscrews. He assured me that the prototypes have been tested and that they will not crack.)

Then Baker took me outside for a walk through the "boneyard," the several fenced-in acres of cast-iron parts—everything from planer bases and bandsaw main frames to tablesaw fences and trunnion boxes. All the castings were stacked in neat piles, some small, others mountainous. Some parts were painted green, some yellow, some blue. "Why all the colors?" I asked. He explained that each month of the year was assigned a color, that when castings came from the foundry to age in the boneyard they were painted so that their age would be apparent at a glance. "This keeps us from bringing a casting into the plant and milling it before it's had time to age for at least three months," he said.

I had been promised a tour of the foundry, so late in the afternoon on my last day there, Baker and I drove the short distance to the place. On the way I asked him what he thought about Rockwell machinery. "I used to work for Rockwell," he replied with a little grin, "and I know their line pretty well, and really can't knock it. But I think Powermatic has the best 14-in. bandsaw in the business."

At the foundry, the patternmaker and his apprentices had locked up and gone home for the day, so I didn't get a chance to talk with them or look around the patternshop. But Baker explained that all of Powermatic's machine parts begin as wooden patterns which are sent out to have aluminum working patterns made from them. The original wooden patterns

are returned and stay in the patternshop. We walked about, winding past long banks of patterns hanging from the wall, past molding and coring operations, past hot, unflasked molds, with their castings cooling inside. On we went by the quaking conveyor that shakes the sand off cold castings, until at last we arrived at the heart of the place—the twin furnaces. I mounted the steel gangway to the little booth where the operator was getting ready to charge the furnace. He was maneuvering an overhead electromagnet that clutched a load of scrap iron, including some rejected machine parts, and he stopped it just above the far furnace, whose thick, iron lid slid slowly back. Red and white light shot from the opening with palpable force. The operator lowered the magnet into the fiery pot and released its load. There was a burst of light, with sparklers flying high into the air and flames leaping up as though to consume the magnet. This is how all machines die and are born again, in the white-hot soup that turns into cold, grey iron.

Foundry practices have come a long way from the time when Bob Johnson's huge machines were made, when strength depended largely on the sectional thickness of a casting and when getting a good batch of molten iron was literally pot luck. With the introduction of the Meehanite technology in the 1950s (and subsequent, more advanced procedures), the entire casting process, from mixing the sand to pouring the metal, came under scientific control. The improved quality of the cast iron meant that sheer mass was no longer needed to achieve strength, and it also meant that the grain structure of the metal could be manipulated to suit the kind of part being cast. Scientific control has almost eliminated hard spots in cast metal, irregularities that make a casting brittle and that can dull and sometimes break metalworking bits and cutters. So now the machining of cast-iron parts can flow at a production pace and the quality of the finished tools can remain fairly consistent.

Nineteenth-century machines were big because they had to be, and ornament could be incorporated into their structure because sectional thicknesses were so great and weight so negligible a consideration that a given part could take almost any shape the millwright fancied, so long as it did its job. The pretty S-curved spokes of Johnson's giant bandsaw wheels were not engineered for getting maximum strength from minimum metal. Rather, they were designed for appearance and to cope with the problem of shrinkage as the castings cooled. But these days the need for lighter, more portable trade tools, along with high-speed spindle requirements, makes stress engineering preeminent. Thus woodworking machines and their functional parts have to look like what they have to do. So what we have lost in mass and stature, we have gained in better machine performance and improved metal quality. Too bad we can't have both. □

On choosing machinery

If someone were to ask me whether I'd buy a Rockwell or Powermatic spindle shaper or whether I'd choose a Powermatic Model 66 10-in. table saw over a Rockwell Unisaw, I couldn't give a simple answer. But here are some general observations. Even though Rockwell jobs-out its castings, they appear a little cleaner and crisper inside and out than Powermatic's castings; on the other hand, Powermatic's castings are a little heavier and thicker in section than Rockwell's; and on the average, a Powermatic machine weighs a little more than the equivalent Rockwell model. The Powermatic 8-in. jointer, for example, is about 50 lb. heavier than the Rockwell 8-in. jointer. As far as I could tell, both manufacturers paid equally close attention to machine-finish tolerances, spindle run-out tolerances and general machine performance. Equally close in every case but one: Rockwell's tolerance for its 8-in. jointer is 0.01 in. end to end; Powermatic's tolerance for its 8-in. jointer is 0.0015 in. end to end—a significant difference. Powermatic's ground table surfaces look a little nicer than Rockwell's, but this has no effect on stock feeding or mechanical performance.

Rudolf Bass Co., in New York, sells more woodworking machines than any other distributor in the country. They handle and service both Powermatic and Rockwell lines. I phoned Richard Bass and asked him which of the two firms made the better machine, and he answered that to choose intelligently one had to check out the machines model for model, compare the features where they are different, and decide on that basis. And, he said, there's a good deal of personal preference involved. For some applications a Powermatic machine would be the right choice, for others a Rockwell model would get the job done better. "It's just not something you can generalize about," Bass said. He then added that to make a good choice one should also take into account the kind of service the dealer can provide for each. "But when you get right down to it," Bass quipped, "Powermatic's machines are green, Rockwell's are grey."

Most distributors I spoke with agree that woodworkers would have less trouble with their machines if they would read their owner's manuals, set the machines up properly and adjust them correctly to begin with. Another mistake a lot of woodworkers make is trying to save a few bucks by skimping on the motor and electrical controls. Too often a person will spend $1,400 on a good table saw and then get the cheapest motor he can and a simple manual switch with no overload protection. A 10-in. table saw should have at least a 3-HP motor; a 5-HP one would be even better. Motors that are underpowered for the work they do can overheat, and they consume more current as well. Having more HP than you need is best, because power consumption is reduced, along with the danger of burning out the motor or causing an electrical fire.

Several years back, when copper got scarce because of political goings-on in Chile and other places, electric-motor manufacturers introduced the T-frame motor, which is now generally sold in place of the old U-frame motors. T-frame motors have formed-steel bodies and steel end bells, whereas the U-frame motors have cast-iron bodies and bells. T-frame motors are smaller and have fewer field windings, and use 30% to 50% less copper than U-frame motors rated at the same HP. This means that T-frame motors can burn out faster and will produce less starting torque than the equivalent U-frame motors. You can still buy U-frame motors, but they're very expensive. This is another good reason for getting a motor whose HP rating is as close as you can possibly afford to the highest rated for the particular machine.

Having said all this about buying new equipment, I'd prefer to own old machines, and if I were getting ready to outfit another shop, I'd beat the bushes to see what bargains I could scare up. Some woodworkers I know seem favored by good fortune, as they always manage to stumble on good pieces of used machinery without really looking for them. The rest of us have to haunt the auctions and pester the used-machinery dealers until at last we find what we're looking for in some dark corner of a warehouse or barn. Though the demand for used equipment is increasing as more woodworkers discover its worth, there are still plenty of old machines sitting around gathering dust all over the country. The trick is to find them, and to be able to tell how much work is needed to restore them to operating condition.

The best table saw I ever owned was a 20-year-old Davis & Wells. Its arbor-raising mechanism was a rack-and-scroll gear, and the arbor assembly rode in gibbed dovetailed ways. When I gave the dealer my $450, the inside of the saw was filled with gobs of pine resin and several thick layers of compacted sawdust. He told me it had been worked hard for years in a factory that made prefabricated buildings and that for the price he couldn't guarantee anything. I loaded the monster in my pickup, took it home and then took it completely apart, cleaned off all the hardened gook, honed and polished the ways and put it back together again. I was surprised at how smoothly the arbor tilted, how easily I could crank it up and down, how accurately it did its work. Davis & Wells (now owned by Rankin Div., PAL Industries, 11090 S. Alameda St., Los Angeles, Calif. 90262) still makes this saw, but a new one will cost you thousands, even without the motor and electrical controls. —J.L.

Used Machinery
Where to start looking

by David Landen

Hand and foot power circular saw,
Carpentry and Building, *1889.*

For a woodworker setting up shop, used machinery is often the only choice. If one knows how to find and assess it, one can buy used machinery for half the price of new, and for considerably less if one is willing to undertake serious repair work. On the other hand, industrial machines usually require three-phase electric power. They take time to find and more time and money to fix, and they eat floor space in the shop. And it is easy to make serious mistakes.

Without three-phase power, one is limited to small machines with small motors in the 2 to 3-hp range, and the price of used single-phase equipment is almost as high as new because so many hobbyists are competing for it. Rewiring for three-phase power is expensive or impossible, unless the building is in an industrial area. Another solution is to purchase a device that converts single-phase current to three-phase. The cheapest phase converters ($100 to $150) will start and run one large machine at about 80% efficiency; more expensive rotary models (about $500) can handle several machines at once at close to full efficiency (all 1978 prices).

To illustrate the possibilities, a man I know in North Carolina found a ripsaw, a planer and a variety saw abandoned in a pasture. He got them running and used them for several years to produce furniture, before selling them for more than the reconditioning had cost him. On the other hand, I once bought a used 36-in. band saw. It is an impressive machine, 8 ft. tall with a huge milled table, 14-in. depth of cut, 32-in. throat, and a 5-hp motor. Moving it required a forklift, a front-end loader and a flatbed trailer. I replaced the bearings and turned a new drive shaft to get it going, and now I use it perhaps four times a year to rip a badly cupped board. Sometimes it cuts firewood. The rest of the time it sits covered with dust, crowding my shop. I'd sell it or even give it away, but I would have to tear out a wall to move it.

Some sources for used machinery:

Want ads. The daily newspaper is a good place to start looking, but frustrating since woodworking equipment is often buried in long lists of other items, or else is mislabeled and inaccurately described. Sometimes more things are for sale than are listed. Time-consuming, but can be rewarding.

Auctions. Trade journals, such as *Furniture Design and Manufacturing* (220 S. Riverside Plaza, Chicago, Ill. 60606) and *National Hardwood Magazine* (1235 Sycamore View, Memphis, Tenn. 38134), are the best sources for information on auctions of woodworking machinery. Internal Revenue Service auctions are publicized on courthouse bulletin boards and by notes nailed to the door at the site. Most auctioneers will send periodic notices of sale if asked by letter.

Obviously, auctions of the equipment of large cabinet shops, mill shops, furniture factories and lumberyards will be worthwhile. But any large industrial auction, farm sale or estate sale is a good bet. In fact, the more remote from woodworking the business, the cheaper the machinery is likely to be, because other buyers come for the primary offerings.

Weekend auctions and flea markets generally don't have much woodworking equipment, and they are attended by amateurs who will bid close to the new price. Midweek auctions of industrial machinery are attended by professional buyers purchasing for factories or resale. Unfortunately, there is no guarantee that auctioned machinery will be anything but difficult to move back to the shop. One must locate all the fences, attachments, cutters, pulleys, sharpeners and guards, and make sure they are included in the sale.

Government surplus. Federal, state and local governments all dispose of used equipment. Some agencies publish bid lists, some sell by lots, some through surplus agencies. For federal surplus, contact the General Services Administration in Washington, D.C., or write your congressman. Most items are sold in large lots via incredibly intricate procedures, but the equipment often is nearly new.

The state-level arrangement is everywhere different, and can be tracked down by telephone to the state capitol; one might also ask highway maintenance men, junkyard owners and used equipment dealers about how the stuff comes to the market. In many states it is possible to visit the surplus depots, inspect the machines and make bids.

The best local source is the school system, which disposes of used machinery through state or county agencies. School vocational shops often replace everything at regular intervals, for accounting reasons or to meet new safety regulations, and their machines can be well worth hunting up.

Industrial equipment dealers. There are companies everywhere that deal in new and used industrial woodworking equipment. Most of it is simply too large for cabinetmakers: gang ripsaws, multiple-head planers, plywood peelers. But these firms usually have such useful items as 16-in. jointers, 24- and 30-in. thickness planers, stroke sanders, band saws and table saws. Prices of course depend on condition, but smaller industrial machines are usually competitive with used cabinet-shop equipment. And they are heavy and durable.

A helpful trade journal is the *Classified Exchange* (1235 Sycamore View, Memphis, Tenn. 38134). More than 100 dealers from 27 states advertised in one recent issue (1978); their ads give a good idea of available items and going prices.

Dealers are generally straightforward about the condition of their machines and usually will offer a warranty if they have rebuilt a machine. Most of the other sources discussed here sell the stuff as is, and let the buyer beware. In general, if the tables and other milled surfaces are true, and castings that house the bearings are sound, one can replace most other parts at reasonable cost, providing the manufacturer is still in business. If not, then having parts made is very expensive. □

David Landen, of Chapel Hill, N.C., has equipped his cabinet shop with used machinery.

Made in Taiwan

Copycat tools give U.S. makers a run for their money

by Paul Bertorelli

Browsing through a gift shop last summer, I came across a shelfful of what must be the classic American roadside souvenir: cheap cedar knickknacks stenciled with an epigraph or the name of a tourist attraction. When I picked one up—a little box whose crudely slotted top suggested a piggy bank—I couldn't help but wonder who makes these things. And at less than $2 apiece, how can the makers survive after the store takes its cut? Stamped on the box's bottom was the not-too-surprising answer: "Made in Taiwan."

Even if the box had been made in the United States, chances are the cedar could have been planed in a Taiwanese planer, sawn on a Taiwanese tablesaw and maybe even glued up with Taiwanese clamps. Though the Taiwanese have earned a reputation as maker of the world's throwaway goods—everything from cut-rate clothes and shoes to cheap radios and watches—they have graduated to more sophisticated and expensive products, including woodworking machine tools, a market once dominated by U.S. companies.

For the past ten years or so, Taiwan has been exporting to the United States a slowly expanding line of the most popular stationary woodworking tools: tablesaws, jointers, planers, bandsaws, lathes and drill presses. Some of these are heavy-duty tools of Taiwanese or European design, but many more are out-and-out copies of familiar trade-tool machines made for years by companies such as Rockwell and Powermatic. Even the ingenious Shopsmith has been cloned. Some copiers duplicate the original machines bolt-by-bolt, even casting in Rockwell's foundry numbers and tossing in a plagiarized owners' manual.

Early knockoffs were so inept that few Americans were willing to gamble, despite absurdly low prices that were commonly as little as one-fifth the cost of the real thing. During the past couple of years, though, the Taiwanese have noticeably improved quality, attracting more customers and a network of dealers willing to offer the service and warranties that the early copies lacked. I couldn't dig up reliable sales figures, but Rockwell seems to have been hit the hardest by the Taiwanese invasion, particularly in the trade-tool market, which is the bread and butter of its power tool division (recently sold and renamed Delta). Determined to win back lost sales, Rockwell has lowered prices through factory rebates, and in the fall of 1983 it asked the U.S. International Trade Commission to bar importation of the most slavish copies.

Taiwan-made tools are sold in the United States through direct importers—companies who buy from Taiwanese factories and then resell to individuals, or to dealers who want to broaden their line of U.S., Japanese or European tools with cheaper alternatives. Some importers, such as Jet Equipment

Crated Taiwan tablesaw.

and Tool of Tacoma, Wash., are big corporations that bring in woodworking equipment with the other goods they sell. Others, such as Conover Woodcraft Specialties and Wilke Machinery, are smaller firms that specialize in foreign-made woodworking tools.

Ernie Conover got into importing in the late 1970s, when he needed metalworking machine tools to produce a wooden threadbox he planned to market. Like most of us, Conover didn't have the money for American-made tools, so he bought what he could afford: a Taiwanese vertical milling machine. The mill worked well enough to convince him that Taiwanese tools, if chosen carefully, were a bargain, so he began importing woodworking equipment to augment his growing tool business.

Conover's catalog shows ten Taiwanese machines, including a couple of 10-in. tablesaws cloned from Rockwell's popular Unisaw and Contractors' saw, and a Rockwell 6-in. jointer look-alike. I'd seen enough cheap Taiwanese merchandise to expect the worst, but I have to admit that the jointer I inspected at Conover's Parkman, Ohio, store was impressive. The table and fence castings were quite clean, the machining was crisp, and the entire machine had an even, gleaming coat of gray paint. At $495, Conover's jointer sells for less than half Rockwell's $1200 asking price.

So, for a $700 saving, how much quality do you lose? Conover believes that the only sure way to tell is to use the machine over a period of time. Even then, he cautions, quality is liable to vary from machine to machine. The other tool sellers I talked to seem to agree. Machines I saw at Conover's and at other dealers generally looked good, with big, beefy castings and smooth, polished machined surfaces. Some fall down under closer scrutiny. The ribbed undersides of a Taiwan-made machine's cast parts, for example, are often rough and malformed. On one tablesaw I inspected, the factory hadn't cleaned the underside of the table but had merely painted over the mess—sand, casting dross and all. Rough castings don't necessarily degrade performance, but details such as access plates, handwheels, pulleys and threaded parts are often similarly dispatched without clean-up or deburring, so some clearly fit and work better than others.

All this seems to suggest that the Taiwanese are generally very good at what the United States used to excel at—basic smokestack work such as founding and smelting, industries that don't require engineering finesse and innovation. They're less adept at the finer points of mass production—the precisely organized assembly steps, jigged setups and automatic adherence to tolerances that add up to airtight quality control. The poor record of Taiwanese electric motors and controls illustrates this point: beefs about motors and electrics lead the

Though generally improving, copycat quality is hit-or-miss, especially in detailing. The photo above shows painted-over sand and dross in the fillets of the Taiwanese planer's table casting. The photo below shows the same detail on the Rockwell original.

If a U.S. company scores big with a hot-selling machine, the Taiwanese are likely to be right behind with a copy. At right above is a Taiwan knockoff of Rockwell's popular Invicta planer, at left, which is itself made in Brazil. The copy is atypically modified: it's 2 in. wider and the depth-adjusting crank has been replaced by a handwheel. (The Rockwell/Invicta name is soon to be changed to Delta.)

customer-complaint list, and none of the importers I talked to would guarantee a Taiwanese motor for more than ninety days. From the outside, the motors look great, often sporting heavy cast housings whose cooling fins make them look like the American-made motors of forty years ago. In use, I'm told, the motors tend to overheat or run erratically, or occasionally burn out after a few hours. They're not always repairable, either. "We just chuck 'em out," says Ted Grieco of Rudolph Bass, Inc., a big machinery house in New Jersey that sells some Taiwanese equipment. "If we get a bad motor, we just eat it. In the import business, there's no returning a motor to the factory for a credit."

I got a look at the guts of a Taiwan-made motor when I visited Rockwell's Pittsburgh headquarters, where the company maintains its own museum of copies in a room adjacent to the product-testing lab. Rockwell technician Fred Weimer ushered me through the collection of clones, which includes a really awful Unisaw copy with a tabletop that looks more carved than cast. Weimer, who's been poking and probing these machines for a couple of years, showed me the wreckage of a motor he had pulled from an 8-in. motorized tablesaw copy. In the Rockwell version, a router-type motor connected through a gearbox drives the sawblade. The counterfeit apes the motor and gear drive faithfully enough, but instead of mounting the shaft in ball bearings, as Rockwell did, the copiers substituted bronze bushings. Spinning at 20,000 RPM, the bushed shaft had so much end play that its cooling fan cut into the motor winding and stopped it dead after four hours of use.

Repairing the other parts of any Taiwan-made machine

may or may not lead to as much grief, depending on which factory built it and which importer brought it in. Taiwanese woodworking tools spew from a group of factories clustered around the industrial city of Tai-chung. Importers say that these factories—which range from garage-sized machine shops to a few modern factories outfitted with state-of-the-art tooling—compete viciously for a share of the North American market. Since they all build identical machines, copycat companies beat out their competition by selling at the lowest price, not by offering better quality. "I can buy a six-inch Rockwell-type jointer from maybe six shops," importer David Wilke of York, Pa., told me. "The cheapest one might be a hundred dollars out the factory door; the best one will be twice that much. But I'll tell you, I wouldn't want that hundred-dollar machine in my shop."

Taiwan's cottage-industry manufacturing approach plays havoc with quality control and parts interchangeability. One foundry might make up accurate patterns to cast an American machine's parts, but another will use actual parts from the original as patterns, ignoring the fact that cast iron shrinks when it cools, thus producing parts smaller than the originals. The assembly shop is left to cope, machining parts one at a time on outdated, run-down machine tools without any set-up jigs to ensure interchangeability.

"On one of my first trips to Taiwan," says Conover, "I went through a shop where they had a little kid making wrenches for the cutterhead bolts in planers. He'd chalk the outline of each wrench onto a piece of steel plate as big as this room, then he'd burn each one out with a torch. When you've got lots of cheap labor and no tools and dies, that's the way you do it. Here, we'd just stamp them out on a hundred-ton press." Low-skill, labor-intensive manufacture doesn't necessarily produce inferior goods, but some lemons are inevitable. "You've really got to be careful of what you buy from Taiwan, and you have to sit on the quality control," says Wilke, who, like Conover, has been importing for about seven years. Wilke has his Taiwanese suppliers bolt rather than nail crates so that he can unpack machines for testing and repair before they're shipped to the customer.

Some Taiwanese factories are capable of excellent work. Besides the look-alike tools, both Conover and Wilke import a line of more expensive machines that the Taiwanese seem consistently good at making: big, heavy industrial tools that are a notch above the trade-tool category but still priced at a fraction of what you'd pay for the equivalent U.S. machines. These aren't copies but generic heavyweights—mostly jointers and planers—of some indeterminate design origin, probably dating to the 1930s.

In addition to generally nicer detailing and finishes, these machines have design features found only on the most expensive industrial equipment. This sophistication suggests that they come from factories more competent than those that do copies, factories that are also clever enough to improve and innovate at the behest of savvy importers. A 12-in. jointer that Conover and Wilke buy from the same Taiwanese supplier has a beautifully made, crank-adjusted fence and fluted table castings that reduce cutterhead noise. One of the nicest Taiwanese machines I saw was a 13-in. planer that Wilke sells under his own Bridgewood label. For $1995, this machine has a cast-iron stand, segmented cast-iron chippers, a segmented feed roller, variable feed speed, and, best of all, a little lever for adjusting the bed rollers, sparing you the hassle of crawling under the machine, wrenches in hand. Compared to the $2500 Powermatic 12-incher (with none of the same goodies) sitting next to it on Wilke's showroom floor, the

Bridgewood looked like a decent buy. Wilke, by the way, says he has been satisfied with Taiwanese motors. Conover, on the other hand, bolts American motors onto his heavier machines.

The fact that some importers have overcome the stigma of cheapness once attached to Taiwanese goods suggests that their market toehold is permanent. Everyone I talked to, including Rockwell executives, seemed to agree that except for occasional lapses, the quality of Taiwanese machines is improving. Rockwell obviously plans to put up a stiff fight. In gathering evidence for its trade-commission maneuvering, the company has been running magazine ads asking purchasers of Taiwan-made machines to report misrepresentations involving look-alikes. This, in fact, is the heart of Rockwell's argument before the trade commission. Most of its patents on copied equipment have long since expired, so Rockwell, wishing to hamstring the Taiwanese in any way it can, is pleading unfair competition. Its main gripe is that copies wear the Rockwell "trade dress," that is, they are not just functional copies, but are gussied up and sold to look like the real thing, thus hurting Rockwell's sales and reputation.

Rockwell has other options. "We could get into bed with a Taiwanese company and have our machines made under license," says Lou Brickner, head of new-product development for Rockwell. Other U.S. firms troubled by counterfeiters have done just that. "It wouldn't take the Taiwanese much to improve their quality to our standards," Brickner says. "They're almost there now. Then again, that would put six hundred people out of work in Tupelo [Rockwell's largest tool plant]...we don't see that as a solution."

It's hard to say how effective Rockwell's tactics will be, but I think we'll be seeing fewer dead-ringers. By midwinter, two of the twenty-two companies named in Rockwell's trade-commission suit (some U.S., some Taiwanese) had agreed to a confidential informal settlement, which probably means that they will stop selling copies altogether, or will change them to look appropriately non-Rockwellish. This outcome is prob-

Some knockoffs are faithful to the original, some aren't. The Taiwanese factory that built this motor substituted bronze bushings for the bearings used in the original. The sloppy fit allowed the motor's fan to slice apart the windings.

ably in everyone's interest. After researching this article and inspecting plenty of credible Taiwan-made equipment, I can't escape the feeling that there is just something sleazy, if not downright wrong, about copying if it extends to matching the color of a machine's paint and duplicating the typeface on the instruction plates. Some copycats push the ruse even further by tacking on U.S.-sounding brand names such as "American" and "Chicago."

When confronted with this moral unease over copying, most importers just shrug and say competition is competition.

Evidently their customers agree—we've yet to get a letter from a reader complaining of buying a Taiwanese copy that was palmed off as the genuine article. Finally, I suppose, it shakes down to money. If buying a copy meant the difference between woodworking and not woodworking, it would be hard to pass up the prices on some of this equipment. I guess I'd strip the "Buy American" bumper sticker off my Japanese pickup truck and take my chances. □

Paul Bertorelli is editor of Fine Woodworking *magazine.*

Tips on buying Taiwanese machines

Compared to the best U.S., Japanese and European equipment, the rough-and-tumble castings and crude detailing on some made-in-Taiwan tools seem undeniably second-rate. Look around carefully, though, and you'll find plenty of bargains, copycat or not. I'm no machine expert, but when I asked tool dealers how they'd go about buying Taiwanese tools, I got enough useful advice to limit my chances of getting stuck with a junker.

First of all, don't buy on price alone. A 6-in. Taiwanese jointer, for example, might sell for $275 through a discount importer, while the identical tool goes for $450 elsewhere. For the extra money, the higher-priced dealer will usually uncrate and test a machine, repairing any damage or defects before shipping it on to the customer. Discounters are less likely to offer such services. They trim their overhead by shipping direct, so if a defective or incomplete machine is sent out from Taiwan, you'll be the first to find out about it. And you may have to wait quite a while for repairs or parts.

Buying a bum machine from a reputable company shouldn't be a problem, since most dealers will take it back or repair it to your satisfaction. But before you buy, get straight on the seller's warranty policy and, if possible, get it in writing. Like quality, warranties on Taiwan-made machines are all over the map: some sellers guarantee the machine and its parts for a year but the motor for only 90 days; others offer only 90 days on both machine and motor. Also find out who pays the freight if you have to send a machine back for warranty work, or if parts must be shipped to you.

If you live near a dealer, go and look at the equipment you plan to buy. Have it uncrated and inspect it for broken, damaged or missing parts. Examine machined surfaces for rust—seawater sometimes leaks into shipped-on-deck marine containers. If you're buying sight unseen via mail order, you can't inspect before you buy, so go over your ma-

chine as soon as it arrives, and if anything is amiss, file a claim right away with the dealer or shipper. Here are some things to look for:

Check a tablesaw by sighting the table casting with a straightedge. You shouldn't find any appreciable hollows or lumps in either the main table or its wings. Test the miter gauge for reasonably smooth travel in its slots, and see if the rip fence locks tightly and parallel to the miter-gauge slots. If it won't lock correctly, be sure it has an adjustment mechanism—some copycats omit or bungle this feature. With a blade on, crank the depth of cut to both limits of travel and angle the arbor to its 45° limit, and see if the blade spins freely without banging into the saw's internal parts. Taiwanese tablesaws have been built with arbors too short to accept a dado blade. For a full ¾-in. dado set, the arbor has to be at least 1¼ in. long.

In jointers, machined tolerances are critical, particularly the flatness of the tables. To check it, crank both infeed and outfeed tables into the same plane, then span the length of both tables with an accurate straightedge. If you see any daylight between the edge and the table surfaces, the tables are not parallel, and may be impossible to repair economically. Use a pair of winding sticks (identical wooden sticks, spanning the tables, spaced so you can sight along their top edges) to check the tables for twist. Also sight the fence; a slight bow is less a problem than a twist. Crank both tables to their travel limits, occasionally spinning the cutterhead by hand, to make sure everything clears. The table lead-and lock-screws should turn smoothly.

A bandsaw has fewer critical-tolerance parts, but if it's to run smoothly, the wheels should be true and, ideally, balanced. To check, remove the blade and the motor belt, and spin each wheel. A warped or bent wheel will wobble noticeably. Spot a lopsided one by chalking a mark on the rim and giving the wheel another spin. If the mark comes

to rest at the same point each time, the wheel may be heavy enough on one side to vibrate at sawing speed. Blade guides are harder to judge. Some Rockwell copies mimic the original faithfully, others only halfway. Just make sure that the machine has guides of some sort and that they are adjustable. Check the blade length, too; it should be a standard size, not an oddball that will have to be custom-welded. Also, make sure that replacement tires are available.

The best Taiwan-made motors are heavier and larger than their Western counterparts, and are likely to provide good service. The worst reveal themselves by overheating and occasionally burning up during the first few hours of use. There's no practical way to pick a good one. You ought to check the wiring, though. A single-phase motor should be wired with a two-conductor cord, plus a ground wire—usually green—through a three-prong plug. The ground should be connected to both the motor frame and the machine itself. A three-phase motor should have a three-conductor cord, plus the ground. Make sure that none of the three-phase legs is grounded to the machine frame, or a shock hazard will exist if the plug is incorrectly wired. Ground wires often get fastened to painted metal surfaces, defeating their purpose. Disconnect them and clean up the mating surfaces with sandpaper.

Finally, don't expect to uncrate a perfect machine, at least not every time, and don't plan on it having much resale value. Besides using cheap labor, Taiwanese factories are notorious for cutting corners to keep prices down. This might mean you'll get a lousy paint job, sand-bound castings, or burred edges left undressed—all minor problems you can fix yourself. But defects serious enough to render a machine useless aren't uncommon, so your best bet is to try to spot a dog before you pay. It's one thing to have to file a few parts to a perfect fit. It's something else entirely to have to remachine a warped casting. —*P.B.*

Basic Machine Maintenance
Regular cleaning and lubrication are essential

by David Troe

Many people mistakenly expect machines to work perfectly from the time they are unwrapped and think they will last forever with no attention, but the life and accuracy of machines are directly proportional to the amount of care they receive. Thoughtful attention and simple preventative maintenance will ensure accuracy, minimize the need for major repairs and increase resale value.

Woodworkers generally don't maintain their equipment as well as they should, and they often don't understand the relationship between various mechanical components of their machinery. Unlike some furniture these days, machines are designed logically—there is a reason why the components are where they are, and they are all there for some reason. Obviously not all equipment is assembled correctly by the manufacturer, but far more damage is done by unobservant protomechanics who fail to recognize the interrelationships of things. If you don't have an exploded assembly drawing of your equipment, try and get one from the manufacturer, or if your machine is an antique, see if a machinery distributor in your area has one on file that you could copy. Assembly drawings are excellent, but often not detailed enough. When you are pulling something apart, if there is any question in your mind about how it goes back together, label the parts, make sketches or take photographs. But before doing any cleaning or repairs, turn off the power or unplug the machine.

Most repairs are not outside the capability of woodworkers. Most of the tools will already be in the shop: screwdrivers, wrenches, pliers and the like. Unlike automobile repair, extremely few specialized tools are necessary. If you should encounter a situation requiring tools that you do not have, do not attempt to use a substitute that might damage the part. Pliers won't replace wrenches, nor will a cold chisel substitute for a spanner wrench. If you cannot completely disassemble a component for repair or replacement, do as much as you can and then take it to a competent mechanic. This will save the mechanic time, thereby saving you money. Ideally you should take the work to a machinery distributor with repair facilities or to the manufacturer's service center, but that is rarely practical. If the job requires more tools, skill or confidence than you possess, it can often be handled by a jack-of-all-trades machine shop, or even by a garage. If the equipment is still under warranty, it will be voided if anyone other than those authorized by the manufacturer works on it.

The regularity with which maintenance should take place depends on how much use the equipment gets. Follow manufacturer's recommendations and establish your own schedule. Unless you suspect a serious problem, such as a new noise or vibration, the only regular maintenance required is to keep your equipment clean, to keep it lubricated, to check for

loose parts and wear, and to check the motor and the power transmission system. Do this at least once a week in a commercial shop, once a month in a one-person shop, and every six to twelve months in a hobbyist shop.

The first rule is to keep your equipment clean. Dust and dirt will accumulate in even the smallest and least accessible places. At the least, brush off your equipment, or better yet, use a vacuum cleaner. Compressed air is effective in blowing out dust from inaccessible areas but caution must be exercised to avoid driving the dust into other components. For this reason a maximum line pressure of 30 psi is suggested. However romantic sawdust and chips scattered around the shop may be, they are harmful both to you and to your equipment. Dust sticking to machine surfaces causes many problems: excessive wear; drying out and premature failure of bearings and ways; sticking of gears, trunnions and all sliding surfaces; *V*-belt and band-saw tire deterioration. All lead to extensive down-time if the situation gets out of hand. Also, accumulated dust is a very real fire hazard, especially in electrical switches and motors. Clean your equipment and your shop regularly and often.

Lubricate your equipment when and where necessary. Remember that excessive lubrication is at least as harmful as under-lubrication. Over-lubrication in bearings causes the lubricant to churn and heat up, which can lead to early failure. Exposed grease and oils collect dust and chips like a sponge, eventually turning into a gummy blob that restricts free rotation and easy movement. It is safer to under-lubricate frequently than to over-lubricate infrequently.

It is difficult to recommend a lubricant if there are no guidelines from the manufacturer or the distributor, but the following suggestions can be assumed to be safe. For bearings that have oil fittings, use SAE 10 to 20 nondetergent machine oil. The SAE rating refers to viscosity, not to motor oil, which should not be used. For bearings that have grease fittings, use a lithium-soda type bearing grease, NLGI (National Lubricating Grease Institute) Grade 2. Do not oil a bearing designed for grease, and do not grease a bearing designed for oil. For gearboxes, use SAE 90 to 140 gear oil. And on drill-press quill and pinion gears, try SAE 40 oil.

As a general rule, use dry lubricants on any moving part that is not subject to high speeds or where movement is for adjustment, such as on tabletops, dovetail ways, jackscrews, trunnions, fences, miter-gauge slots, tailstock spindles and the like. Wherever possible, use dry lubricants such as hard wax or graphite. Avoid silicone or Teflon-based sprays—they are extremely expensive and adversely affect wood glues and finishes. My favorite is plain old hard wax, which is inexpensive, easy to apply, and as far as anyone knows doesn't cause cancer or affect the ozone in the atmosphere. Wax provides longer service on cast-iron surfaces because it fills up the microscopic pores in the iron. You can use any paste wax or

David Troe owns Advantage Machinery in S. Yarmouth, Mass., where he designs and makes woodworking machinery.

liquid wax that does not contain cleaners, because the abrasive action of cleaners would cause lapping and excessive wear. Rub in the wax well and remove any excess.

Another way to lubricate surfaces upon which wood must slide is to apply a Teflon-impregnated tape or adhesive-backed sheet. Thoroughly clean the surfaces with a grease solvent to ensure a strong bond, and extend the Teflon over any edges where it might catch on a piece of wood. The covering need not be solid—several strips of tape running parallel to the direction of feed and spanning the wood are often adequate. Planer beds, saw tables and fences are good candidates for this treatment. Look in the Yellow Pages under "Plastics" for a specialty supply house.

When lubricating with grease or oil, make sure that both the lubricants and the fittings are clean. Often oil cups and grease nipples are coated with gummy sawdust, which must be cleaned before lubricating. Oil levels are generally set by visible marks on oil cups or by the saturation of fiber wicks, but grease levels are more difficult to ascertain. Do not overlubricate. Common sense is essential in determining the correct amount of lubricant to use. Never force grease into a bearing and its housing more than half full.

Bearings

Bearings cause woodworkers the most confusion and grief. Different kinds of bearings require different treatments. Sleeve bearings, usually oil-impregnated metal but sometimes plastic, rely on a very thin lubricating film to reduce sliding friction. It is interesting to note that sleeve bearings are used both in inexpensive applications and in situations where precision is a prime requirement: at one end the lowly $9.95 drill and at the other end a metal-machining spindle costing many thousands of dollars. The difference is in the materials used, the precision with which they are made, and the complexity of the bearing lubrication system. Before modern metal-hardening technology and precision machin-

ing, which made the manufacture of ball bearings feasible, all bearings were of the sleeve type. That is why Babbitt bearings are so often found on old machines. Sleeve bearings are either full or split, and worn ones are relatively easy to replace by pushing them out of their housings. Press evenly on the rim of sleeve bearings when replacing and be careful not to roll an edge or raise any burrs. Babbitt bearings can be repoured, but this should only be attempted by someone who knows how to do it properly—it is hazardous.

Antifriction bearings are bearings in which rolling members reduce friction. These bearings fall into four categories: ball bearings, roller bearings, tapered roller bearings and needle bearings. Ball bearings are the most frequently used. Needle bearings, because of their smaller size, are used in portable power tools. Tapered roller bearings, because of their inherently high-thrust load capacity, are used in some high-quality portable drills and in lathe headstocks. Many machines have bearings that are said to be "lubricated for life" or "sealed for life," but this refers to the life of the bearing itself and not to the life of the machine or to the life of the owner. The life of a bearing can be quite short if it is improperly handled during installation, or quite long if treated with care. Sealed bearings are so named because they have a shield that seals the lubricant in and the dirt out—at least that's the theory. Care must be exercised not to damage the seals in any way. Sealed bearings can be relubricated by prying out the seal, cleaning the bearing, relubricating and replacing the seals, but this requires a bit of expertise to avoid damaging the seal so I can suggest it only to those who have patience, confidence and the skill to be gentle. For the general lot of us, when a sealed bearing needs lubrication (you'll know by stickiness, roughness or strange noises), it must be thrown out and replaced with a new one.

While most people can replace bearings, care must be exercised not to damage either the bearing or its housing. Any pressure above that which you can supply with your fingers

Rolling members reduce friction in antifriction bearings. Clockwise from above, tapered roller, needle, roller, ball bearing.

Pressing bearings

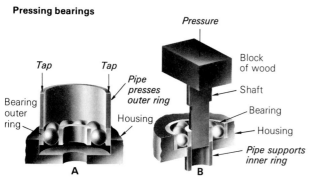

When removing or replacing a bearing, apply pressure to the ring that is fixed to the shaft or set in the housing, never to both rings at once. To replace a bearing in a housing (A), a pipe the diameter of the outer ring will distribute the force of the tapping evenly over the ring. When the shaft is then set in (B), a pipe supporting the inner ring will prevent distortion of the bearing.

V-belts

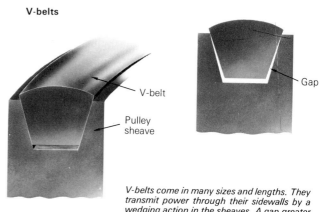

V-belts come in many sizes and lengths. They transmit power through their sidewalls by a wedging action in the sheaves. A gap greater than 1/32" between the pulley and the side of the sheave means that the pulley is worn and should be replaced.

must be evenly applied to either the inner or the outer ring, never to both at the same time and never between the rings. If you don't have a section of pipe, a socket wrench or other suitable cylinder of the right size, you can turn a wooden one on a lathe, but if you are replacing the lathe bearing, you are up the proverbial creek. An uneven force on the bearing can dent the bearing races and/or ruin the trueness of the housing. Don't try to free a stuck bearing from both the shaft and the housing at the same time. If the bearing is tight, try spritzing some penetrating oil around the ring. Or heat the housing to about 250° F—the expansion will usually do the trick. If that doesn't work, the bearing can be removed with a gear puller, but that always ruins the bearing and it then must be replaced. If in doubt, take it to a good repairman.

Manufacturers use standard "in stock" bearings whenever possible to reduce costs. Because stock bearing dimensions have long been standardized, a bearing from one manufacturer can replace a bearing of the same series from any other manufacturer. All a supplier needs to know is the bearing identification number, which is etched on the side of the bearing. Tapered roller bearings have two numbers you must know—one on the cup and one on the cone. If you can't find an identification number, measure the outside and inside diameters and the width, get the speed (rpm) and phone a bearing distributor. Check in the Yellow Pages under "Bearings." You will save money by dealing with a bearing-supply firm rather than with the machine manufacturer.

When replacing a bearing, follow the reverse order from that used to remove it. Sometimes bearings are not symmetrical, so be sure to replace it in the same orientation as the original. Keep the bearing wrapped until you install it.

Neither ring on a bearing should fit so loosely as to allow it to rotate independently of its assembly. If the rings are loose, they can be temporarily fitted with an anaerobic sealant, such as Loctite. This delays the necessity of replacing the worn component. Heating to about 350° will soften the Loctite when you want to remove the bearing. Clean off all foreign material from the spindle and the housing before replacing a bearing to prevent scoring them.

Open or unshielded bearings should be cleaned once a year or as your specific situation requires. Some bearings can be cleaned while in place, but usually a more complete job will be had if the bearings are removed from their components. Never use water to clean a bearing: Wash out all the old lu-

bricant in clean kerosene, degreasing fluid or other commercial solvent, and rinse with fresh, clean solvent. An old soft toothbrush is excellent for scrubbing the parts. After cleaning, allow the bearing to dry dust-free by wrapping it in a clean lint-free cloth. As soon as the bearing is dry, rinse it in a bath of clean, light mineral oil. Until you are ready to replace it, protect it from contamination by putting it in a plastic bag. Never spin a dry bearing, and never use compressed air to dry or spin a bearing. Check the cleaned bearing for any sign of wear or damage, and replace if necessary. When you are ready to replace a grease bearing in the machine, grease the rolling elements by squeezing the correct grade of grease into the bearing with your clean fingers. The housing and the bearing should be packed no more than half full with grease. Check all bearings for adequate lubrication before running.

Unless otherwise stated by the manufacturer, lubricate the components at rest. This is especially true with electric motors, where stray oil can splash into the windings and harm the insulation. More detailed guidelines can be found in the references cited at the end of this article.

Belts, pulleys and chains
If you are experiencing vibration or a loss of power at the cutter, the problem is most likely in the power transmission system. V-belts are the most common means of transmitting power from a motor to a cutter. V-belts transmit power through their sidewalls by a wedging action in a pulley sheave. They are manufactured in standard cross-sectional sizes. It is imperative to replace belts with ones of the same series, because the different series are not interchangeable. V-belts are marked as to their series and length, but sometimes the marking wears off. Some parts lists state what series and length belt to use, though more typically they give only a replacement-part number. If the belt is old and you have no idea what to replace it with, a power-transmission supply house will be able to figure it out. Since there is some latitude in the length tolerances allowed in the construction of belts, it is essential, when replacing a belt in a multiple-belt drive, to replace all the belts, and to replace them only with a matched set of belts guaranteed to be of the same length.

If you have a machine with no belts on it, or if you are replacing a leather-belt drive system with V-belts (which there isn't really any reason to do), you can approximate the proper belt length by adding twice the distance between the centers of the shafts to half the sum of the circumferences of the two pulleys. Or wrap a steel tape around the pulley rims and give the supplier this measurement. Fractional-hp drives use the outside distance around the pulleys for belt length. Multiple-belt or heavy-duty drives use the pitch diameter. When this yields a nonstandard length, go to the next longest belt and adjust the components for proper tension.

Proper tensioning is important for both maximum power transmission and maximum life of the components. Excessive tension stretches the belts, causes heat buildup that accelerates deterioration and places unnecessary strain on the bearings, leading to premature bearing failure. Insufficient tension results in belt slippage, loss of power, vibration, whip, excessive noise and accelerated wear of the belt and pulley sheaves. Belt tensioning is a matter of feel. One method is to strike the belt with your fist—if it feels dead, it is slack. A properly tensioned belt will feel alive and vibrate. On multiple-belt drives, if you can push down on one belt so that its top face is flush with the bottom face of an adjacent belt using moderate pressure (10 lb.), then the belts are properly tensioned. Ideally belts should flex about 1/32 in. for every inch of span between the centers of the driving and driven pulleys.

Old belts wear pulleys more severely than belts in good condition, so it is advisable to replace belts that are worn, frayed, cracked or split. Time and money are not saved by trying to get additional service from a worn belt. Dirty belts can be washed with soap and water. Rinse thoroughly and dry completely before replacing.

Flat-belt drive systems are found on old equipment—the trusty old leather belt—or on equipment that is run at very high speeds such as industrial overarm routers and portable power planes, both of which use a belt of synthetic rubber. Only leather belts should be treated with a belt dressing at three to six-month intervals. This dressing keeps the leather reasonably supple and improves the transmission of power. Replacement belts are available from belting suppliers and, if possible, should be purchased already spliced into an endless loop. Splicing a leather belt on a machine is difficult for the inexperienced. If you insist on doing it yourself, go to the library and read all you can about the various techniques.

The greatest problem of belt drives is misalignment of the driving and driven pulleys. Proper alignment is essential to realize maximum power, and the longest possible pulley, belt and bearing life. Angular and axial misalignment and loose pulleys all place unnecessary strain on the drive system. Use a straightedge to line up your pulleys and make sure they are secure on their shafts. If the pulley appears to wobble on its shaft, either the shaft is bent and must be straightened or replaced or the bore of the pulley is worn oversize and the pulley must be replaced. Do not try to shim an oversize pulley bore as it is almost impossible to control the concentricity of the pulley. Pulleys should also be replaced when the sides of the sheave have worn to the point where there is a gap of 1/32 in. or greater on either side. The belt must not touch the bottom of the pulley sheave.

Pulleys are almost always "keyed" to their shafts, most commonly with a short piece of square keystock but sometimes with what is called a Woodruff key. Replace missing keys with the same size keystock (available at all hardware stores) and don't rig a temporary replacement out of nails. When so provided, tighten the pulley setscrew(s) but be careful not to overtighten—it is easy to strip the threads in pulleys, rendering them useless. Unless you are an engineer or a mechanic, replace worn pulleys with ones of the same size. Any variation in size from the original will affect the speed at which the equipment runs.

The same general suggestions regarding alignment, tension and cleanliness apply to variable-speed belt drives. Since these are relatively new, it should be possible to contact the drive manufacturer to get lubrication recommendations. Remember that in drives of this type it is important to change speeds only when the equipment is running, so as not to damage either the belt or the pulleys.

Roller chains transmit large amounts of torque at low speeds and that is why they are often found in the feed-drive mechanisms of thicknessers. The same general suggestions concerning belts apply to chain drives, except that chains must be lubricated to operate freely. Keep the chain taut but not tight if you can adjust it. Make sure the links are free and not sticking to each other, and that the chains are reasonably clean. Since grease attracts dust, I prefer to use a dry lubricant on chains, but this also means that the chains must be lubricated more often. Roller chains, just like their bicycle-chain cousins, usually have a removable master link that allows the chain to be taken off for thorough cleaning or replacement. Chains can be cleaned with kerosene or other degreasing solvent, in much the same manner as bearings. Replace chains that show signs of rust. When the chain is off, check the sprocket teeth for wear. If they are worn, or if one side of the chain is riding on one side of the teeth, most likely the sprockets are not properly aligned. In any case, replace worn sprockets and chains.

Unless you are familiar with electric motors, do not attempt to do anything to them other than to keep them clean and, if fittings are provided, to keep them lubricated. Dust should be frequently cleaned out of motors, electrical junction boxes and electrical switches to minimize the hazard of fire. Repair or replace electric cords that are cut, cracked or abraded. Always make sure that the power is cut off when you are working around electrical equipment.

Regular maintenance need not take a great deal of time, but should be thorough and comprehensive. A little time invested on a regular basis will minimize major repairs and lost time by catching problems before they become serious. □

Further reading

Some useful shop maintenance references:

Power Tool Maintenance by Daniel Irvin (McGraw-Hill, Inc., 1221 Ave. of the Americas, New York, N.Y. 10036, 1971).

Machinery's Handbook by Erik Oberg and Franklin D. Jones (Industrial Press, Inc., 200 Madison Ave., New York, N.Y. 10016; 22nd edition, 1984).

Millwrights and Mechanics Guide (Theodore Audel & Co., distributed by Bobbs-Merrill, 4300 W. 62nd St., Indianapolis, Ind. 46206, 1975).

Selecting and Using Electric Motors by L. H. Soderholm and H. B. Puckett (U.S. Government Printing Office, Farmer's Bulletin No. 2257, 1974; out of print, but useful if you can find it).

Woodshop Tool Maintenance by Beryl M. Cunningham and William F. Holtrup (Chas. A. Bennett Co., Inc., 809 W. Detweiller Dr., Peoria, Ill. 61614, 1974).

Misalignment

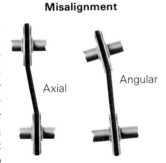

Axial

Angular

Restoring a Rusty Titan
Far from easy, but worth the group effort

by Jim Haber

Early in my woodworking endeavor I noticed an obvious correlation between a person's work and the tools he or she uses. I am speaking not only of the quality but also of the kind of work. So when I gained some insight into the work I wanted to pursue, I knew what machines would help. I wanted a 12-in. jointer and a planer of about the same size, but, most important, I wanted a good, tough, somewhat large band saw. One day at the mill site of my favorite wood supplier (the man who owns the place is a story in himself), I noticed a large band saw standing in the middle of a field. Upon inquiry I found that it had stood there like a statue in a park for the last six years. Believing as we do, my wife and I had prayed that God would provide the machines I needed. So as I walked toward the old saw I felt as if the answer to my prayers was standing before me. When I was within touching distance of the old machine I was impressed by several things, most notably its size and condition: huge and awful, respectively.

Later that week I enticed a friend to go down and see the old saw and help me decide if I should buy it. As we inspected it we learned the following: Rust covered it like frost, the trunnions supporting the 36-in. by 40-in. table were broken, and, worst of all, the shaft of the direct-drive motor had snapped at the shoulder of the Morse taper that held the lower wheel. I enthusiastically paid the paltry sum the mill owner was asking.

Jim and Kathy Haber (foreground) and friends. Behind the saw, from left to right: Joe Reynolds (Haber's father-in-law), Tom Reynolds (brother-in-law), Frank Edwards and Dale Clark.

My first obstacle in what later turned out to be a seemingly endless list was to get it home. As my buddy, my wife and I began to dismantle the monster, I gained firsthand knowledge of another quality of this titan—its mass. The main table weighed approximately 320 lb. and proved to be quite sufficient to smash my friend's big toe. We loaded all that we could easily dismantle onto a trailer with some wood I had bought and drove the 60 miles home. It took two more trips to get all the pieces. On the first of these, my brother-in-law, yet another friend and I spent most of the time yanking the motor from the main casting, and on the subsequent trip my father-in-law, brother-in-law and I managed to bring back the 1-ton main casting with the help of a whole slew of machine rollers, jacks, chains, blocks and a come-along.

Once home, we deposited the casting in the prone position in the middle of our driveway. I now began to jump the long row of hurdles before me. With wire brushes and a wire wheel, my wife and I removed the layer of rust that covered everything. The tables were sent to the sandblaster and finished up beautifully. I took the trunnions to school and brazed them together. And finally, a machinist friend of mine bored the rotor, pressed in a new shaft, pinned it and then turned the appropriate taper and thread onto the end. This was all done after the motor had been rewound to fit the phase converter I needed to run the saw off of single-phase current. This process of cleaning, fixing and assembling it in my garage took the better part of six months.

After I had the machine basically together, I balanced both wheels as best I could, started up the motor and bottom wheel and sanded the tire to a crown. With the installation of the blade, tracking it and some other final adjustments, I was ready for the big moment. I pressed the starter. The saw emitted a groan that grew to a sound not unlike a galactic ship out of *Star Wars*. By the time the saw reached full speed (the blade travels at 120 MPH), my 2-ton monster was shaking mildly, while the blade tracked unpredictably. With a crash the blade untracked and ripped into the custom-made stainless-steel blade guards. My heart sank; a lot of time, money and hopes had gone into this project. Seething and frustrated, I left the room.

I had too much invested at this point to give up. Upon analysis, I decided the saw needed modern blade guides and the 38-in. cast-aluminum rim of the upper wheel turned to a slight crown. After spending another $250, I had my saw back together, ready for another trial run. This time it ran beautifully and the tracking was solid. I was delighted with the cuts, though I did have to add a vacuum to eliminate the clouds of sawdust that the high speed of the blade produced.

The saw is used only once per piece, but the fine resawn matched panels, stiles and sides it cuts make it indispensable. My work is richer because of this machine, but the help and friendship of friends and relatives is richer still. □

Repouring Babbitt Bearings
A low-tech way to rescue old machines

by Bob Johnson

What woodworker hasn't dreamt of having a 36-in. or 42-in. bandsaw in the shop, a machine that can saw the thinnest stock one minute and then slab a 12-in. log the next? Most of us recoil from the price tags on such new machines. For the craftsman who would like industrial-quality machinery without paying new-machine prices, one answer is to seek the machinery of the 1880-1930 era.

Machines of that era are generally massive and well-made, and since most of them were built with babbitt bearings, industrial buyers are scared off, making such used machines available for surprisingly low prices. Aside from cleaning and painting, very often the only work required to put such machinery back into practical service is the rebabbitting of its bearings.

Modern ball and roller bearings have ended the age of babbitt in woodworking machines, but its heyday is still recent enough for there to be thousands of babbitt-bearing woodworking machines still in use and many more that are out of service and in used-machinery emporiums which can be restored. Babbitt bearings last a long time and will continue to function even when worn. But best of all, when they do need replacement, the job can be done cheaply with a minimum of tools.

The principles of rebabbitting bearings are the same whether for a toy engine or a submarine propeller shaft. The metal is melted and poured, using the machine's bearing shells and shaft as a mold. When the assembly cools, the shaft is removed, if required, and the bearing surface is dressed with hand tools for a good running fit. Holes and grooves to supply and hold oil are cut in the finished babbitt.

Why babbitt?—Throughout the 19th century and well into the 20th, machine bearings were cast in a variety of alloys that have all come to be called babbitt. The name itself comes from Isaac Babbitt, who invented the recessed bearing box and lined it with metal alloy. Today, babbitt refers generally to a low-melting-point alloy made from some mixture of lead, copper, tin, zinc, antimony and/or nickel—a blend soft enough not to wear shafts and easy to renew when worn.

Most of the babbitt bearings in woodworking machinery are made with two-piece cast-iron housings that have a con-

Old babbitt bearings are easily renewed by pouring molten babbitt, above, into the mold formed by the bearing shell and shaft. A torch warms the shell, keeping the metal from hardening prematurely. Babbitt, replaced by ball and roller bearings in new machines, still does its job in restorable, older machinery.

siderably larger inside diameter than the shaft they will support. The molten babbitt is poured into the space between the shaft and housing to form the bearing. The hot metal runs into holes, slots or lips drilled partway into the housing, and this locks the bearing in place.

Some bearings, particularly those for vertical shafts, are one-piece and so are a bit more troublesome to pour. Machinery designers often did not allow much space for the babbitt, or for pouring it in between shaft and bearing shell.

One-piece bearings are not adjustable for taking up play, but a two-piece bearing can be adjusted by adding or removing shims until the cap is tight against the base (figure 1, page 20), while still allowing the shaft to rotate freely. Many people try to adjust by tightening or loosening the bearing cap nuts until the shaft rotates freely, instead of by removing or adding shims. This is a poor practice, as it allows the cap to move, and usually causes the bearing to heat and wear rapidly.

How do you know when to rebabbitt? A quick inspection should tell. With two-piece bearings, tighten the cap bolts until the shaft won't turn, then back them off until it can be spun freely. Grab the shaft and give it a shake. There shouldn't be play in any direction. If the machine can be run, examine the end of the shaft while it's turning. If it wobbles instead of just rotating in place, new bearings are probably needed. Before you decide to rebabbitt, try eliminating the play by removing any shims left in the bearing.

Materials—In addition to standard shop tools such as wrenches, screwdrivers and hammers, you'll need some other tools and supplies for rebabbitting. First, you'll need a way to melt the babbitt and to heat the bearing castings, both for removing old babbitt and for pouring new. An oxyacetylene rig is best for both jobs, although a propane or MAAP gas torch can do small jobs. An ordinary household gas or electric stove gets hot enough to melt babbitt. Be sure to use an old heavy iron or steel pot—a 2-qt. saucepan is ideal. If you have a big bearing to pour, a plumbers' pot—a stove and crucible for melting lead—will save time and is more convenient. Hardware stores sell cast-iron plumbers' ladles in several sizes. These ladles have long handles and pouring lips. Each bearing

Fig. 1: Typical two-piece babbitt bearing

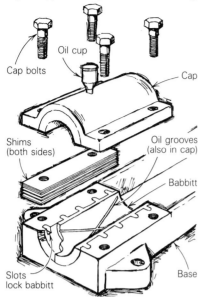

Cap bolts

Oil cup

Cap

Shims (both sides)

Oil grooves (also in cap)

Babbitt

Slots lock babbitt

Base

Lug for mounting bearing to machine, or bearings can be cast in machine

Restoring the bearings in an old machine takes but a few tools. You'll need a torch (propane will work, but oxyacetylene is better), a container to melt the babbitt in and a ladle to pour it. Babbitrite or other damming material contains the metal while it hardens in the bearing shell, light machine oil keeps the babbitt from sticking to the shaft, and the popsicle sticks are used to test the temperature of the babbitt before the pour.

After disassembling the bearings, Johnson's assistant melts out the old babbitt with a torch, above left, making sure he gets it out of all of the recesses, slots and holes in the bearing shells. The old babbitt is saved. With the addition of some fresh metal, it can be reused. Setting up a bearing for the pour calls for some artful placement of supports and damming materials. Above right, Johnson has placed wood blocks that will level and support this sawmill arbor exactly in the center of its bearing shells;

Babbitrite, a damming material, has been placed at both ends of the bearing to contain the molten metal until it has cooled. With the bearing shell braced on a level surface and the shaft firmly supported and centered in it, below, the molten babbitt is poured until it slightly overfills the shell. The shell is kept warm during the pour with an acetylene torch. Johnson pours two-piece bearings, such as the one shown here, in two separate operations—one for the bearing base and one for its cap.

must be made in a single pour, so make sure the ladle is large enough to do the job.

In 24 years of pouring bearings, I've never found that I couldn't reuse the old babbitt melted out of a machine simply by adding a little bit of new babbitt to make up the quantity required. If you're a perfectionist, you may decide not to take chances with an unknown old babbitt mix and to use all new. Babbitt is locally available from hardware stores or industrial supply houses and most sell two types, a high-lead alloy for slow-speed bearings and a high-nickel mix for high-speed ones. For most woodworking machinery, the high-nickel babbitt, or high-speed babbitt, is worth the cost—about $9 a pound (1982) from my supplier. We always use it on machine shafts that run at several thousand RPM, such as jointer and planer heads and tablesaw arbor bearings. We save money by using the old melted-out babbitt of unknown alloy only for slow-speed bearings, such as the drive gear and feed roll bearings on planers or bandsaw wheel shafts.

Babbitt is sold by weight in bar form, and some dealers will break a bar for you. Be sure you have enough. Nothing is more frustrating than to almost finish a perfect pour and run out of babbitt—you have to do the whole job again.

You'll need to seal the bottom, ends and oil holes of the bearing shell to stop the molten babbitt from running out. The handiest material is fireproof clay made for babbitting, which can be worked like modeling clay. There are various proprietary names—Babbitrite and Dambabbitt are two. The stuff is reusable and a can seems to last forever. Wood, cardboard, sheet metal, cloth, rope, string and other materials can supplement the damming material.

Preparation—Some machines have non-removable bearing shells cast right into their frames, others are made with a removable cap which bolts to a base that's cast into the machine, and others have both removable bases and caps. Whichever the case, before rebabbitting, all the old babbitt must be removed, and the bearing shell and the shaft must be clean and dry, free of all traces of loose rust, grease and oil.

If the bearings are removable, tip the bearing up and support it so that the old babbitt can run into your ladle or melting pot. Play the torch on the babbitt, starting at the bottom, allowing the babbitt to flow out. When the shell cools, inspect the surface to be sure that you've melted out all the corners, slots, and keyways provided to lock the babbitt in.

Machines with cast-in bearing shells are harder to clean. These will often have the babbitt-locking holes at the bottom of the bearing; if so, the holes can be used as drains for emptying the old babbitt as you melt it out. If there are no holes, you can sometimes drill one. Failing this, you'll have to chip the old babbitt out with a chisel, a task made easier by playing the torch on the metal so it flows and accumulates in a lump at the bottom, where it can be removed.

Machinery that has been out in the weather often has rust under the original babbitt. This should be removed by sandblasting, wirebrushing, or scraping and sanding after the old babbitt is out.

The shaft that will ride in the bearing must be clean, straight and polished to a bright, smooth finish. Flaws in the shaft will be reproduced in the bearing. Check the roundness of the shaft with a micrometer; it may require remachining if it is worn out-of-round or deeply pitted. We put old, worn shafts in a lathe and take a very light skim cut, and then

polish them with fine sandpaper followed by crocus cloth. This is especially important in finely-fitted high-speed bearings. If you are dealing with a very long shaft or one that you can't prop into position for the pour, you'll need to make a babbitting mandrel—a piece of shafting the same size and finish as the original and long enough to extend beyond the bearing to some means of support at both ends.

Setting up—If there's an art in rebabbitting bearings, it's in the setup, wherein the shaft is secured in the exact position it will occupy in the finished bearing. You need room to pour the hot metal around the shaft, and it must not move during the pour and while the babbitt is hardening. Each machine requires its own special setup, so you have to be resourceful. Pour two-piece bearings in two steps, one for the cap and one for the base. Single-piece bearings are done in one pour. Here are some general guidelines for setting up:

With two-piece bearings, start by making up the shims that go between the bearing halves. I make brass shims of assorted thicknesses for each bearing, so play can be adjusted in variable increments. The shims can range in thickness from 0.1 in. to 0.001 in. Hard-finish paper will work for the thinnest shims. Use as many shims as you can, in equal numbers and thicknesses on each side, so your bearing will be thick and will last a long time before rebabbitting is required.

If the bearing shells are removable, place the bearing bases on a level surface; if they can't be removed, wedge and brace the machine so the bearing base is level in both horizontal planes. This will keep the babbitt from running to one side or one end when poured. When you're satisfied that the bearing is level, locate the shaft precisely in the center of the bearing, and in the final position it will be in the machine. Use dividers, sheet-metal guides, wooden wedges or whatever to measure and mark the location of the shaft. There are various methods for securing it there. You can sometimes support the shaft with small wooden blocks beyond each end of the bearing, or you might have to build a jig or cradle. Each situation is different. Use common sense, and remember that the shaft and shell must be in the relationship you ultimately want them, which usually means that the shaft is centered inside and parallel to the bearing base. Small, light shafts and mandrels can sometimes be supported by Babbitrite alone, but it is better to use a solid support.

There will be space between the shaft and the ends of the bearing shells, and this is where Babbitrite comes into play. Wrap it around the shaft and press it against the bearing shells to prevent the escape of molten metal. Holes in the bearing castings can be filled with Babbitrite, or with small dowels. Plugging oil holes with dowels saves drilling them out after the bearing is poured. Make certain that there is no unwanted egress for the molten babbitt.

Sometimes bearings are made in pairs or sets, such as on some jointer head assemblies. You must set up all the bearings at once, though the actual pour can be done a bearing at a time, without moving anything between pours.

One-piece or sleeve bearings are likely to be more successfully poured vertically. Brace your shaft or mandrel and make sure it is plumb—check on two sides 90° apart with your level, and secure it in position. If you have a large pulley that fits the shaft, it can be used as a base with small wedges under the rim to plumb the shaft. Slide the bearing housing over the shaft and support it at the point where the bearing will actually be. I find that the easiest way to support such a bearing is to bore a shaft-sized hole in a block of wood, split the block and then snug it to the shaft with a C-clamp. Put a layer of Babbitrite between the block and the bearing, and nail small pieces of wood to the block to center the bearing.

As it cools, the babbitt will pinch the shaft if you don't provide running clearance. Hard-finish letter paper is just thick enough to create enough clearance. Apply a light coat of oil to the shaft so the paper will stick to it, or use tape beyond the ends of the bearing. Instead of using paper, you can scrape the running clearance by hand after the pour. But be sure to oil the shaft in either case so the babbitt doesn't stick to it.

Check over your setup. Make sure the shaft is accurately positioned and braced, and that you've dammed every place where the babbitt could run out. You are now ready to melt the babbitt.

Bearings that are not adjustable, or that have a limited range of adjustment on the machine, should be set up together with their shaft in place, and then poured. Pouring the bearings individually off the machine allows less margin for error, so that when they are replaced they may pinch the shaft. If misalignment is not severe, scraping can often cure it.

The pour—Babbitt alloys contain metals that rapidly oxidize when heated, so it's unwise to leave the babbitt on the burner for long periods while you adjust the setup. We shorten the melt time even more by playing an acetylene torch flame directly on the lumps of babbitt in the melting pot. Impurities rise to the top of the molten babbitt and must be removed. Old-timers and old books sometimes suggest that you skim off the dross with a wooden stick, and this will work. However, the clean surface is an unstable composition that will quickly skin over again. It's better to leave the impurities floating on the top until you are ready to pour, then push them to one side and dip your pouring ladle in. Some old texts suggest putting powdered charcoal on the surface of the molten babbitt to help retard oxidation. Such things as pumice powder, fine sand, plaster or even shop dust can also be used. Each will retard oxidation and will float, making it easier to sweep aside with a stick before pouring.

Before you pour, you must heat the bearing shells. If you omit this step the babbitt coming in contact with cold metal is liable to chill and start to harden, giving rise to all manner of problems, from bearings of uneven, spongy texture to bearings with cavities, or those not filled by the pour. More babbitting problems arise from failure to perform this step than from all others combined, and those words—*heat the bearing shells*—should be branded on the brow of anyone pouring babbitt.

While your babbitt is melting, play your torch gently and evenly over all the bearing's exterior. You want it much too hot to touch, but nowhere near red-hot. The less space you have between shell and shaft, the hotter the shell should be, to ensure that babbitt will flow into all corners. This is especially true when you are pouring one-piece bearings. If the shaft is large, warming it with the torch will help. If you are pouring a bearing without the paper wrap, then you definitely should heat the shaft as well as the bearing shell, though take care—overheating can cause warping.

The time-tested way to check temperature is to insert a stick of soft wood (we use a popsicle stick) into the melted babbitt. If you can feel the stick wiggling, the babbitt is too hot. After three or four seconds in the molten babbitt, the stick should char on the end, but not burst into flame.

Put on heavy gloves and eye protection (molten babbitt splashing about causes nasty burns) and quickly dip up a ladleful, pushing the dross and impurities out of your way with your testing stick. Pour the babbitt into the bearing. Move quickly. Ideally, your pouring ladle should hold enough babbitt to fill the bearing shell in one go, but if you must pour another ladle, do so as rapidly as possible. With a helper and two ladles, you can pour from diagonally opposite corners of a horizontal bearing. Watch for overflows and especially for babbitt running out of openings you failed to plug. If babbitt is running out where it shouldn't, stop pouring, fix the leak and start over. Pour until there is a slight excess on the top. When you see the poured babbitt begin to harden, however, do not pour any more.

The pour is done. Now leave the assembly alone until it cools—when you can hold your hand on it, you can disassemble the setup and learn the degree of your success.

Finishing the bearing—If all's well, when you remove the shaft you will be greeted by a uniform, smooth, shiny, silvery babbitt surface. It will have no specks, streaks, blowholes or other irregularities. Some of these, if present, can be removed in finishing up, or ignored, depending on the size of the bearing and the degree of precision required. In most woodworking machinery bearings, you can ignore slight irregularities, especially those at the ends of the bearings, or those where oil grooves will be cut. Glaring irregularities will require a repour. How to decide? Check for the following problems.
Frosty patches: Usually in the center of a bearing, frosty patches can be caused by babbitt trapping air that didn't escape fast enough, or by impurities that got into the metal. If these don't cover more than a third of the bearing, you can still use it. Some small pockets in the center will act as oil reservoirs. If you feel grit on the babbitt surface, the babbitt must be removed, skimmed more carefully and repoured. If the babbitt is frosty all over, the metal was too cool when poured or the casting was not hot enough. Sometimes, uniform frostiness can result from impurities that did not rise to the top. The bearing will be spongy and weak, and should be repoured, with careful skimming after the melt.
Streaks or layers: This means the babbitt was not hot enough when poured, or more likely the casting was too cool and the babbitt began to chill. Light streaks may be removed by scraping and the bearing used; if they are deep, repour.
Looseness: If the babbitt is loose in the bearing shell when it cools, you probably left some oil in the bearing shell or housing, or some got in the babbitt itself, or some other contamination was present. You can repour, but you might be able to tighten the babbitt in the bearing shell by peening it gently with a ball-peen hammer, expanding the babbitt slightly. Peen from the center outward to the edges. This will leave dents in the bearing that you will have to scrape out.
Incomplete babbitt: Voids usually occur at the ends, and in most cases impair only the bearing's appearance. You can use the bearing anyway, or repour it. Sometimes there is a cavity in the bearing center—not a hole but a gentle depression, often not visible until you test the bearing. The cause could be a shaft that was too hot, or trapped air. Leave a small cavity to act as an oil reservoir, but one large enough to reduce the

shaft/bearing contact by a third or more should be repoured.

Clean up the bearing by paring away excess babbitt with a chisel. Pare away the surplus babbitt protruding above the top and beyond the ends, drill out any oil holes and cut oil grooves. Though old books carry a bewildering variety of designs for oil grooves in babbitted bearings, you can use the originals, if they were visible, or cut a V-groove from the oil holes along the length of the bearing, stopping ¼ in. short of the ends so that oil will not run out.

Special tools are made for cutting oil grooves, but as these are hard to find nowadays, you can make one from a piece of ⅜-in. iron rod, as shown in figure 2. The corner of an old flat file will cut oil grooves; small chisels and even pocketknives can also be used. The edges of these grooves and the points where drill bits have emerged through the babbitt are usually a little ragged, so smooth them off or chamfer them.

Final fitting of the bearing is done by scraping, the aspect of babbitting that many beginners fear most. It does take time and some judgment, but there is nothing mysterious or difficult about it. The amount and method of scraping depend on the speed of the shaft, the load on the bearing, and the degree of precision desired. Ideally, all bearings should be hand-scraped (or machined) to a perfect running fit. In practice, many bearings will fit their shafts well enough right after the pour, needing little or no scraping. Our rule of thumb is that woodworking machine heads that turn at high speeds, and parts requiring a perfect fit, such as a lathe headstock or the cutterhead of a large planer, should be scraped. However, the wisdom of taking the time to scrape rough, large or slow-speed bearings is questionable.

If you decide scraping is required, you'll need bearing scrapers and a small bottle of Prussian blue (machinists' layout dye), available from industrial supply houses. Lacking Prussian blue, ink or shoe polish could be used. Bearing scrapers can be purchased or made—they look like a 3-cornered file with the teeth ground off. Homemade scrapers of other shapes are often more useful than the store-bought kind. A flat file with the teeth ground off one face and one edge makes a fine scraper for large bearings. Babbitt cannot be sanded or filed. Not only will it gum, but abrasive sandpaper particles will become embedded in it.

Begin by coating the shaft with layout blue. Lay it carefully in the bearing, rotate it a couple of turns without sliding it lengthwise, then remove it. If the shaft is a perfect fit, the bluing will evenly cover the surface of the babbitt. More likely, though, you'll see blue spots where the shaft is making contact and the rest of the bearing will be shiny babbitt. Scrape gently at the blue spots, and try the shaft again. Shave gently rather than digging at the babbitt. Each time you try the shaft you should see more blued babbitt, meaning that the bearing is making better contact with the shaft. Continue in this fashion to any desired degree of finish.

A perfect fit is not impossible but requires much patience, and is not, in most cases, worth expending much time over. If a bearing must be that perfect, better to machine it with a reamer, a hone or a rotary cutter in a lathe or drill press—a job best done by a machine shop. Since babbitt is soft, it is somewhat forgiving, and after a period of time shafts will run in and wear the babbitt to a running fit. With or without scraping, however, if your bearing makes at least 50% contact with the shaft, pat yourself on the back and say well done.

Most woodworking machinery will have bearings con-

When the bearing is cool, Johnson uses an old woodworking chisel to trim the babbitt flush with the mating surface of the shell. Next he'll check shaft/bearing contact with machinists' layout dye and scrape out the high spots for a good running fit. He'll finish by scraping an oil groove along the bearing's length.

Fig. 2: A homemade oil-groove cutter

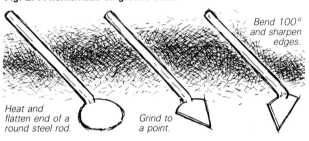

Heat and flatten end of a round steel rod.

Grind to a point.

Bend 100° and sharpen edges.

structed as I've decribed, but occasionally you may see an insert bearing—similar to car-engine connecting-rod bearings. These are often made of bronze or iron. Rather than making a new bearing of these metals, it's cheaper and easier to bore out the old shell to a diameter larger than the old insert, and pour a babbitt bearing in its place. For flat rubbing or sliding bearings, follow the steps—clean, set up, level up, heat and pour. Use an old plane to level off such a flat surface—grind a steep bevel on the iron as you would for very hard wood, and take light cuts. Or make a jig to hold a long scraper made from an old file.

Newly babbitted bearings require running-in. High-speed shafts will often heat new babbitt bearings until they have worn the bearing in. During this period, they should be oiled liberally with any kind of motor oil, and the caps kept snug against the shaft. But watch for overheating. In woodworking machinery, no babbitt bearing housing should get too hot to touch. If a bearing heats excessively, it will melt some of the babbitt at the running surface, and some of the components in the alloy may separate out and scratch or mark the shaft. If this happens, clean the shaft, lightly scrape the bearing, and check the fit of the cap.

If you take the time to restore, adjust and lubricate the babbitt bearings in machinery, you'll be amazed at how long the bearings will last. Being able to repair them easily and cheaply when they do wear out only adds to the enjoyment of owning and using these fine old machines. □

Bob Johnson restores vintage woodworking machinery and sells exotic hardwoods. He lives in Rossville, Ga. Photos by the author.

The Dial Indicator

by R. Bruce Hoadley

An indispensable tool in our shop is a dial indicator with a magnetic base. Although this tool is usually associated with metalworking, we routinely use it for a host of jobs, from aligning equipment and setting up cutterheads to precise measuring of wood samples and deflection in joints.

The dial indicator works by coupling a plunger-type spindle through internal gearing to a sweep hand. When the instrument is held firmly in position, any slight in-and-out movement of the spindle results in greatly magnified movement of the hand around the dial. The spindle is lightly spring-loaded so its tip will follow variations in the surface it contacts, and it can be fitted with a variety of contact points for special situations. Our instrument has a full inch of spindle travel, and its dial is graduated in units of 0.001 in. Indicators are made with greater accuracy, but the trade-off is a smaller measuring range.

The indicator comes with a universal-jointed arm that holds it in virtually any position relative to its magnetic base, which can be demagnetized by the push of a button. When the button is "off," the base retains only a whisper of magnetism, just enough so it will rest snugly against a steel surface. Once in position, the magnet is turned "on," whereupon it locks with about 50 lb. of force.

When the base is locked to a drill-press table and the indicator positioned perpendicular to the quill, the trueness of quill rotation can be measured. Similarly, measuring against the shank of a drill will reveal whether the chuck is centered. Out-of-round, out-of-center and bent shafts and mandrels of all kinds can be checked this way. By setting the base on the outfeed table of a jointer, the height of each knife can be gauged, and measuring across to the infeed table will tell whether the two tables are parallel. A hand-plane iron could be set in the same way. The indicator is invaluable in setting the bedrolls, outfeed roll and pressure bar of a thickness planer. On a table saw, the indicator will measure tooth height as well as set. Of course, the machinery must be electrically disconnected and revolved by hand. Never attempt to gauge cutting edges at operating speeds.

By setting up on a flat surface such as a saw or jointer table, the indicator becomes a comparator-type of measuring device. It will check the diameters and roundness of dowel pins, or the thickness of veneers. The magnetic base also has angled surfaces which will lock against a cylindrical shaft, and because of its weight the base will set firmly against a flat wooden surface as well. By laying an accurate metal bar across a large flat surface, the surface can be "scanned" to gauge overall flatness and locate irregularities. The base holder by itself also has many uses around the shop. Locked to the saw table, it makes a convenient end-stop for crosscutting multiple pieces. I often use it to position an air hose or to hold excess electric cord out of the way.

Dial indicators are quite similar among reliable brands, although a variety of backs are available for mounting to different holding devices. A good indicator costs $40 to $80, and a magnetic base is about $40 (1980 prices). □

The dial indicator easily measures minute variations—here, it is set up for checking chuck concentricity on a drill press. With the dial's spindle bearing against the quill, it will measure bearing runout. Setting it against the shank of a bit will tell whether the bit is centered or bent.

The dial indicator can also gauge surface flatness—here, it checks the height of a jointer knife. Revolving the cutterhead by hand will tell whether all the knives are cutting the same circle. Moving the indicator across a knife will show whether it is parallel from end to end. The spindle can also be extended to the infeed table to check if infeed table and outfeed table are parallel.

Photos: Bruce Hoadley

Converting to 3-Phase Power
More surges per cycle can save you money

by Mac Campbell

Recently I had the basement of my house wired to supply the power that's required to drive both the single-phase and 3-phase machines I need to run a one-man, custom woodworking shop. From a two-pole, 60-amp fuse box, I get enough power to drive portable hand tools as well as my standing shop machinery. I have a 10-in. table saw (2 HP, single phase), a central dust-collection system (3 HP, single phase), a 14-in. jointer (2 HP, 3 phase), a 24-in. thickness planer (7½ HP and ¾ HP, 3 phase), a stationary belt sander (1½ HP, 3 phase) and a 30-in. band saw (5 HP, 3 phase). I use a phase converter to provide the power I need to drive the 3-phase machines. This converter takes the 220-volt, single-phase, alternating current that's supplied to my house and changes it to 3-phase electricity, as is normally found in commercial and industrial zones.

Before saying more about the advantages of 3-phase power and about making a phase converter, a warning is necessary. Electricity must be treated with respect, deliberation and caution. Improper planning, poor layout or failure to observe those safety standards set forth in the National Electrical Code (NEC) or the Canadian Electric Code (CEC) can result in blown fuses, burned-out motors, shop fires, personal injury or death. So if in the process of setting up your shop and installing your electrical system you have doubts or run into problems you can't readily solve, call in a licensed electrician. You may have no choice in the matter because in many cities and towns only licensed electricians are authorized to do the kind of electrical work I describe here.

In addition to observing standard safety practices when wiring your shop, you'll need to put each machine on its own separate circuit, which will protect the individual motor from overload with either a fuse or circuit breaker. Each machine will also require its own power switch that's rated to match the voltage and current draw of the motor. And for maximum safety, especially on concrete floors, each motor circuit should be equipped with a ground-fault interrupter. This device senses current leaks and breaks the circuit before the leakage gets powerful enough to cause a harmful electrical shock.

Next to safety, the efficient use of energy should be your chief concern, and here's where 3-phase electricity is important. Consisting of three separate sources of single-phase alternating current, 3-phase electricity is generated so that the voltage peaks of each phase follow one another at regular intervals, dividing the duration of one cycle of single-phase current (⅟₆₀ second) into even sixths. So instead of two voltage peaks every ⅟₆₀ second, you get six, each ⅟₃₆₀ second apart. Electric motors get their driving force from surges of electromagnetic energy, a power surge occurring with each voltage peak (one positive, one negative). At 60 cycles per second, an 1,800-RPM motor running on single-phase current will receive about four power surges per revolution. But an 1,800-RPM, 3-phase motor will get three times as many power surges per revolution, and will produce smoother, more efficient rotary power and higher starting torque. Single-phase electric motors are to 3-phase motors as two-cylinder gasoline engines are to six-cylinder engines. Aside from getting more energy efficiency, the woodworker who's supplied with 3-phase power has ready access to the used machinery market and can equip his entire shop, if he wishes, with superior industrial-duty machines, most of which have 3-phase motors. Such machines sometimes can be purchased for what it would cost to buy new consumer-grade tools with single-phase motors.

Three-phase wiring requires three insulated conductors plus a ground wire, rather than the two conductors plus a ground needed for single-phase wiring; the practical advantages of 3-phase are numerous. Three-phase motors contain fewer internal parts. They do not, for example, require a separate starter winding and centrifugal switch or a starting

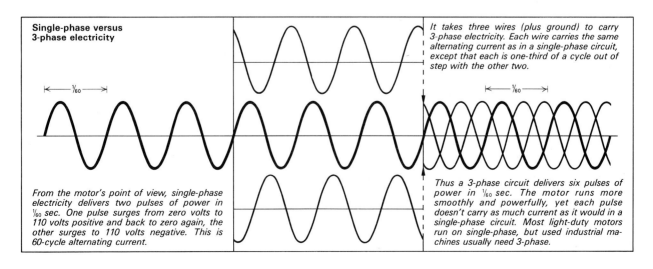

Single-phase versus 3-phase electricity

It takes three wires (plus ground) to carry 3-phase electricity. Each wire carries the same alternating current as in a single-phase circuit, except that each is one-third of a cycle out of step with the other two.

From the motor's point of view, single-phase electricity delivers two pulses of power in ⅟₆₀ sec. One pulse surges from zero volts to 110 volts positive and back to zero again, the other surges to 110 volts negative. This is 60-cycle alternating current.

Thus a 3-phase circuit delivers six pulses of power in ⅟₆₀ sec. The motor runs more smoothly and powerfully, yet each pulse doesn't carry as much current as it would in a single-phase circuit. Most light-duty motors run on single-phase, but used industrial machines usually need 3-phase.

Jim DiVeto

220-volt, 3-phase output

220-volt, single-phase input

Belt-tensioning lever

Large, 3-phase, 220-volt motor

Flat belt

Idler

Single-phase starting motor

Once started and with no mechanical load, a 220-volt 3-phase motor will run on 220-volt single-phase current. You tap two power legs from the same wires that feed the motor, while its rotation generates the third phase via its third wire. With a small converter in a heated shop, the starter motor can be eliminated: Just wrap a rope around the motor shaft, give a smart tug to start the rotor turning and then switch on the electricity.

A phase converter is simply a large, 3-phase motor coupled to a smaller, single-phase starter motor. In the setup shown (photographed at an upstate New York shop), the starter motor is mounted on a hinged plate attached to a lever. This does the same job as an idler, allowing the V-belt to be disconnected when the converter reaches operating speed. Wall-mounted breaker-box controls power to both motors, while the large cable at right takes 3-phase current to shop machinery. Since this converter is in an unheated room, it's housed inside an insulated box (photo, right) along with a light bulb connected to a timer. This setup holds enough heat to prevent the grease from freezing, else the motor wouldn't start on winter mornings.

capacitor; consequently they are less likely to break down, and they're cheaper to repair if they do. Because they're simpler they are usually more compact, a useful feature if you want to increase the horsepower of a given tool and not the space taken up by its motor. They are much more efficient in terms of power consumption (see Table 1, facing page) and cheaper to install, though this is partially offset by the requirement of the fourth wire. Because of its increased efficiency, switch components for 3-phase are usually comparably priced to those for single-phase motors of the same horsepower. An added bonus is that any 3-phase motor is reversible simply by transposing any two lead wires.

There are two ways to obtain 3-phase power. The best way is to buy it directly from the power company, but this may not be possible in many locations because of zoning restrictions. Or you can produce your own 3-phase electricity, as I have done, with a phase converter. Of the several kinds available, I prefer the rotary type because it's the most durable and efficient. Mine is still going strong after 15 years' use in a dry-cleaning plant and another year's duty in my shop. Basically a large, 3-phase motor, used like a generator, this unit puts out the same voltage that's fed into it; so when you drive the converter with a 220-volt, single-phase current, you'll get 220-volt, 3-phase current out of it. (Since it's not running under a mechanical load, single-phase power is sufficient to keep it turning.)

If you want to make your own phase converter, you'll need

to buy a 3-phase motor whose rated horsepower is twice that of the largest motor you'll run in your shop. If, for example, your most powerful machine motor is 5 HP, you'll need to obtain a 10 HP, 3-phase motor as your converter.

Because the converter won't start itself on single-phase power, you need a way of mechanically bringing this 10-HP motor up to operating speed. The simplest is the slack-belt and idler-pulley system diagrammed above. Old-fashioned flat belting is ideal, and the pulleys can be made of plywood discs, bolted and glued together and turned on the lathe. Crown the pulley faces slightly, and space the bolts evenly around the center to maintain balance and reduce vibration. You can, however, use a V-belt and pulleys. A fairly small single-phase starting motor (1 HP or less) should work, since the load is applied gradually with the lever and only after the starting motor has come up to operating speed.

To start and run the converter, first start the single-phase motor. After it reaches full speed, gradually tighten the belt and bring the 3-phase motor up to speed. When it reaches full speed, release the belt tension, shut off power to the starting motor, and apply single-phase power to any two legs of the 3-phase motor. It will continue to turn by itself, and will generate 3-phase power, which is available from the three motor leads as shown. □

Mac Campbell designs and builds cabinets and furniture in Harvey Station, New Brunswick.

Shop wiring: switches and breakers

Whether you are wiring your own workshop or contracting to have it done, you'll need to understand the principles and practices involved. Here is some information that I consider especially important to the woodworker who operates electrically powered machinery.

Because of the increased current needed to start (as opposed to run) a motor, simple toggle switches or light switches won't do. While Table 1 shows the current required to produce the motor's rated horsepower, the current required to start the motor under load, as in most woodworking machinery, is about three times this figure. A switch should carry a current rating of at least three times the full load amperage (FLA) of the motor it controls. An ordinary light switch rated at 15 amps is too small to start even a ¼-HP motor safely. The danger is that the contacts will arc each time the switch is thrown and will become less efficient, building up heat and creating a fire hazard. Another danger is that the heavy starting current can generate enough heat to weld the switch contacts together, making it impossible to shut the machine off. Lastly, this type of switch provides no overload protection for the motor.

There are two basic kinds of motor switches—manual and magnetic. The manual switch has an amperage and/or horsepower rating equal to or greater than that of the motor it controls, and the current used by the motor runs through the switch contacts. A magnetic control uses a momentary contact switch (usually push buttons) at a reduced current and voltage to control heavy-duty, magnetically operated contacts, which in turn conduct power to the motor. The magnetic control is safer because the push buttons, even if they operate at full-line voltage, do not carry the heavy current of the main contacts. Magnetic switches also make remote control, as in a dust-collection system, safe and easy.

Either type of switch requires two or three heaters to provide burnout protection for the motor. These heaters are small lengths of wire or flat strips of metal that screw into receptacles in the starter. They are made so they will conduct their rated current and remain fairly cool, but any increase in current beyond the rated amount, as when a motor is overloaded, causes them to heat up very quickly. This heat trips a built-in circuit breaker. The size of these heaters is determined by the FLA rating of the motor. If the nameplate is missing, use the values in Table 1. If your motors don't have built-in overload protection, the money that protective switches cost is well spent. The control switch should be mounted so it is easy to reach, yet out of the way of cut-off pieces, heavy streams of chips and dust.

For the actual wiring, stick to copper; sizes can be obtained from Table 2. Aluminum wire requires considerable care and expertise for safe installation. While local code requirements vary, the general rule of thumb is that BX (metal-covered) cable or conduit is necessary only where the wire is liable to receive mechanical injury. For most shop wiring NMD-7 Romex cable is perfectly satisfactory (NMD-7 means non-metallic covering for dry location with temperature below 90°C.). Fasten Romex to the wall with staples designed for this purpose, but don't drive them so hard they pinch or cut into the insulation. BX cable and conduit must be attached to walls and floors with metal straps. Most wire connections are made with twist-on connectors. But when there are too many wires for these, use a junction box with a fully insulated bus bar mounted on the inside, or use a split bolt and wrap it securely with several layers of electrical tape. All of these supplies can be purchased from building and electrical supply stores, discount stores and wholesalers.

All your shop wiring should comply with NEC regulations and with local electrical codes. You can purchase a copy of the NEC from the National Fire Protection Assn., Batterymarch Park, Quincy, Mass. 02269. Ask for the latest version of NPFA No. 70-84. Obtain the CEC from Canadian Standards Assn., 178 Rexdale Blvd., Rexdale, Ont. M9W 1R3. I also recommend H. P. Richter's *Practical Electrical Wiring* (McGraw-Hill, 1978). —*M.C.*

Table 1: Approx. current draw (amps) for different motors

Single-phase 110 volts

Single-phase 220 volts

3-phase 220 volts

3-phase 110 volts

HP ¼ ⅓ ½ ¾ 1 2 3 4 5 6 7 8 9

Table 2: Wire size required to maintain 3% voltage drop for given length of copper wire

Motor current (full-load amperes)	Fuse (amps)						
3	15						
4	15						
5	15			14			
6	20						
7	25						
8	25						
9	30			12			
10	30						
12	40						
14	45			10			
16	50						
18	60						
20	60			8			
25	80						
30				6			
110 volts		30	45	60	75	90	105	120
220 volts		60	90	120	150	180	210	240

Length of run (ft.)

Once you know a motor's horsepower, these tables allow you to plan wire and fuse sizes. Suppose your biggest motor puts out 1½ HP at 220 volts, single phase, and your shop is 200 ft. from the main electrical panel. Table 1 tells you the motor will draw 10 amps under load. Table 2 tells you to protect the motor with a 30-amp fuse, and

to run at least No. 10 wire to carry the current from the main panel out to the shop. If the motor were 3-phase, you'd need only No. 12 wire, saving expensive copper. In reality, main-panel-to-shop runs must be figured by adding the current draw of all motors and lights that might be on at one time, and to be safe, be generous.

Comments on "Converting to 3-Phase Power"

Mac Campbell's article on 3-phase conversion (pages 25 to 27) contains some misconceptions that, while they won't prevent his converter from operating properly, should be corrected.... First is an apparent confusion between power, voltage and current.... The instantaneous 3-phase power is constant rather than sinusoidal like single-phase power. This is why 3-phase motors run smoother—there are *no* power surges. Second, the reason that single-phase power is sufficient to keep the conversion motor running is because its total load (electrical plus mechanical) is less than two-thirds of the motor's power rating....

—*Tony Armendariz, La Honda, Calif.*

...3-phase power is more economical for the industrial user as it comes from the power company but Campbell's system introduces inefficiencies that will make his overall system use more, not less, energy.

The smartest thing one can do with a 3-phase motor and only single-phase power is sell the 3-phase motor and use the money to buy a single-phase motor. Or, in a real bind, a 3-phase motor can be run single-phase up to about two-thirds of its rated capacity if started by some external means.... The solid-state converters available are expensive and have poor efficiency and usually poor starting torque. A motor-generating set—single-phase motor driving 3-phase generator—would give the best power and performance, but is also expensive and has efficiency losses. You just can't get something for nothing. —*Mike Graetz, Lakeland, Minn.*

...There are numerous types of single-phase motors; there are also a lot of types of 3-phase motors. These motors differ in many ways such as full-load efficiency, speed regulation, etc., and 3-phase motors don't necessarily have higher starting torque. For example, a single-phase repulsion-induction motor would start a much heavier load than a normal 3-phase motor. Furthermore, starting torque is quite pointless in woodworking machinery; I know of no examples where the machine must start under working load.... Rather than allow the converter to run with no mechanical load, Campbell might really be able to save some power by using it to drive some permanent load like the fan of his central dust-collection system.... He could get rid of the motor that drives his fan, eliminating one motor—and its losses, which now must be supplied by the converter....

—*E.W. Jones, Wilkes-Barre, Pa.*

...To illustrate the efficiency advantages of 3-phase motors over single-phase motors, the article used a chart of motor currents. The electrical to mechanical power conversion efficiency of a motor is a function of current, voltage and power factor, and it is not valid to compare currents alone and expect a meaningful result. For example, an average 1-HP, 110-volt single-phase motor draws as much as 16 amps at full load, versus 3.8 amps for a 1-HP, 230-volt 3-phase motor. In terms of power consumption, however, the single-phase motor will use about 1,040 watts versus 960 watts for the 3-phase motor. Thus the single-phase motor draws about 400% more current but only 8% more power. If the motors were on a small saw, run at full load for one hour per day, and electricity cost 5¢ per kilowatt hour, the single-phase motor would use about a dime more energy per month than the 3-phase motor. Even the dime would disappear if the user had to convert single-phase to 3-phase because of the energy consumed by the converting equipment....

—*T.J. Cotter, Mauldin, S.C.*

...When using a 3-phase motor as a converter as described, a second motor is not needed to start it. Simply place a motor-starting capacitor (about $10 in 1982 from electrical suppliers and sources such as W. W. Grainger, Woburn, Mass.) in series with a push button as shown in the diagram below. After turning the power on, pushing the button will cause one winding of the converter to act as a starting winding. A 3-phase motor can also be used directly on 220-volt single-phase in this manner, with an output of roughly two-thirds its rated output. Capacitor size ranges from about 150 μfd for a 1-HP motor to 650 μfd for a 5-HP motor.

—*Bruce Fortier, Essex, Mass.*

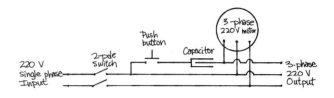

EDITOR'S NOTE: *Fine Woodworking* magazine received a dozen letters discussing conversion to 3-phase power, several of them from electrical engineers who took the time to explain the intricacies in exhaustive detail. The excerpts printed here are the points on which the engineers agree. To validate their advice, *Fine Woodworking*'s New England correspondent, Richard Starr, explored the question with Eric LaWhite of South Royalton, Vt. LaWhite is a mechanical-engineering consultant with well-equipped metal and woodworking shops; for 20 years he has run about half of his machines on 3-phase current supplied by a small idler motor. Starr's report:

"LaWhite's idler, a 3-HP, 3-phase motor, sits inconspicuously in a corner of his woodworking shop. To get it running he spins its shaft with the rubber sole of his shoe (up to about half its rated 1,200 RPM), then switches on its 220-volt single-phase power supply. The biggest 3-phase motor in the shop, which drives a pedestal belt sander with 5 HP, caused the idler to buzz slightly as it generated the third leg of the sander's starting current. His 3-phase-powered equipment includes the sander, a table saw, a wood lathe, several machinist's lathes, a surface grinder and a dust collector. All these tools can run simultaneously without overloading the idler.

"LaWhite explained that the function of an idler is to generate the third leg of 3-phase current. Any motor in the circuit can do it. If your idler seems to overload while starting or running a large motor, you can augment its capacity by running a second or third motor in the circuit—for example, run your idler and disc sander to start your table saw. In fact, as long as any two motors are running, they are both operating on 3-phase current. But take care using this method; there is risk in running power tools unattended. The advantage is that you don't need to waste current operating an over-sized idler. LaWhite suggests using a conversion motor whose horsepower rating equals the average shop motor. The diagram (page 29) shows the circuitry LaWhite recommends, with Fortier's capacitor starter included. Note that each leg of the 220-volt input requires its own circuit breaker, that the starter circuit for the idler motor should be enclosed in a metal box (capacitors can explode if something goes wrong), and that each additional motor should have its own starter switch with heaters for overload protection.

"Considering the conversion losses and the nuisance of setting up a second wiring system, why bother with 3-phase power? A major advantage to machinists, says LaWhite, is the instant reversibility of 3-phase motors. Single-phase equipment can be run backward by reversing the wires in the starting circuit, but the motor must first be stopped. When you switch a 3-phase motor into reverse at full speed, it is like hitting a brake. This is very handy on lathes and milling machines, and could be useful on woodworking tools. Reversing drum switches are about $15 at electrical supply houses (1982).

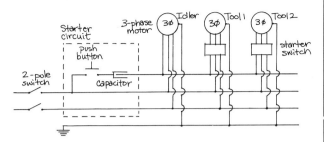

"New 3-phase motors sell for 10% to 30% less than the price of comparable single-phase motors, require less maintenance because they are simpler, and can be had in much larger sizes. They are slightly more efficient than single-phase motors.

"But for the small shop, the main advantage is in the purchase of used 3-phase equipment, and the advantage is twofold. First, the motors and the tools they power are built to industrial standards and are far more durable than 'home-craftsman' models. Second, since these tools are not in demand they can be had for bargain prices. LaWhite prowls the classified ads, used-tool shops and auctions.

"Consider these points when shopping for used 3-phase motors:
—Recent motors are usually more efficient than old ones; they have better magnetic properties. Ball bearings usually indicate a newer motor. Ball-bearing motors will run freely when spun by hand; they have grease fittings or permanent lubrication, while sleeve bearings have oil cups. When shopping for an idler, get a modern motor.
—For use as an idler, choose a lower RPM motor. It is easier to start, will run quieter and have fewer internal losses. There's no need to match speeds among motors and idlers. But whatever starting method you use, be sure that your motor is running at rated speed once started. Always start in the same direction; a reversed idler will run the other motors backward.
—You will seldom (if ever) find a 3-phase motor with a ground lead, so don't reject a motor if one is not present. Three-phase equipment is usually wired to metal conduit or BX cable, which provides grounding. If you wire with plastic-sheathed cable, be sure to ground the frame of each motor.
—Check the motor with an ohmmeter. Three-phase motors have either three or nine leads, and there's usually a wiring diagram on the housing or inside the cover of the wiring box. None of the leads should show a connection with the frame of the motor. A motor with a current leak is dangerous.
—Run the motor. It should sound right without excessive hum or grumble.

"Commercially built converters come in two types—static and rotary. The static variety generally consists of a box of capacitors tuned to a particular motor, which supply the starting current and then drop out of the circuit. It's designed for running a single motor under constant load. A rotary converter, which consists of a matched motor-generator set with capacitor start, is much more suitable for woodworking machinery. It works the same way as scavenged equipment, except it's designed for the job rather than cobbled together. One model, rated to handle a total of 9 HP and to start 3 HP under load, lists for $428 (1982). Both static and rotary converters are sold by Ronk Electrical Industries, 1208 E. State St., Nokomis, Ill. 62075; Arco Electric Corp., PO Box 278, Shelbyville, Ind. 46176; and Cedarberg Industries, 521 W. 90th St., Minneapolis, Minn. 55420.

"In most conversion setups, two legs of current are supplied directly from the power lines at full-line voltage. LaWhite found that his idler was supplying only 160 volts on the third leg. Motors run on unbalanced 3-phase start slower and lose efficiency. Most 3-phase motors can be wired to run on either 220-volt or 440-volt. By wiring the output leg of his idler to 440-volt, LaWhite found that it would supply close to line voltage. But he warns that this reduces its current-carrying capacity, increasing the likelihood of overloading.

"Finally, LaWhite advises craftsmen to keep in mind that electricity is deadly, and wiring of this sort should not be attempted by inexperienced persons. In many jurisdictions, local codes make it illegal to wire without a licensed electrician. In any case, it pays to have a competent electrician check your system before you use it."

Q & A

Understanding motor horsepower ratings—*It seems to me that the horsepower ratings on electric motors used to be straightforward. If you wanted a ¾-HP motor, that's what you bought. Now there's all this talk of "developed" horsepower, and I get the impression that when some manufacturers say they've got a motor with 2½ HP at full development, they really mean 1 HP straight on. Are we, as motor users and buyers, being lied to?* —Matt Olsson, Pekin, Ill.
MICHAEL REKOFF, JR., REPLIES: You aren't being lied to, but you aren't being told the entire truth, either. In the past, motors were given horsepower ratings based on their capacity to deliver that power on a continuous basis without burning up from excessive heat build-up. Induction motors, the type used for most woodworking equipment, will actually deliver as much as 3½ times their rated power. But at these peak power levels, the motor is unable to dissipate the internal heat generated and it will soon burn out—in as little as a minute or two in some cases—or it will blow its own internal circuit breaker.

Confusion arose when advertising hype got ahead of the laws of physics. Manufacturers of some tools began quoting the developed or peak power of the motors they used rather than the rated or continuous power. Their claims are, of course, not strictly false. The motors will develop the higher horsepower figures, but they won't last very long. It's easy to tell when inflated claims are being made by judging the size of the motor. If a 2-HP motor looks suspiciously small, read the fine print and see if the rating is quoted as developed horsepower. If so, the motor is capable of delivering less power continuously—say ¾ HP. Generally, the more power a motor has, the larger it must be. The larger size gives the motor sufficient surface area to quickly dissipate the heat it generates when delivering its rated power.

European electric current—*I'm a U.S. serviceman stationed in Belgium, where I can buy European woodworking machines at considerable savings. Unfortunately, they are designed to run on the 220-volt, 50-Hz current provided in Europe. I can rewire my shop at home for 220 volts, but it will be at 60 Hz. Will this be a problem? I don't want to spend my savings buying new motors and switches.* —Charles L. Carpenter, APO New York
MICHAEL REKOFF, JR., REPLIES: There's no reason to replace the motors and switches on European equipment that will be operated in the United States. In fact, a 50-Hz motor operated at 60 Hz will run cooler and more efficiently because its core has more iron than it really needs to run at the higher frequency. The European motors will turn 20% faster, but for most machines this should pose no problem. If it does, just change the pulley diameters to get the right speeds. I'd buy the pulleys in Europe, where metric sizes are readily available. As for the switches and fuses, they couldn't care less what frequency flows through them. Just make sure that the voltage and current ratings are right. One caution: Don't try to run a 60-Hz motor on 50-Hz current. The motor won't have enough core iron, and will likely overheat and burn up.

Substitute compressor—*If you can't afford a compressor and spray gun but want to spray lacquer finishes, buy the best electric (airless) sprayer you can find. It will work almost as well as the air-compressor, and it has several advantages: It's portable, produces fewer fumes, comes with a number of accessories, and isn't attached to a cumbersome tank. Mine is a Wagner No. 300, and I use a #6 nozzle for spraying lacquer.* —Michel Chevanelle, Acton Vale, Quebec

Precision
Tips from the die-making trade

by Fred J. Johnson

As a package designer, I am fortunate to be associated with some extremely skilled woodworkers—the steel-rule die makers who make the cutting dies used to produce folding cartons out of boxboard. Many of these cartons, beverage carriers for instance, require incredibly complex cutting dies made to tolerances usually associated with metal work. The dies are made from ¾-in. thick hardwood-plywood blocks, which separate the steel cutting and scoring rules. Solid birch is used for the really tiny pieces of wood. I have discovered that it pays to watch others at work. Each craft and each woodworker has distinctive methods of getting the job done. Having learned from die makers a number of ways to be safer and more accurate in my own woodworking, I would like to share some of them here.

Proving a table saw

It is so easy to be a good craftsman when all of your sawn pieces are perfectly rectangular—every edge an exact 90°. Achieving this state sometimes seems difficult, but here is an easy way to check your saw to see if it is cutting squarely.

Take a piece of scrap with parallel edges and crosscut with the board flat on the saw table. Turn one of the pieces over and put the sawn edges back together. Align one side against a straightedge and examine the cut. Any error will be doubled. When you have set the miter gauge or sliding table so that only a line shows, the saw will be cutting truly square.

To see whether the blade is set at 90° to the table, crosscut with the scrap on edge. Crank the sawblade to its maximum height and make a cut, then check as before.

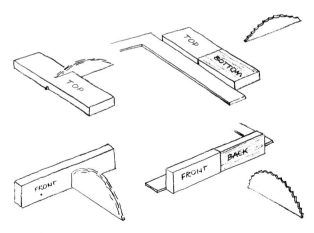

Proving a jointer

To prove that the jointer fence is set exactly at 90° to the table, joint two pieces of scrap and mark the machined edges. Stack them with jointed edges together and check their faces with a straightedge. Then turn the top piece around, keeping the same edges together, and recheck the faces. If they are not flat, then what you see is twice the error.

When edge-gluing stock, it is not imperative to have the jointer set at 90°. Anything close will do—providing the boards have relatively straight grain. Mark their faces and run alternate faces against the fence. They will edge-join flat; the error cancels.

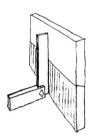

Adjusting band saws and jigsaws

Here is a simple way to ensure that the blades of band saws and jigsaws are cutting at a true 90° to the table. Set the top blade guides at the height that you are going to cut. Then take a scrap of wood an inch or so wide and cut across the width to its center. Turn it around and make another cut up to the first, stopping about ⅟₃₂ in. short of cutting through. Turn the block over and examine the two kerfs. Any offset will be double the error—adjust the table and try again. It pays to recheck after changing the height of the blade guides.

Accurate measurement

To measure really accurately you need a good ruler and a draftsman's pricker, or else one made from a dowel and needle. I use an 18-in. Starrett adjustable square blade in satin chrome. Stand the ruler on edge and slide the pricker down the ruler's engraved grooves at the desired dimension, being careful to hold the pricker perpendicular to the face of the ruler. Using this technique, you can accurately space lines one hundredth of an inch apart, if your ruler is so graduated.

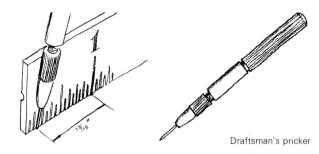

Draftsman's pricker

Illustrations: Fred J. Johnson

Cutting to precise dimensions

Here is a technique for sawing wood to precise dimensions, invaluable when reproducing a previously sawn piece. Place the piece to be reproduced against the rip fence of the table saw. Leave enough space between it and the blade for a safe cut. Hold some scrap wood against the piece and run the scrap through the saw. Then replace the piece with the scrap. Now the distance between the blade and the scrap is the same as the piece to be reproduced.

Steel-rule die makers use this technique to saw blocks of plywood to precise dimensions. They keep precut and marked blocks and strips, usually made of Micarta, aluminum or precision-ground steel. If they want to cut a block to $3^{13}/_{16}$ in. wide, they will stack pieces measuring 3 in. and ¾ in. and also a ¹⁄₁₆-in. steel strip against the rip fence and then cut the scrap block. This technique also saves setup time.

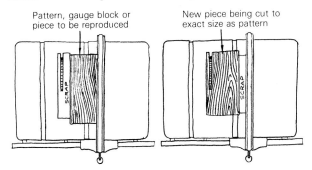

Pattern, gauge block or piece to be reproduced

New piece being cut to exact size as pattern

Precision crosscutting

The mark of precision crosscutting on a table saw is perfect edges that are smooth and straight all the way around. Some blades (carbide and dado blades are the worst offenders) chip splinters off the trailing edge of the cut. To prevent this, always place a solid backup behind and under the workpiece. Stand a piece of straight scrap on edge and screw it to the miter gauge so that it extends beyond the sawblade, for good support. The saw kerf in the scrap is also a precise way to align your cutoff mark because it represents exactly where the saw is cutting, even if there is a slight wobble to the blade.

The same principle holds true for the saw slot in the table. For super-precise cutting where you cannot tolerate any splintering, the sawblade should fit the slot exactly. Make a wooden table insert and hold it firmly in place with a stick. Then crank the blade through the insert to the depth of your cut. Now the edges of the work will be supported right at the tabletop—especially important in dado work.

The same techniques apply to other tools. Shaper cutters, even if sharp, often tear giant splinters off the end grain. If you can't leave enough scrap on the work to trim later, glue a piece of scrap to the edge and trim it off afterwards.

Step-and-repeat

Step-and-repeat is what die makers call the process of accurately spacing holes or cuts. It is ideal for doweling. The basic setup consists of spacing blocks cut equal to the desired spacing, and stop blocks that define the end spaces. The work is held against a stop block and is then drilled or cut. The work is moved away from the stop block, and spacers are put between stop block and work, one at a time.

Fred Johnson, of Long Beach, Calif., is filling his house with his reproductions of 18th-century antiques.

This technique has three advantages: It will space as accurately as you make your spacing blocks, you can make any number of pieces exactly the same, and you can make mating parts with exactly the same spacing. Be careful not to get sawdust between the blocks or inaccurate spacing will result.

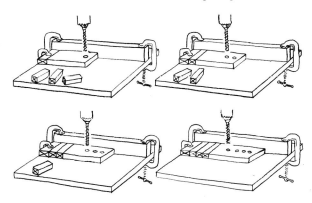

Ice-pick technology

One of the more difficult things to do on a table saw is to cut small pieces of wood precisely and safely, especially when using the rip fence. The die makers solve this problem with ice picks. They hold the workpiece securely in the jig or fixture, or firmly against the rip fence, with the point of an ice pick. They use the pick to guide it carefully past the blade.

On rare occasions an accident chews the end off an ice pick and sends a blade or cutterhead to the sharpening shop. But consider the alternatives. Ice picks are made of excellent steel that can withstand the pressure needed to control the workpiece. Square-handled picks are best because they don't roll.

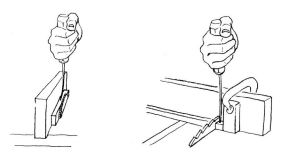

Miter gauges

The play of the miter-gauge bar in its slot can be annoying as well as contribute to inaccuracy by causing wide, long planks to jerk through the blade. To cure this, remove the bar from the protractor part. Put it on an anvil or stout piece of steel, and peen the top edges slightly with a hammer. Go lightly over both top edges, being careful not to hit it at much of an angle. Check the fit and peen until it fits the way you want it to. If you overshoot, file the fat parts. To set a miter gauge, mark the required angle on the underside of the board to be cut. This can often be scribed directly from the work. Set the miter gauge against the same edge that will be used when cutting. Now swing the bar to align exactly with the scribed line and lock it. It is now set perfectly. ☐

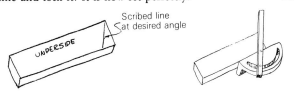

Scribed line at desired angle

UNDERSIDE

Circular Saws
How to keep them sharp and running true

by Eugene Roth

Circular saws must be kept sharp. When a saw does not cut easily, it is usually dull or has lost its swage or set. Forcing the feed in these conditions will heat the rim of the saw, and the metal may expand and crack. The saw may also lose its tension and bend or break over the collar. A saw that wobbles and does not cut straight is dangerous to use and should be sent out for professional repair.

With practice and careful attention to detail, however, a woodworker can learn to sharpen and maintain circular saws in tip-top shape. The set and rake of the teeth can be adjusted to suit the type of work. The basic tools for sharpening are a good saw vise, which can be homemade, a setting stake and hammers, the correct files (mill bastard, round, cant, square mill and triangular tapered) and grinding wheels. The 60° triangular file is familiar to most craftsmen, but the cant saw file is not. It is also triangular in cross section, but with a 120° angle and two angles of 30°. It is used for sharpening saws with a very steep gullet angle, and for filing the face bevel of dado and combination blades. The square saw file is also used on dado and combination blades.

Circular saws are usually described by the type of cut they are designed to make, as crosscut, cutoff, rip, miter, dado, combination or planer. But to prevent binding in the wood, all circular saws are widest at the very rim. This clearance is obtained in one of three ways: setting, swaging or hollow grinding. Most common rip and crosscut saws are set, which means the tips of the teeth are alternately and uniformly bent to the right and left. Cutoff and ripsaws designed for use in green lumber are usually swaged, which means the point of each tooth is spread by hammering with a small anvil. Combination and planer saws are usually hollow-ground, which means the tips of the teeth are as thick as the hub of the saw, and the metal in between is ground thinner to provide clearance. When a new blade is purchased, it is wise to trace around it, or make a carbon-paper rubbing, to serve as a pattern later on.

There are four operations in sharpening all flat circular saws: jointing, gumming, setting or swaging, and filing sharp. To know when the saw is getting dull, watch the corners of the swage or set. They may seem sharp to the touch, but close examination will reveal a slight roundness, which will make the saw feed hard and not cut properly. Although the set seems full, the saw will bind just back of its points. The saw must be jointed below the rounded corners, and each tooth brought back to a nice, keen point.

A common error is allowing a saw blade to accumulate gum and pitch on the sides, which may cause it to run hot and snake. The best way to remove the gum is to soak the saw for a while in a strong warm solution of Oakite in water, and then rub it clean in a small box of sawdust. The gum will come right off, and the Oakite solution can be kept in a covered jar and used over and over. Never scrape off gum with a sharp tool because this will mar the finish and make the blade more susceptible to buildup.

Jointing

The first operation in sharpening by hand is jointing, to make all the cutting teeth the same height. If every tooth does not do the same amount of cutting, the unequal strain on the high teeth may cause cracks. If several teeth are unusually high, they may break off upon encountering a hard knot.

Professional saw-jointing equipment includes a powered grindstone mounted with a fixed center on which the blade can pivot. Lacking such a machine, the craftsman can joint

The saw-filing bench. Equipment shown here includes flat, triangular, cant and square files, swage (among files), setting hammer and anvil-and-stake (right). Conical stake accepts blades for various sizes of arbor, adjusts up and down, and moves along slot to position teeth over anvil.

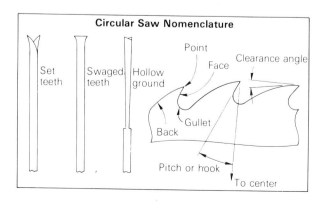

Circular Saw Nomenclature

Set teeth
Swaged teeth
Hollow ground
Point
Face
Clearance angle
Back
Gullet
Pitch or hook
To center

Eugene Roth has retired as foreman at Huther Bros. in Rochester, N.Y., once a leading manufacturer of circular saws and carbide-tipped blades. Huther still makes and repairs special-order saws as a minor sideline; its main business is grinding knives for industry. The hands in the photos are those of Eric Michaud, before his retirement the only craftsman left in Huther's once-bustling filing room.

right on the table saw by using a flat vitrified medium jointer stone or a piece of broken emery wheel. The blade is reversed on the arbor and revolved at full speed, and the stone is lightly but firmly pressed against the points of the teeth. Lower the blade below the surface of the table, press the stone over the slot in the table, and slowly raise the blade. Raise it enough to grind a small shiny flat at the top of each tooth.

Gumming

Repeated filing is bound to make the teeth shallow, and grinding the gullets deeper is known as gumming, although a saw does not need to be gummed every time it is sharpened. A blade is gummed on a bench grinder with a grade 1-6 VL emery wheel, with its edge dressed round, or use an 8-in. or 10-in. round second-cut file. To keep the saw in balance, all the teeth should be gummed to the same depth. It is easy to make a simple wooden compass with a dowel center to fit the saw's arbor hole, as shown in the drawing on the next page. Use a colored pencil to mark a circle the proper distance below the points; the distance can be gauged from the tracing made when the saw was new. Then grind until the bottom of every gullet just touches the edge of the circle. Generally, gullet depth is two-fifths of the distance between the points of the teeth.

When gumming, go around the saw several times so as not to crowd the wheel by taking too deep a cut. Taking out too much metal at one time will heat the gullets and stretch the rim, and the saw will then need expert hammering on an anvil to restore its original tension. Crowding the wheel will also blue and burn the gullets, and often glaze the metal so hard that a file will not touch it. From these hard spots small cracks begin, at first invisible but gradually enlarging until they become dangerous fractures.

After gumming, the saw should be lightly jointed before continuing with the sharpening, to make sure it's still round.

Setting

A uniform, even set is most essential for an easy-running, smooth-cutting saw. An uneven set places a greater strain on some teeth and may crack them. Too much set not only puts an unneccessary strain on the rim of the saw, which can result in cracked gullets or broken teeth, but also causes it to chatter or vibrate, resulting in a rough cut. Vibration heats the rim and gullet cracks appear. If the teeth are set more to one side than to the other, the saw will lead to the side with the heavier set and may break.

There are two ways of setting teeth: with an anvil and stake, or with a saw set. The anvil and stake consists of an adjustable, conical center post that slides on iron ways to allow the edge of the blade to rest precisely over the beveled edge of a small anvil. Different anvils may be used, depending on the size of tooth and amount of set required. A special setting hammer, which has a small, flat face, is used to bend alternate teeth over the anvil. Then the blade is turned over and the process repeated.

A saw set bends the teeth by leverage rather than by pounding. It consists of a series of slots for different lengths and thicknesses of teeth, and is mounted on a handle with an adjustable gauge for regulating the amount of set. When placing the set on the tooth, permit it to drop until the point of the tooth touches the bottom of the slot, then bend the tooth over until the gauge touches the side of the saw.

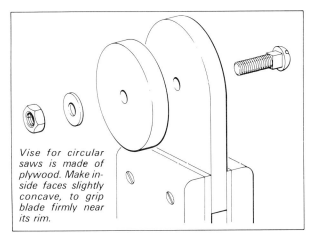

Vise for circular saws is made of plywood. Make inside faces slightly concave, to grip blade firmly near its rim.

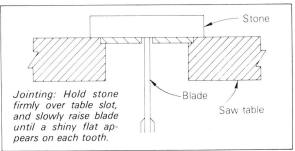

Jointing: Hold stone firmly over table slot, and slowly raise blade until a shiny flat appears on each tooth.

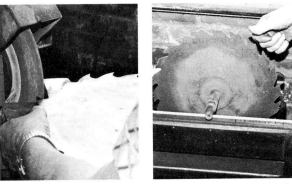

Thin, round-edge grinding wheel (left) is used to gum a saw blade. Balance is checked, right, by mounting blade on dummy arbor and rolling along parallel knife edges.

With anvil and stake, one sharp tap per tooth sets the saw.

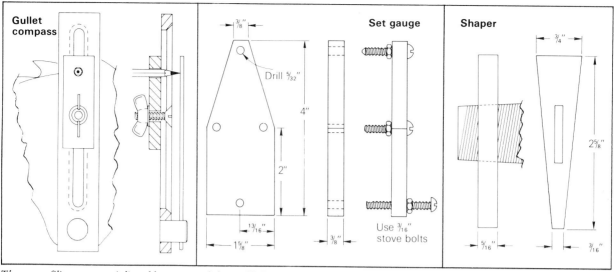

Three saw-filing gauges. Adjustable compass, left, establishes uniform gullet depth for gumming. Set gauge, center, checks the set of each tooth. The top screw is first filed sharp, then the point is flattened to about 3/64-in. dia. Adjust the bottom screw to the desired set. Right, a shaper holds the file at the correct angle for regulating the set of swaged teeth. Its long side slides on the face of the blade.

Swage, top, is placed on each tooth of ripsaw and tapped sharply to spread point. In close-up, left tooth has been spread with convex die, right tooth has then been squared with straight die.

Filing a crosscut saw: Both hands push the file in long, rhythmic strokes powered from the shoulder to ensure uniform teeth.

Since only the points of the teeth do the cutting, the set should not extend more than one-fourth of the distance down the tooth. If the set extends too far down the tooth, the blade will vibrate and cut roughly. The amount of set, as measured from the plane of the blade, varies according to the type of wood and the smoothness of cut desired. A fine set does fine work; dry hardwood requires less set than green hardwood, and softwood requires more set than hardwood. The amount of the set is always less than the thickness of the blade, and usually less than half the thickness. For dry hardwood, the set is usually .012 in. to .015 in.; for green hardwood, .015 in. to .018 in. Electric hand saws, because of the rough work they have to do, require a heavy set—around .02 in. or even more.

After determining which set works best for a particular type of cut, it is well to make a simple side gauge, as shown in the diagram, to check the set of each tooth.

Swaging

Swaging is spreading the point of every tooth. A swaged saw will cut more wood than a set saw because every tooth is cutting on both sides, and it will take a faster feed and more power. On the other hand, the cut is rough. Ripsaws for green lumber and production saws are generally swaged. Any type of saw may be swaged, although if the blade is too thin the swaged corners will be needle-pointed and fragile. If it is too thick so much pressure will be needed to spread the metal that it may crack.

Before swaging, joint, gum and file all teeth sharp, using an 8-in. or 10-in. mill bastard with two rounded edges. Swages, which are hand-held anvils with two dies set in the face, are sized according to the thickness of the saw blade. One of the dies is convex, one is flat. Use the convex die first and keep a drop of oil on it. Set the swage atop the point of the tooth and strike several light, quick blows with a small setting hammer. Keep the swage straight, so the die centers on the tooth. Then use the straight die to square up the cutting edge and give body to the swaged point.

Lightly file the sides of the teeth with a shaper, to even up the swage. A shaper can easily be made from a scrap of hard-

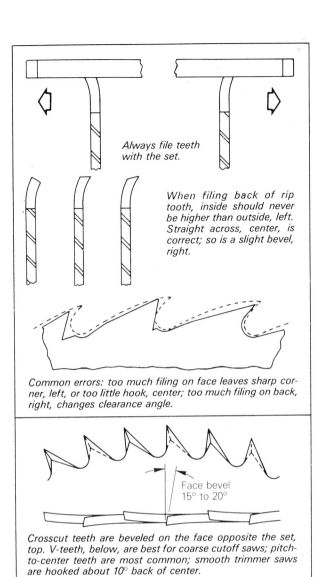

Always file teeth with the set.

When filing back of rip tooth, inside should never be higher than outside, left. Straight across, center, is correct; so is a slight bevel, right.

Common errors: too much filing on face leaves sharp corner, left, or too little hook, center; too much filing on back, right, changes clearance angle.

Face bevel 15° to 20°

Crosscut teeth are beveled on the face opposite the set, top. V-teeth, below, are best for coarse cutoff saws; pitch-to-center teeth are most common; smooth trimmer saws are hooked about 10° back of center.

V-teeth

Pitch to center

Pitch back of center

10°

60°

Raker

1/64"

30° back of center

10° back of center

20°

90°

Combination blade, cross section of cut

wood, as in the drawing. Its long side slides on the face of the blade, to guide the file at the proper angle. Use the set gauge to keep the swage uniform. Then file straight across the underside of the tooth and across the top, very lightly, with an 8-in. or 10-in. mill bastard. Be careful to maintain the original angle of the tooth and avoid dubbing off the swaged corners, as this will reduce side clearance and cause the saw to bind and burn in the cut. Finally, use a round 8-in. or 10-in. second-cut file to clean out the gullets.

Filing ripsaws

For a rip saw to cut fast and easily, the teeth should be hooked so that a line along the face passes halfway between the center of the saw and the rim (about 30° and known as 1/3 hook). When filing a ripsaw with set teeth, use an 8-in. or 10-in. mill bastard file, and maintain the original hook, shape and angle by taking the same amount off the back and front of the tooth. Usually the backs are filed straight across, though some prefer a slight bevel (about 5°). Too much bevel produces a lateral motion that causes the teeth to chatter and vibrate in the cut. When filing the backs, file every other tooth on one side all around the saw, with the set; then reverse the saw in the vise and file the other teeth, with the set. This is the only way to file the backs uniformly, either straight or with a slight bevel. The inside edges should never be higher than the outside ones.

Keep the gullets round with an 8-in. or 10-in. round second-cut file. Cracks are most often caused by sharp corners in the gullets.

Filing crosscut saws

Joint, gum and set the saw. For coarse-tooth cutoff saws use an 8-in. or 10-in. mill bastard with two rounded edges; for saws with a pitch of 5/16 in. to 3/8 in. use an 8-in. cant saw file; for pitch 1/4 in. or finer use the cant saw file or a slim triangular file. The flat file used on large saws can sharpen only one face of a tooth at a time, but the cant saw file and triangular files catch the face of one tooth and the back of the next on each stroke. A face bevel in the 15° to 20° range is usually recommended for hardwoods. A somewhat longer bevel is sometimes used in softwoods, and a slightly shorter bevel in very hard woods. Must cutoff saws are made with pitch-to-center teeth and some are pitched slightly back of center, while others have V-shaped teeth. Try to keep the gullets round.

Planer saws

Planer saws are hollow-ground, and are designed for precise, smooth cuts both with and across the grain. Their teeth are in groups of three to six crosscut-type cutting spurs, followed by a deep gullet and a rip-type raker tooth. The raker is sharpened flat across the back, 1/64 in. lower than the cutting spurs. The spurs sever the wood fibers on each side of the kerf, then the raker comes along and cleans out the core of the cut. Flat-ground novelty and combination saws cut in essentially the same way, and it is particularly important with all saws of this type to make an accurate template when the saw is new, as a guide for sharpening.

To file a planer saw, you should have a special raker gauge to keep the rakers a uniform 1/64 in. lower than the spurs. Without such a gauge, joint the blade on the circular saw, then take the rakers down by filing the same number of strokes square across the back of each. Then file the spurs

All the spurs in a group on a dado blade, left, are alike. In blade blank above, right gullet is typical, left is correct.

with a 20° face bevel, maintaining the original hook (usually 10°), using the 8-in. cant saw file or the square mill file.

A block of hardwood can be used as a gauge to keep the raker teeth uniform. After jointing, leave the blade on the saw arbor and adjust the height until it can be locked by jamming a piece of plywood into a gullet and clamping the plywood to the saw table. The top raker should be very close to parallel to the table surface—adjust the height until it is parallel. Now make a block a fat sixty-fourth lower than the back of the raker, and rest the mill file on it to shape the tooth. Moving the plywood stop to the next gullet should index the next tooth, and so on around the blade.

Dado heads

First, joint the entire dado head, including all the inside cutters. File the spurs on the outside saws with a 10-in. square mill file, keeping the original bevels and stopping when the teeth just come to a sharp point. Then file the rakers and inside cutters across the top until the flat left by jointing is just gone, and finally take the same number of strokes on each raker and inside cutter. As with planer saws, the rakers and inside cutters should finish about 1/64 in. lower than the spurs, but the precise amount is not nearly so important as uniformity—use the whole length of the file on each stroke, and follow through from the shoulder. Do not touch the face of these teeth except to remove the burr left when the tops are filed.

Saw manufacturers and repair shops commonly joint all the spurs just enough to remove the dull points, then set the stop on their machine 1/64 in. deeper. They joint all the rakers and inside cutters just enough to remove those joint marks. After repeated sharpenings, it becomes necessary to gum the saw and reset the spur sections.

The spur sections of most dado heads manufactured for the home craftsman are ground straight across, with no face bevel. They will cut much better if all the spurs in a group between a pair of rakers are beveled about 20° one way, and all the spurs in the next group are beveled the same amount on the other side. Use the square file at a steep angle (about 30°) to the face of the blade, and be careful to keep all the teeth the same length. □

Sources of supply

Saw-filing tools are usually sold by large hardware stores and industrial hardware suppliers. For mail order, consult the catalogs of Woodcraft Supply Corp., 313 Montvale Ave., Woburn, Mass. 01801, and Silvo Hardware, 2205 Richmond St., Philadelphia, Pa. 19125. Brands to look for include Nicholson (files), Disston (setting tools) and Simonds (all saw tools).

Q & A

Sawblade speeds—*I have a Rockwell 10-in. tablesaw that is rated to operate at 5,500 RPM. Rockwell recommends using blades rated at 6,000 RPM. I've had trouble finding blades rated this high; in fact, most manufacturers don't advertise the RPM rating of their blades. What happens if I use a blade rated at 4,500 RPM on my saw?*
—*Mike Conner, Juneau, Alaska*

TOM MILLER REPLIES: You are wise to consider the RPM of your machine when purchasing blades. Most blades don't have a blade body that can run at 6,000 RPM (which is also 100 revolutions per second) without experiencing metal fatigue and deformation, and they also tend to deviate or flutter at that speed. A faulty blade could even fly apart.

All blades are tensioned to run at a given RPM, and they will likely wobble or run out if they're run at a substantially different speed. Only the better-quality blades are hand-tensioned in the first place, so finding one will probably involve paying a bit extra. My firm, Winchester, hand-tensions its sawblades to run as fast as 6,500 RPM.

As a general rule, 10,000 SFM (surface feet per minute) is the desirable speed at which to run a sawblade. SFM is a measure of the distance a saw tooth will travel in a straight line in one minute. In special applications, a different speed can be used. Most people, however, shoot for 10,000 SFM for general usage, and the chart gives these figures. In the general shop, all blades

Recommended sawblade speeds *(10,000 SFM)*	
Blade diameter	RPM
6 in.	6,622
8 in.	4,830
10 in.	3,831
12 in.	3,184
14 in.	2,732
16 in.	2,398
18 in.	2,123

should run at the speed recommended in the chart, but a coarse-tooth ripping blade can run 10% to 15% slower.

Radial-saw front fence—I used a table saw for years, then shifted to the radial saw. I am more comfortable with the radial saw, mainly because the saw is always in plain sight.

Twenty-five years ago I installed a hardwood fence (see sketch) across the front of the table. It can be quickly raised to any height and clamped by nuts on two bolts that project from the front edge of the table through two vertical slots. Keeping your thumbs on the outside of the fence holds your hands away from the saw, so you can saw very narrow stock without your fingers slipping toward the blade.
—*Allen L. Cobb, Rochester, N.Y.*

Rip fence for radial-arm saw

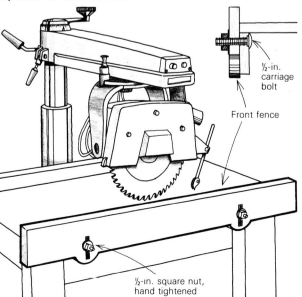

½-in. carriage bolt

Front fence

½-in. square nut, hand tightened

Using the Tablesaw
Some basic rules for safe, accurate results

by Ian J. Kirby

Ripping is the tablesaw's forte, but it's a versatile machine, used for dimensioning wood as well as for cutting joints. The tablesaw is so simple and universal that it is frequently used without the operator's ever having taken the time to learn its common-sense fundamentals. In most small shops the tablesaw usually has improper guards and an inadequate rip fence. In the interest of keeping fingers attached to hands, a review of tablesaw basics may be of value.

The ordinary tablesaw is nothing more than a steel table with a circular blade projecting through its surface. The blade projection is adjustable for cutting wood of varying thicknesses. The blade can be fixed perpendicular to the table, or it can be tilted for cutting wood at an angle.

For safety's sake, tablesaws need a blade guard, though even the best guard can't keep fingers out of the blade. A guard should serve as a visual reference to the blade's location, warning the sawyer of the danger zone—any point within 9 in. of the blade. The best guard is mounted on an arm suspended above the blade. The guard should not be attached to the riving knife or splitter, and it should be adjustable, set as close as possible over the stock being sawn. There are several variations of this mounting method and any guard is better than no guard.

The machine's electrical power switch should be easy to reach, mounted on the saw cabinet just under the table or on a nearby wall or post. When switching on, place one finger on the start button and a second on the stop button. This allows for a quick shutoff if something goes wrong. A foot-activated switch allows the sawyer to control the wood with both hands while operating the switch. Many saws have mechanical or electrical brakes that stop the blade quickly when the switch is turned off. In the absence of a brake, use two push sticks— one rubbing each side of the blade—to stop its coasting. When changing rip-fence settings never stick a tape or rule between a moving blade and the fence. Wait until the blade has completely stopped. The saw depth of cut should be set so the blade protrudes about ½ in. out of the workpiece. Carbide-tipped blades should be adjusted so the entire tooth projects above the wood during the cut. A 10-in. saw should be operated at 3,000 to 3,500 RPM at the arbor, or at a speed that runs the blade's periphery at 10,000 feet per minute.

Noise can be a major barrier to safe machine operation. The racket muddles thought and can force the operator to adopt timid and unsafe working practices. So ear protection—as well as goggles—should always be worn when using the saw. To concentrate without the distraction, the novice woodworker can develop safe habits by practicing moving wood past the blade with the machine switched off.

Ian J. Kirby directs Kirby Studios, a school of woodworking and furniture design, in Cumming, Ga. Drawings by the author.

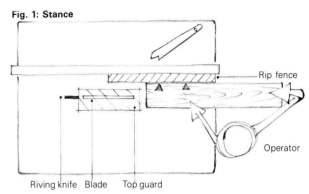

Fig. 1: Stance

Rip fence

Operator

Riving knife Blade Top guard

Stand to one side of the blade when ripping. Hold the work against the fence with the left hand, feed with the right.

Fig. 2: Guard, knife and fence

Guard can be adjusted to suit stock thickness.

Fence ends at center of blade.

Riving knife should be just below top of blade arc.

Proper stance is also important to safe tablesaw operation. When ripping or crosscutting, the operator should stand with his weight equally distributed on both feet. Stand to one side of the sawblade to stay out of harm's way and to have a better view of the cut. Figure 1 shows a good position—during ripping, kickbacks can be hurled from the saw like spears and you could be skewered.

Because the tablesaw is at its best when used for ripping, the rip fence is its most vital attachment. The fence should be mounted parallel to the blade. Whether it's used on the right or left side of the blade is the preference of the operator. Virtually all of the tablesaws sold in the United States have rip fences extending the full length of the saw table. This fence forces the wood to remain in contact with the back of the blade during the rip, thus inviting binding, burning and kickbacks, particularly when cutting refractory wood. The fence should end at the front of the blade, just where the cut is completed. This allows both pieces to move clear of the blade for safer, cleaner results. The quickest fix for tablesaws equipped with a full length fence is to fit them with a board ending at the center of the blade, as in figure 2. Actually, it's good practice to mount a board on the steel fence of any machine. This will prevent damage if the blade accidentally touches the fence.

To keep the kerf from closing up and pinching the blade during ripping, tablesaws should have a riving knife or splitter mounted in line with and just beyond the back of the blade. The knife is a fin-shaped piece of steel, tapered in sec-

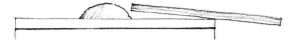

Feed the stock angled to the rear or flat against the table, above.

Never start the cut with the front of the board elevated, below.

Fig. 4: Push stick

90°
12 in. to 15 in.

Make push stick of solid wood or plywood, ⅜ in. to ½ in. thick.

Fig. 5: Crosscutting

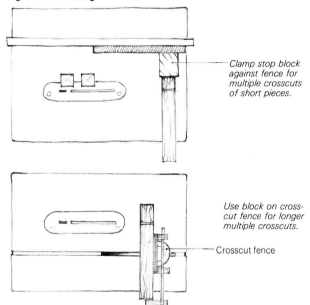

Clamp stop block against fence for multiple crosscuts of short pieces.

Use block on crosscut fence for longer multiple crosscuts.

Crosscut fence

Fig. 6: Miters

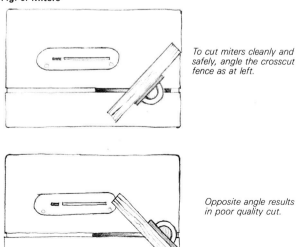

To cut miters cleanly and safely, angle the crosscut fence as at left.

Opposite angle results in poor quality cut.

tion and as thick at its back edge as the kerf is wide. It should be permanently mounted at a height just below the top of the blade's arc, as in figure 2. The knife should maintain this relationship to the blade for every cutting depth. Some saws, particularly the cheaper variety, have no riving knife at all, but the payback in safety and improved cutting makes it worth the effort to install one.

When ripping, the wood should be offered to the blade very gently at first, especially when using carbide-tipped sawblades, whose teeth are brittle and can break under heavy impacts. Feed the board into the saw flat against the sawtable or angled as in figure 3. Never touch the board to the blade with its front end tilted above the table, or the blade will grab the stock and slam it to the table. Make sure a push stick is handy before starting any cut; keep one on the sawtable on the opposite side of the fence. Figure 4 shows a simple push stick design. Keep plenty of sticks around—their absence is no excuse for a missing finger. With the cut started, hold the wood against the fence with your left hand (if the fence is to the right of the blade), while feeding the stock into the blade with your right hand. As the rip progresses, make sure you hold the board firmly against the fence. Keep your eye on the contact point between board and fence—some wood may tend to run away from the fence during the cut. Feed into the saw at an even rate. If fed too slowly, the blade will burn in the kerf, while too quick a feed will stall the saw. Never move your left hand beyond the leading edge of the blade. This is unsafe and merely pushes the waste to the blade, not the stock to the fence. As the cut nears its end, remove your left hand from the wood and use a push stick to complete the rip.

If the saw stalls during a rip, withdraw the wood quickly, or turn off the saw immediately—a good reason to have a foot-operated switch. It isn't advisable to rip warped or twisted boards, but when you must, crosscut the stock into the shortest lengths possible, and then rip with the concave side of the board up, so the wood is level with the table as it meets the blade. Rip a cupped board as close to its center as possible and exert even pressure, to minimize rocking during the cut. Long boards or large panels should be cut with the help of a second person, or use a table or roller on the saw's off-feed side for support. The sawyer's helper should clearly understand that his job is only to support the stock (keeping it level with the table and parallel to the blade) as it comes off the saw and not to pull it through—he could pull the sawyer's hands into the blade. When the cut is complete, the takeoff man then takes control of both pieces.

Wood is crosscut on the tablesaw with the miter gauge or crosscut fence. This angle-adjustable attachment usually runs in grooves milled in the table surface parallel to the blade. The fence must slide smoothly in the grooves. A board about 12 in. in length can be attached to the crosscut fence to offer more support to the stock. Crosscut fences are sometimes equipped with clamps to stop the work from slewing as it is fed through the blade.

Crosscutting should be done from the same stance as ripping. To test 90° crosscuts, cut a test piece and check it with a square rather than attempting to square the blade directly to the crosscut fence. With the crosscut fence set, hold the stock firmly against it while advancing the wood evenly into the blade. Only practice will reveal the best way to grip the stock against the fence. When the cut is complete, move the crosscut fence beyond the back edge of the blade or back to the starting point. To avoid binding the stock against the blade, slide the wood slightly away from the blade as the crosscut fence is returned. Small stock may have to be clamped to the crosscut fence to be crosscut safely. To crosscut many parts to the same length, clamp a stopping block to the rip fence ahead of the blade as in figure 5, or attach a stop block to the crosscut fence. Never bring the rip fence over to stop the length of a crosscut, as the cut piece is liable to lodge between the fence and the blade, and bind or kick back.

For 45° miters make a test cut to set the crosscut fence accurately. Grip the stock firmly and feed it into the saw as shown in figure 6, the blade shearing with the grain. Because of the fibrous nature of wood, mitering it from the opposite direction results in a cut of lesser quality. □

Choosing a blade

Which blade for which cut? That's the first problem the woodworker faces when using the tablesaw. You want to rip and crosscut, leaving smooth, tear-out-free edges on solid wood or plywood. No blade does everything well. Many types of blades are available but you need only a few to start out.

There are two categories of readily available sawblades: those made of carbon steel alloyed with nickel and chrome and those of steel with tungsten-carbide tips brazed on to form the teeth. New steel blades are inexpensive, and although they dull quickly, you can resharpen them yourself. For information on sharpening, see pages 32 through 36. Carbide blades cost more and cut smoother, but you must send them out for sharpening. You have to weigh cost against use—carbide blades are preferred for repeated high-quality cuts.

Alloy steel blades—There are three basic types of steel blade: rip, crosscut and combination. These blades can have spring-set or hollow-ground teeth. Teeth on most steel blades are ground in the same way—with the tops of the teeth alternately beveled, and the fronts left flat or beveled. Set—the alternate and uniform bending of teeth to the right and left—creates clearance for the blade during cutting. This keeps the blade cool and prevents binding and burning. For ripping heavy wood to rough dimensions use a hefty alloy steel rip blade (figure 1) with a lot of set and 20 to 40 teeth. The thicker the wood, the fewer the teeth. This blade will produce a quick but fairly rough cut with little binding or burning. Rough crosscutting can be done with a steel crosscut blade with 40 to 60 teeth (figure 2), but a combination blade (figure 3) will do the job just as well. Combination blades, designed to rip and crosscut, are a good value for the money. They have four alternating front-beveled teeth followed by a flat or raker tooth with a deep gullet to clear sawdust quickly and prevent overheating. Properly sharpened and set, a combination blade will work well for most general purpose work.

The hollow-ground combination blade (figure 4) tends to be a smoother cutting blade than the spring-set. This blade has about the same number of teeth as the combination, but its teeth have no set. The body of the blade below the gullets is ground thinner than the teeth so the saw won't bind. Tolerances for a hollow-ground blade are small—it must be accurately cut and sharpened to work well, otherwise it will bind and burn.

Tungsten-carbide blades—Plywood, particleboard and solid wood impose different loads on a sawblade. Carbide blades are better for plywood and particleboard. For a given type of blade, sharp carbide almost always produces a smoother cut than sharp steel, and because it is harder, carbide stays sharper longer than steel does. Carbide blades don't have set, and usually the tops rather than the fronts of the teeth are ground. A good general purpose carbide combination blade for solid wood and man-made boards (figure 5) should have between 40 and 60 teeth ground in a series of four alternately top-beveled teeth, followed by a flat or raker tooth. If you can afford only one carbide blade, this is the type to buy.

For ripping only, a 24-tooth carbide blade with flat-ground teeth (figure 6) is excellent. If you need to cut plastic sheets or laminates, choose a 50 to 70-tooth carbide blade that has alternating triple-beveled teeth with a raker tooth in between (figure 7). Properly sharpened and maintained, all carbide blades leave a smooth, almost finished surface. For more information on saws and blades, see "Carbide-Tipped Circular Saws," pages 40 to 43. —*I.J.K.*

Alloy steel blades

Fig. 1: Rip blade

Teeth are set.

20 to 40 teeth

File teeth faces perpendicular to blade.

Fig. 2: Crosscut blade

40 to 60 teeth

File teeth faces with alternating bevels.

Fig. 3: Combination blade

40 to 60 teeth

Raker tooth, with deep gullet, clears chips.

Fig. 4: Hollow-ground combination

Blade body below teeth is ground thinner (here exaggerated). Teeth have no set.

Carbide-tipped blades

Fig. 5: Carbide combination

40 to 60 teeth

Four alternating top-beveled teeth are preceded by flat-ground, raker tooth.

Fig. 6: Carbide rip

24 flat or raker teeth

Fig. 7: Carbide triple-chip

50 to 70 teeth

Triple-chip tooth alternates with raker tooth.

Carbide-Tipped Circular Saws

Alloy's hardness is its weakness

by Simon Watts

Most woodworkers now own a carbide-tipped sawblade or have at least considered getting one. The advantages are many. The teeth are accurately aligned so they make a cleaner and more precise cut, producing a good gluing surface directly from the saw; the tooth form stays practically the same after each sharpening; carbide-tipped blades can cut teak and other abrasive materials, and they last about 40 times as long between sharpenings as steel-toothed blades.

The main disadvantage of carbide-tipped blades is the cost. Not only is the initial cost substantial—$75 to $125 for a 10-in. blade—but also since you cannot file them yourself you have to send them out for sharpening, which now averages 25¢ a tooth, about $15 for a 60-tooth blade. A good sawblade can be ground more than 30 times before it has to be retipped, so you can expect to spend $450 on sharpening over the life of the blade—three or four times your original investment. Because saw manufacturing is a highly competitive business, a substantially lower price inevitably means inferior materials and poorer workmanship. The cheaper blade will need more frequent sharpenings, which soon will swallow up the original savings. (All prices are 1980 estimates.)

Woodworkers use their saws for cutting a wide variety of materials and for a number of different operations. Few of us can afford a different saw for each use and so we usually buy combination blades, which may do everything claimed for them, or may not. Carbide-tipped saws come in a bewildering variety of tooth shapes and configurations. How does one choose the right blade for ripping and crosscutting? For hardwood and softwood? Is price the only indication of quality? Is a retipped blade as good as new? What about cutting veneers, plywood, particle board and plastic laminates? Can the same blade be used on a radial arm saw and a table saw? What are the differences between a high-quality blade and an inferior one, and how can one tell?

Before getting into these and related questions, let's take a look at carbide itself and at how a modern carbide-tipped circular saw is manufactured. The alloy tungsten carbide, to give it its full name, can be made only by a process known as sintering, in which powdered tungsten and carbon are mixed together and heated under tremendous pressure. The carbon atoms penetrate the crystal lattices of the metal, creating one of the hardest synthetic materials known. This new alloy retains the granular structure of the original metal powder but the individual grains now have a hardness that is second only to diamond.

It is important to remember that tungsten carbide, although immensely hard, is also extremely brittle. It can be chipped easily by vibration or rough handling and can be used for cutting only when backed by another metal having the tensile strength it lacks. It cannot be drawn to thin edges with very acute angles, cannot be ground thin, and must not be left overhanging and unsupported. It must not be vibrated against a grinding wheel because the particles of carbide will be torn out.

The body of the saw (shown below in figure 1) is made from heat-treated alloy steel, which can be harder and tougher than an ordinary all-steel saw because the teeth don't require filing or setting. Slots are cut in the plate to allow its rim to expand without buckling. To reduce the danger of cracking, the slots end in round holes, which sometimes cause an annoying whistle. This whistling can usually be stopped by plugging the holes with a soft metal such as copper. Pockets are cut into the teeth of the saw, and the little grey blocks of carbide are brazed into them. The carbide tips are then

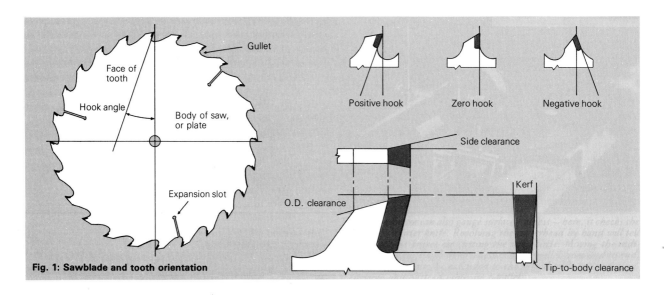

Fig. 1: Sawblade and tooth orientation

Gullet

Face of tooth

Hook angle

Body of saw, or plate

Expansion slot

Positive hook

Zero hook

Negative hook

Side clearance

O.D. clearance

Kerf

Tip-to-body clearance

ground on a diamond abrasive wheel to the required shape and bevel.

All circular saws are subject to centrifugal forces, which tend to make the blade fly apart. These destructive forces are directly proportional to the radius but increase as the square of the speed in rotation. These rotational loads cause the saw to expand unevenly across its diameter, giving it a tendency to buckle. If uncorrected, these forces can prevent the saw from running true, cause noise and vibration, and can even crack the saw body.

To minimize these effects, all good-quality circular saws more than 6 in. or 8 in. in diameter are put through a manufacturing process known as tensioning. This consists of hammering the bodies to an extent determined by their thickness, diameter and operating speed. The work, done with curved hammers on a crowned anvil, puts the middle in compression to compensate for tension of the rim at high speed. Machining done on finished saws (enlarging bores, drilling mounting holes, etc.) will upset the tension and should not be attempted by anyone unfamiliar with this technique. Warped saws can be made flat by hammering, but it is highly skilled work and likewise should be left to the experts.

The thinner the saw body, the more crucial tensioning becomes. Very thick saws have little or no tension added by hammering. Large saws, 20 in. or more, are usually tensioned three times at different stages in their manufacture. Three common types of saw bodies are shown in figure 2. The straight body is the cheapest and most widely used. The other two styles have one or both sides ground away to reduce the width of the saw kerf and are mainly used for cutting thin, non-ferrous tubing and plastics.

The most common tooth form is the flat top (figure 3) also called plain tooth, rip tooth or chisel tooth. The advantages of this tooth form are that since each tooth cuts the full width of the kerf, it has twice as many effective teeth as a staggered-tooth saw. Also, the cutting forces are balanced on the body, the tooth form is easier to maintain, square bottom cuts are ensured and each tooth carries an equally distributed load. The disadvantages are that the chip drags the sides of the cut, reducing the freedom of the chip flow. Chisel teeth can be damaged more easily by side thrust or twisting of the work than can staggered teeth, and the square corners are dulled when cutting abrasive materials. Tooth drag can increase power consumption significantly. Chisel-tooth blades are good for ripping, but when used for crosscutting, they leave a ragged end-grain surface.

All other basic tooth forms (except scoring saws) need more than one tooth to complete the cut. The alternate top bevel (figure 4), known also as a crosscut tooth or simply A.T.B., has the tops of adjacent teeth ground at alternating angles. It makes a very smooth crosscut, particularly across stringy fibers. Its disadvantage is that the leading-point edge is fragile and wears relatively quickly. Also it cannot make a square bottom cut. Crosscut-tooth blades can be used for ripping but easily become overloaded if the work is fed too fast.

To prolong the life of the blade between sharpenings by reducing wear, a rougher tooth, or lead tooth, is introduced. Its function is simply to open a path for the following raker teeth, which take only a finishing cut on the sides of the kerf. Rougher teeth have one or both corners ground at 45°. The raker teeth are usually square, as in figure 5, but they may have the alternate top bevel as in figure 6. Note that the

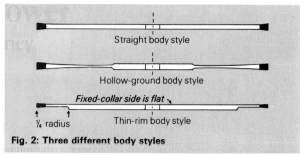

Fig. 2: Three different body styles

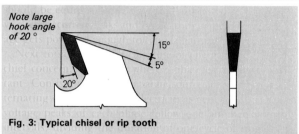

Fig. 3: Typical chisel or rip tooth

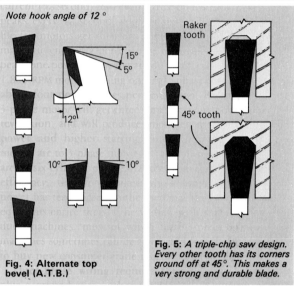

Fig. 4: Alternate top bevel (A.T.B.)

Fig. 5: A triple-chip saw design. Every other tooth has its corners ground off at 45°. This makes a very strong and durable blade.

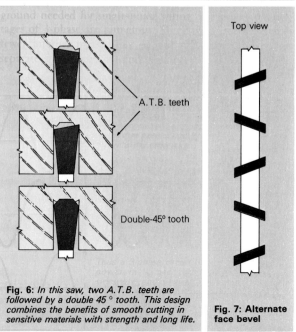

Fig. 6: In this saw, two A.T.B. teeth are followed by a double 45° tooth. This design combines the benefits of smooth cutting in sensitive materials with strength and long life.

Fig. 7: Alternate face bevel

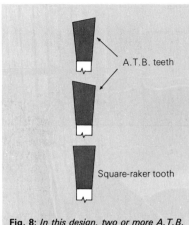

Fig. 8: *In this design, two or more A.T.B. teeth are followed by a square raker.*

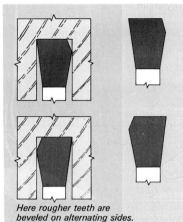

Here rougher teeth are beveled on alternating sides.

Fig. 9: Alternating corner tooth form

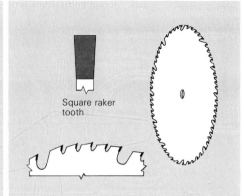

Fig. 10: *Typical combination blade designed for both ripping and crosscutting. Four A.T.B. teeth are followed by square raker.*

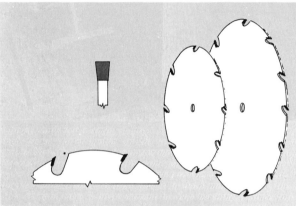

Fig. 11: Limited-feed combination blade

Distance between teeth determines maximum rate of feed.

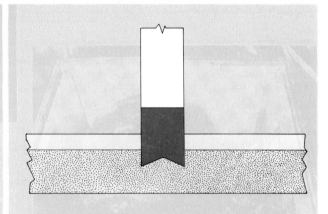

Fig. 12: *A scoring saw is used for cutting thin veneers. Usually its depth of cut is very shallow.*

rougher tooth makes a slightly deeper cut, in order to protect the tips of the rakers.

For abrasive, brittle materials like particle board, the faces of the teeth are slanted alternately right and left (figure 7, previous page), a configuration that reduces chipping out. This arrangement is achieved by placing the teeth in the plate at the required angle or by grinding them.

There are many other possible tooth configurations. For example, every second or third tooth in an A.T.B. can be followed by a square raker (figure 8), or the rougher tooth itself can be beveled first on one side and then the other, as in figure 9.

Figure 10 shows a typical combination blade. It has four alternating beveled teeth followed by a square raker and is designed for both ripping and crosscutting.

Another general-purpose saw is shown in figure 11. It is designed to limit the feed to a predetermined chip load and can be used in portable electric saws, table saws and radial arm saws when smoothness of cut is unimportant.

Most carbide blades can be used on both radial arm saws and table saws. However, as the hook angle increases (figure 1, page 40), so does the danger of a radial arm saw grabbing the work (self-feeding). Positive hook angles of 13° to 15° are usual, although some blades designed for swing-and-pivot saws may have a negative hook. Heavy-duty ripsaws go to the other extreme with a 25° positive hook.

Figure 12 shows a scoring saw, which is designed to cut cleanly through fragile veneers. It usually cuts only about 1/16 in. deep.

Chip loads — For a particular tooth configuration, there are four factors that govern the performance of a circular saw: speed of rotation, number of teeth, rate of feed, and chip load. Chip load is nothing more than the thickness of the chip removed by a sawtooth. There is a simple relationship between these four variables which can be expressed by the following equation:

$$\text{Chip load (in./tooth)} = \frac{\text{feed rate (in./min.)}}{\text{RPM} \times \text{no. of teeth}}$$

As one would expect, halving the rate of feed or doubling the number of teeth reduces the chip load by half, and it is easy to see that a smooth cut requires a low chip load—either a slow rate of feed, lots of teeth, or both. What is not so obvious is that increasing the chip load increases the life of the blade. This is because the greatest wear on the tooth occurs when the cutting edge strikes the work at high velocity. Therefore, the larger the chip load per tooth, the fewer times each tooth has to separate a chip from the material, and the fewer impacts the tooth withstands in cutting a given length of material. Maximum attainable chip loads are affected by the condition of the machine, the thickness of the blade relative to its diameter and the nature and thickness of the material that is being cut. Accurate alignment of the sawblade with the path of feed makes a considerable difference in the performance of the blade.

Choosing a blade — Once you have decided on the tooth configuration you want, how do you select a good blade? Much of the work that goes into making a high-quality carbide blade is invisible (tensioning, for example), and it is difficult to make an intelligent choice between competing brands. In general, the price, the terms of the warranty and the manufacturer's reputation are the best indicators, but here are some other things to look for: A good blade should be flat. When placed on a true arbor, the total indicator runout of the blade body should not exceed 0.005 in. for a 10-in. blade, and outside-diameter runout should not exceed 0.002 in. With a hand lens, check the quality of grind on the sawteeth. If the carbide looks smooth and shiny, it's good, but if it has deep and irregular grind lines, the teeth will dull rapidly. The teeth should be notched in and neatly brazed to the body of the saw (figure 13). There should be at least ⅛ in. of carbide on each tooth of a 50-tooth saw.

Sharpening — Carbide blades are sharpened on special machines using diamond grinding wheels, and only about 0.005 in. of carbide should be removed each time. This requires skill, and blade life can be considerably shortened by careless or improper grinding. Saws sometimes come back from being sharpened with the tips missing carbide particles on one side because the tip was not properly supported and the pressure between the wheel and the sawtooth produced vibration. Another common way of losing carbide particles is to use coarse-grit wheels for finish-grinding. It may cost less, but the results are expensive. The peaks and valleys left by these wheels leave unsupported particles that can easily be knocked off during the cut, rapidly dulling the saw.

Broken and damaged teeth can be replaced and ground to the exact size and shape of the others. If properly cared for, a good blade can be sharpened 30 to 40 times before it needs to be retipped.

Retipping — When there is not enough carbide left to grind, the remains of the teeth are removed with a torch. The notches are ground out, new teeth are brazed on and then ground to the same shape as the original ones. Next, the body of the saw is checked for flatness and, if necessary, straightened by hammering. The result should be a blade equal in quality to the original one. There will not be a great savings in money, but you will have the satisfaction of making a small stand against our throw-away economy.

Care of blades — Ruining a carbide blade is much easier than you think, and I have been guilty of most, if not all, of the following abuses. Saws are most frequently (and most seriously) damaged by overheating. This is usually caused by continuing to use a blade that is dull but can also happen by trying to feed stock too fast. Saws warped by overheating have to be straightened by hammering and sometimes retensioned as well. When the teeth are very dull they have to have more carbide ground off to make them sharp, and this shortens the life of the blade. Like steel saws, carbide blades gum up when cutting resinous woods. The best way to clean them is by soaking them overnight in kerosene or paint remover.

Faulty alignment is another major source of trouble. To get

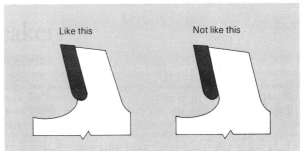

Fig. 13: *Carbide tips should be brazed into pockets in the saw body, not stuck on the leading edge of a gullet.*

a clean, accurate cut, the sawblade must not only run true (no wobble) but also be parallel to the direction of feed, which means parallel to the miter-gauge slots in the saw table. Getting proper alignment (if you don't have it already) usually requires loosening the trunnions and moving the arbor assembly slightly.

Once the sawblade is trued up with the line of feed, you should align the rip fence with the blade, and on this there are two schools of thought. One argues that the blade and fence should be exactly parallel. The other maintains that the fence should be canted slightly away from the line of feed (about 1/32 in. or less) on the outfeed side of the table. This ensures that only those teeth on their downward cutting arc contact the workpiece. Too much of a cant will result in a "heel-and-toe" condition, make feeding difficult and possibly cause the blade to overheat and distort.

To see whether the saw is running true, clamp a machinist's dial indicator to the saw table. Mark a spot near the perimeter of the blade and rotate it slowly through 360°. If you cannot get a dial indicator, clamp a piece of smooth steel almost up to the blade and check the distance between it and the blade with feeler gauges as you rotate the blade. If the indicated runout exceeds 0.005 in., find out the reason. First take the saw off the arbor and make sure the saw collars are clean and not worn. Try the blade on another machine. If the trouble is in the blade and it is not flat, do not take a ball-peen hammer to it, but send it out for correction. Never try to put shims between the saw collars and the blade. This can distort the blade and damage it permanently.

Other factors that will affect a saw's performance, if not its health, are throat plates (table inserts) that are not close enough to the saw or not level with the table, vibration from loose arbors or bearings, tables not flat, and mismatched or loose *V*-belts. Never try to slow down a saw by pressing something against its side. This can generate enough heat to distort the body. Don't drill holes in a blade or enlarge existing holes. This will upset the tension. Keep it on a wooden peg or rack all by itself when not in use. When shipping make sure, if there is a bolt through the arbor hole, that it is not putting pressure on the body. Finally, never lay a carbide saw (or any other edge tool) down on a hard surface like a cast-iron saw table. Remember, the teeth are made of grains of tungsten carbide bonded together—super hard but vulnerable to mistreatment. □

Simon Watts, of Putney, Vt., is a cabinetmaker and a writer. This article was prepared with the help of Steven A. Segal of North American Products in Atlanta, Ga.

Mitering on the Table Saw

Scribe reference lines for accurate alignment

by Henry T. Kramer

Recommendations for cutting good miter joints rarely include using the table saw, although we commonly use this machine to crosscut 90° angles. While it is cheerfully conceded that the Lion Trimmer and other shearing cutters are best for many miter cuts when their fences are properly adjusted, these are expensive single-purpose tools and can't perform many of the operations a table saw can, such as blind or shoulder cuts, or dadoes at 45°. Because the only difference between setting up the table saw for miter cuts and for 90° crosscuts is a change in the angle on the miter gauge, logic tells us that there ought to be a way of setting the gauge to produce a true 45° cut.

The trouble usually lies in the degree markings, positive stops and pointer on the miter gauge, which are usually too far off to be of any use. Given the dynamics of angular measurement, they would still be hard to set accurately even if their calibrations were precise and true. Some manage by trial and error, and while trial is the ultimate check, there is a better way to get set. The answer is to establish a long reference line on the saw table at an accurate 45° to the gauge slots, and with the aid of a long fence and a 3-ft. straightedge, to use the line to set the miter gauge. The principle is straightforward: the longer the radii forming the angle, the less chance for error. In the case of an angle of five minutes of arc, radii 24 in. long define a chord of about ⅟₃₂ in., as shown in the sketch below. Now five minutes of arc is the finest reading on the best vernier bevel protractor available, so if you can work within a lineal error of ⅟₃₂ in., you can establish a very accurate reference line.

Before describing how to establish reference lines, I need to point out possible sources for error when crosscutting with a table saw and how I would correct them. First, the blade must run parallel to the miter-gauge slots; if it doesn't, loosen the trunnion bolts and carefully reposition the arbor assembly to true up the sawblade. Heel and toe (a condition when the blade is not parallel to the line of cut) can cause binding, which will burn the wood and produce a bad cut. Second, most miter-gauge guide bars don't fit snugly in their slots, and this play introduces error. You can fix this by holding the gauge firmly against the side of the groove nearest the blade when setting up and cutting, or you can eliminate the play by peening the guide bar or soldering a shim to it.

Third, since most miter gauges have short work-contacting surfaces, you should attach a longer fence to the gauge. You can make one from a carefully jointed strip of wood. In fact, it's a good idea to have on hand several of them of different heights and lengths for different jobs. The long fence provides for more accurate alignment and gives support directly behind the cut, which prevents thin or narrow stock from bowing and binding. A fourth possible source for inaccurate mitering is the tendency of the workpiece to creep into the blade, causing binding, burning and an uneven cut. You can remedy this by gluing a sandpaper strip to the wooden fence of the gauge and holding the workpiece tightly against it during the cut; or you can clamp the work to your auxiliary fence.

Having done away with these probable causes of error, you are ready to scribe three layout lines on your saw table (extension wings excluded) so you can accurately set your miter

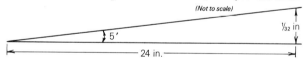

(Not to scale)

5'   ⅟₃₂ in

24 in.

Fig. 1: Layout of alignment marks

A   E   D   -¦- = Punch marks

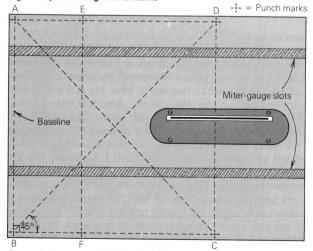

Miter-gauge slots

Baseline

45°

B   F   C

Four points at corners (A,B,C,D) define square and diagonals. The two additional points about 7 in. up from baseline (E,F) are used to align gauge for 90° crosscuts.

Fig. 2: Aligning the miter gauge   ← Straightedge

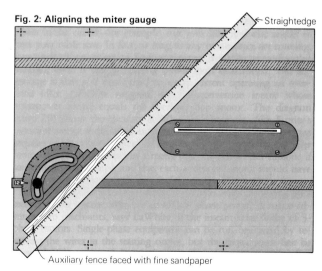

Auxiliary fence faced with fine sandpaper

Even a cheap table saw, at 20 in. by 27 in., can become an accurate mitering tool using this technique.

gauge at 90° and 45°. To begin, you'll need a 36-in. straight-edge, an accurate framing square and a strip of wood sized to fit snugly into the miter-gauge slots and to sit proud of the saw table. Because the most reliable way to produce a 45° angle is by drawing a diagonal in a square, you should establish a square on the table. You don't need to scratch these lines into the table; locating the corners of the square with punch marks is sufficient.

The most difficult part of the square to construct is the base, running along the front of the table. The baseline must be perpendicular to the miter-gauge slots (if the slots are not parallel, get a new saw). Use as much of the table for this square as you conveniently can; its sides should be roughly ½ in. from the edges of the table, but don't use the edges for reference, only the miter-gauge grooves. Place the strip of wood in the right-hand groove and hold one leg of the square against it. Lay the straightedge against the other leg of the square, and draw the baseline using a very sharp pencil. Better yet, scribe this line with a machinist's scriber and layout dye. If you want to make a permanent line, use a machinist's scratch awl. Put the strip in the left-hand groove, flip the square, position the straightedge and complete the line so it runs the whole width of the table. Now you have a baseline that is exactly 90° to the miter-gauge grooves.

To establish the top line at the far end of the table, use the straightedge for a rough initial measurement of the height of the sides (precisely the length of the baseline). Then with a pair of dividers set to the exact distance from one groove (the one with the strip in it) to the end of the baseline, transfer this distance up to the top line, just above the expected height of the side. Now measure the length of the baseline carefully with trammels or by scribing the unmarked back of a 36-in. steel rule. With this and your dividers, locate one of the upper corners. Repeat this process to find the other corner, and the square is laid out. Now check all your measurements, beginning with the diagonals, which must be exactly the same length. When everything is right, locate each corner with a punch mark. If you haven't used a centerpunch much, practice first on some spare or scrap cast iron. The punch has to be held upright and hit dead on with a dead blow. A deliberate "rap-whap" will do it. When you're satisfied that you can strike the punch properly, punch-mark the four corners.

To align the miter gauge for 90° crosscutting, you'll need to mark out another line parallel to the baseline and about 7 in. up from the front edge of the table. Punch-mark the points where this line intersects the two vertical sides of the square. To get the most accurate setting you must hold a straightedge against the face of your miter gauge to set it for both 45° and 90° cuts. This straightedge must, of course, be long enough to be lined up on both punch marks at once. Keep in mind that the longer the auxiliary fence on your miter gauge, the more precise the alignment you'll get.

The approach of using long reference lines laid out on the surface of the table lends itself to other geometric constructions for other desired angle cuts. But if you scribe additional reference lines, you'll have to label them to avoid confusion. The key to this system is the length of the lines; the longer they are, the more accurate the results they'll give. In angular measurement, put not your trust in protractors. ☐

Henry T. Kramer, of Somerville, N.J., is a retired reinsurance specialist and amateur woodworker.

Aluminum Miter Jig
by Pope Lawrence

Here is a sliding miter jig for the table saw. Made from aluminum plate, with aluminum guide bars and a standard miter-gauge protractor head, it can be used to cut accurate miters, as well as 90° crosscuts. It is especially useful for mitering wide, thick stock and is adjustable so that other angles may be cut quickly, accurately and repeatedly. To make the base of the jig, get a piece of ¼-in. aluminum plate from a salvage yard or metal supply house and cut it about 18 in. long and 14 in. wide. The size will vary from saw to saw. An ordinary carbide-tipped blade in your table saw will do if you use prudence and care.

Using aluminum instead of plywood for the jig gives it greater rigidity, durability and accuracy, and makes a stable base for other table-saw jigs. Aluminum drills easily and cuts well enough with a carbide-tipped blade, but you must be cautious as it sometimes grabs the tool, especially a drill bit, as it penetrates the stock. Clamp the pieces down when drilling and wear safety glasses when cutting. You can also band-saw aluminum plate with an ordinary woodcutting blade.

Rip two strips from the plate for the guide bars and file their sawn edges for a snug but sliding fit in the miter-gauge slots. File a little chamfer on their two outer edges. Affixing the guide bars to the plate requires careful measuring and marking. Use ¼ x 20 flat-head machine screws, and tap the plate to receive them. Bore and counterbore the bottom of the guide bars so the holes are slightly oversized. This will allow you to make minor lateral adjustments to get the exact spacing between the bars. With the base complete, attach the protractor head and screw to it an auxiliary wooden fence, which you can equip with one or more toggle clamps (available from De-Sta-Co Division, Dover Corp., 346 Midland Ave., Detroit, Mich. 48203) to hold the workpiece against the base during the cut. Also you can clamp a stop block to the auxiliary fence for repetitive cuts of the same length.

When you've finished assembling the jig, mount a carbide-tipped blade on your saw arbor, set the jig in the slots and saw a kerf in the aluminum base plate so that it runs a short distance past the fence on the miter gauge when it's set for an acute 45° cut. This completes the jig and it's ready for use. ☐

Pope Lawrence is a cabinetmaker in Santa Fe, N. Mex.

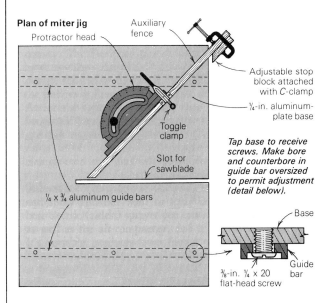

Plan of miter jig
Protractor head
Auxiliary fence
Adjustable stop block attached with C-clamp
¼-in. aluminum-plate base
Toggle clamp
Slot for sawblade
¼ x ¾ aluminum guide bars

Tap base to receive screws. Make bore and counterbore in guide bar oversized to permit adjustment (detail below).

Base
Guide bar
⅜-in. ¼ x 20 flat-head screw

Tuning Up Your Lathe

Mass and rigidity make clean cutting easier

by Del Stubbs

Most lathes I've seen, in both amateur and professional shops, do not function as they could. Yet improving them is simply a matter of understanding and putting into effect the basic principles of lathe operation. The idea is to have no play anywhere, not in the mounting of the stock on the faceplate or between centers, not in the bearings or the shaft, not in the tool-rest base or the tool rest. Then the lathe needs to be mounted on a base so solid that the vibration of an out-of-balance piece or the jarring of an improperly used tool is immediately damped.

A common misconception is that the less serious you are about turning, the less of a lathe you require. The reverse is true. The beginner has enough problems, without a poorly built lathe adding to the burden. A skilled turner can cope with a sloppy lathe and get by, though there's no question vibration slows down the rate at which he can work and makes clean cutting more difficult. Vibration in a beginner's lathe can drive him to quitting. It should be pointed out, though, that in small-diameter turnings the stock has so little mass and leverage against the tool that a very solid lathe is not so necessary. Faceplate turning and large spindle work are the real test of a lathe.

Though the base is perhaps the most neglected part, it is the first priority in tuning up your lathe. For a test, grip the headstock and see if you can move it. It shouldn't budge. If yours is a sheet-metal base, so common on smaller, less expensive lathes, it will probably have to be braced or replaced. Price, though, is no sure determinant of a lathe's quality; I've seen $2,000 lathes whose mass was not proportioned effectively. One quick, inexpensive and removable way to keep the lathe fixed to the floor and to damp vibration is to use sand. Contain it in boxes or gunny sacks as close to the headstock as possible. Take care that grit doesn't get loose and into the bearings of the motor or lathe; wrap the sand first in a plastic trash bag.

For my lathe I bolted together some old 6x12s into a base that is so massive (it weighs about 500 lb., which I consider a minimum) it must be disassembled to be moved. Timbers damp vibration (without sending it back, as steel may). But putting timbers together rigidly, as they must be, involves a disadvantage: If the base is not sure-footed (if one corner is slightly higher), the whole lathe can rock, causing vibration. The solution here is to wedge and shim carefully until each corner carries the same weight. I also use felt pads to separate the wood from the concrete floor—these stop the lathe's tendency to walk around the shop while an unbalanced piece is turning.

What about bolting the lathe to the floor? If the floor is wood, the whole building may shake as well as the lathe. If the floor is concrete, well, as an old millwright told me, "If you bolt a rigid lathe to a solid floor and turn a heavily unbalanced piece, it could tear up your lathe—something's got to

give." The alternative is not a lathe that walks around, but a base that absorbs vibration and deadens it. That's what's ideal about sand: Bang a steel bar and it resonates, punch a bag of sand and it's dead. Wood and cast iron have similar advantages. An old cast-iron lathe has so much mass that it will not resonate like a light steel one. If you build out of wood, triangulating the structure will help achieve rigidity. Set the legs out at an angle and cross-brace them.

One addition that's rare on lathes is a foot-operated clutch; I consider one important. A clutch allows you to start the motor under no load, which saves the motor and electricity, and makes for quicker starts and stops. A clutch is also a safety feature. Out-of-balance pieces can be started slowly—if a corner hits the tool rest, it just stops, and you have the chance to see if the lathe will shake. A clutch also is a foot release, if ever your hands can't get to the switch.

The most important advantage for me in having a clutch is that by slipping it I can modulate speed readily while cutting—mostly to slow down to help stop chatter in difficult or delicate cuts. I often use speeds about 200 RPM to 300 RPM in getting that final clean-up cut in some faceplate and spindle work, the foot on the clutch constantly adjusting the speed as the cut changes. I also experiment with slower speeds, especially if I'm having trouble with a particular cut. If the tool isn't cutting right when the stock is turning slowly, it won't cut any better at high speed. Adding a handwheel to the outboard end of the lathe and turning the stock by hand so the tool cuts at about the speed of a pocketknife through a piece of whittling wood is one way to see if you're getting the shear cut you want. With a clutch you can move the stock almost this slowly, and still have both hands on the cutting tool.

Probably the simplest clutch is to have some way of lifting the motor and thus lessening the tension on the belt. This method uses only the weight of the motor on a hinged motor mount to provide belt tension. A pulleyed cord, moved by a hinged foot pedal, raises the motor mount and releases tension. There should be enough travel for the belt to slip, but not so much for the belt to come out of the pulley grooves. I include a small turnbuckle in the cord that raises the motor to allow fine adjustment of the clutch. With one foot under the plywood pedal and the other pressing it down, I adjust the clutch to release just as the pedal touches my foot.

Belt quality is important. An unevenly manufactured or worn belt creates vibration. For smooth, positive power I've found a notched *V*-belt best. In some cases, though, these will grab even when tension is relaxed; a solid, stiffer belt should then be used. Old-style flat belts slip best and an adjustable idler pulley can be used as a clutch with these, or with any belt if the motor is too heavy or inconvenient to lift. If in heavy-duty cutting you find a belt slipping, use a cam to lock the motor down or add weight to the motor mount. If

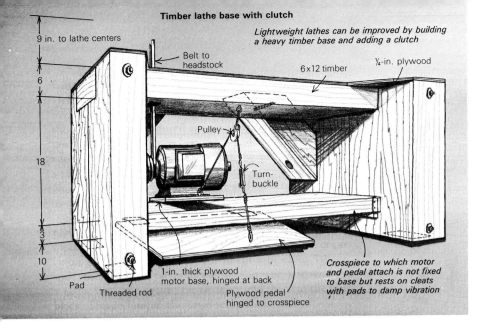

Timber lathe base with clutch

Lightweight lathes can be improved by building a heavy timber base and adding a clutch

9 in. to lathe centers

Belt to headstock

6x12 timber

¼-in. plywood

6

18

Pulley

Turn-buckle

3

10

Pad

Threaded rod

1-in. thick plywood motor base, hinged at back

Plywood pedal hinged to crosspiece

Crosspiece to which motor and pedal attach is not fixed to base but rests on cleats with pads to damp vibration

possible mount the motor separately from the lathe, to reduce transferred vibration. If not, include a damping pad between the motor and the lathe.

Testing for play in your shaft and bearings can be a lesson in sensitivity. Have the shop completely quiet. Take the belt off the pulley, and grip the shaft. Try to rock it from side to side and in and out. Listen and feel very carefully for any knocking. End play is as much a problem as side play in faceplate work. All end play and some side play are eliminated in spindle work by the pressure of the tailstock. You felt a knock—now what? If it's end play, the problem might be solved by tightening an allen screw, moving a collar, adding a shim or tightening an outboard faceplate. Side play probably means shot ball bearings, worn sleeves or Babbitt bearings, or a loose fit between shaft and bearing or between bearing and headstock. If it's a ball-bearing lathe, turn the shaft (belt disconnected) and feel for any catch or roughness. Also give it a spin and, with your ear pressed to the headstock, listen for rumble. If you sense either of these, plan on getting new bearings. In lathes with external grease fittings, play can be temporarily reduced by filling the gaps with a shot of grease; don't overdo it.

If you have to replace the bearings, try first to get an assembly drawing of your headstock from a tool supplier or from the manufacturer. Also take care not to apply pressure or impact to any part of a bearing except the inner sleeve (see "Basic Machine Maintenance" on pages 14 through 17). I pound on my bearings with a piece of hardwood drilled out to just fit over the shaft and turned down at one end to just the thickness of the sleeve. I replace the bearings every 1,000 to 1,500 hours of lathe time, and this has become a routine operation.

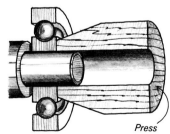

Press

Shaft size is important in selecting or in building a lathe. Flex in a small, ¾-in. shaft is significant, especially in faceplate work. I would recommend 1½ in. as a minimum for serious bowl turning. Not that fine bowls can't be turned on a smaller shaft; I'm talking here about ease of cutting quickly and cleanly. I'd not recommend taking a small lathe and

rebuilding it for a bigger shaft or bearings, as the lathe would still be no more rigid than the rest of it you hadn't souped up. The "weakest link" principle should also be kept in mind in fabricating a lathe.

The mounting of the stock on the lathe is another area that should be checked for play. If it's faceplate turning you're doing, first make sure the faceplate sits securely on the spindle—check for bright spots on the mating surfaces that will indicate only point contact. Next make sure the mating surfaces between faceplate and wood blank are perfectly flat and free of particles. Chamfer the holes in the stock into which the screw or screws will be driven, so the screws raise no splinters that will keep the faceplate and blank from meeting flush. Looseness can also be caused by voids sometimes found in plywood glue blocks. After the blank is mounted, grip it and test-pull it in several directions, checking for movement between the work and the faceplate. Solid mounting is critical for smooth cutting.

In spindle work check the spur center to see that all four spurs are sharp and the same length and that the point extends no more than ⅛ in. beyond the spurs—if it's too long, it will prevent the spurs from making solid contact. I use a small Dremel grinder to true up the spurs while the lathe is turning. Wear safety glasses and grind no farther than the shortest spur. Then take the center to the bench grinder and get the spurs sharp. Thin spindles will be remarkably less flexible if all four spurs are in solid contact. If you have a ball-bearing center, check it with a spindle in place and replace the center if there's play.

The weakest part of most lathes is the tool rest and tool-rest base. To test yours hold one end of the tool rest and press down firmly. If it gives, it will give also under a heavy cut, causing dig-in or chatter. If possible, get a heavier model tool rest and base than is standard for your lathe. For years I had to use a lathe whose tool rest wasn't rigid. I adapted by staying away from using the end of the rest and by applying considerable pressure down on it when cutting. It also taught me to take a lighter, more careful cut, an advantage after all.

Nicks in a tool rest make smooth travel across the workpiece impossible. They are caused by chatter and other impacts, but also by sharp edges on a skew chisel cutting a groove as it is pushed into the work. Check all turning tools for sharp edges and round them over with a stone. Also file the tool rest smooth, then wax it. Be sure the bearing surfaces between the tool rest, its base and the lathe bed are smooth and that they can be tightened together securely. Use a longer wrench for more leverage, if necessary.

If you understand the principles, you can make most lightweight lathes a good deal better than they come straight from the manufacturer. I still use a small Rockwell (with the timber base) for most of my small spindle and faceplate work. If you decide to stick with a sheet-metal base, do a lot of bracing to stop flexing and add weight, at least 100 lb. □

Del Stubbs is a professional turner in Chico, Calif.

Router Tables
Build one you can't buy

by Wallace M. Kunkel

We have three completely equipped shops at our woodworking school, yet there's no spindle-shaper in any of them. We have so many ways of getting around its inflexibility that we've never succumbed to buying one. For a lot of operations a shaper can't do (and was never meant to do), we are addicted to 1-hp portable routers—hanging their motors under table surfaces of all kinds, on radial drill presses and radial saws, and in the usual over-arm devices. For heavier moldings, straight or irregular, as are required on bonnet-top highboys and tall-case clocks, we rely completely on shaping with a DeWalt radial arm saw of one size or another, using a Rockwell 3-knife molding head.

Router tables can go from the ridiculous to the sublime—the really ridiculous being ready-made of fabricated metal with a table about 12 in. square. The four types of tables you can build, described later, work miracles as straight-line shapers, as large-capacity dadoing machines, as splining machines, and as irregular shapers, especially for small parts, using a ball-bearing pilot. We've gone a step beyond these simpler tables, putting the router table into what we call the "sublime" category.

A few pointers about router features seem necessary before discussing tables. I've learned that the fewer gadgets, the more useful the router. The versatility of being able to use a router motor without its base is defeated by the switch-in-handle variety. The motor must be a self-contained unit—the base only as an accessory. When it comes to the motor and long life, I've found the old Stanley model #90008, with the dome top, to be the finest. It costs a little more, but the unit is Model-*T* simple and unbeatable. My next choice is the Rockwell #6300—probably the best buy for the money. However, we've been having trouble with their collets allowing bits to creep out—a very dangerous surprise.

A simple and accurate router table can be made from a 3-ft. square piece of ½-in. thick phenolic (the same material used for router bases). The surface is flat as a die and with the router base (better yet, an extra router base) secured under the surface in the center (take off the disc that comes with it), this table is rigid. It can be clamped to a workbench and allowed to cantilever over the edge toward the operator, or quickly clamped to a pair of sawhorses. (When not in use, hang it on the wall.) For a fence, use a hardwood 2x2 with a jointed face, about 4 ft. long, and clamp it wherever you choose. For working over the bit, using partial profiles of bits, a 1¼-in. wide dado, ¾ in. deep, cut across the underside of the fence, will allow chips to pass through, not clog up around the bit. Recutting clogged chips will affect the quality of your cut.

A piece of phenolic, which can be purchased from large plastics distributors, is rather expensive, but it's worth it. However, a reasonable substitute can be made of high-density particle board (Novaply), laminated with ¼-in. tempered Masonite. It must be strengthened underneath with straight 1x2s, at least. Good dimensions for the table are 30 in. by 60 in., with the router base centered at the 40-in. mark nearest the operator. If you're using a Stanley router, a hole must be cut out of the particle board large enough for the router base to go through. The base is then suspended under the Masonite, which is the work surface. For a Rockwell router, bore a 1½ in. hole through both the particle board and the Masonite, and suspend the base under the particle board.

The wood fence should be straight and rigid, and works best if it is 6 ft. long, pivoted on a bolt at the far corner of the table and clamped in position at the short end. The size of the table and the sweep of the fence determine how many parallel dado cuts you'll be able to rout across panels. In every case, your fence will need to be of ample length, so it can be clamped to the table edge at any position.

In the category of simple router tables, the best of all is a router base secured to a 12-in. square of ¼-in. tempered Masonite, laminated with Formica. This square is then inlaid into any large, flat work surface in the shop. This is convenient

Best of simple router tables, left, is a square of Masonite inlaid into a large, flat work surface, under which a router motor is hung. Fence is clamped to edge of table and supported at the bit by scrap board. Chips escape through opening in fence. Center, router table clamps into the three vise openings of a Scandinavian-style workbench, and was the genesis of Kunkel's convenient, 'sublime' table, which clamps almost anywhere. Right, underside of table. Block in upper right-hand corner strengthens stud bolt on which fence pivots.

and economical. All adjustments are made above the bench, then the power cord is thrust ahead of the router as the square is put into place. The only time you have to reach under the table is to turn the motor on or off.

The category that we call "sublime" is our latest adaptation of these tables. It all started when we came across the plans for a Scandinavian-style workbench designed by Tage Frid. We made four of them—the bases for our own later refinements. The benches have two vises, and the end-vise on the right has two openings. In fitting the vises, we insisted that both openings in the right vise must securely clamp a piece of paper when the vise was closed. This raised a question, "When, if ever, would you use both openings at the same time?" Late one night, we realized that if all three vise openings were used at once, we could clamp a fine router table into a fine workbench without impairing the bench.

As our table design developed, certain requirements became obvious and the answers possible. We wanted a fence that could be adjusted and clamped without having to move bodily to the back side of the table. The answer: Secure ⅜-in. strips of maple along the inside top edges of the tool trough, which act as guides for a large maple block that carries the pivot point and clamping device to the desired position. The strips don't extend to the left end of the trough—for entry of the pivot block. This operation is controlled from the front of the fence. The pivot stud for the fence rides in a ½-in. slot, and is ⅜-in. machine bolt threaded up through an undersize hole. The exposed threads are covered by a ½-in. o.d. bushing made of copper pipe with a ¹⁄₁₆-in. wall. A T-shape in the slot is for adjusting the fence across the router bit.

The router table is 27 in. by 42 in. by 4 in. deep, with a surface of matte-finish Formica. The maple piece that extends into the front vise opening measures 1½ in. by 3¼ in. The router is centered 20 in. from the right end and 10½ in. from the front edge. This table has a 12-in. width capacity for dadoing, but a second router base can be positioned on the left side, giving a 36-in. width capacity. Shims must be used if the faces of the end vise don't contact the structural members under the table with the same pressure.

What we call the "sublime" in router tables is also our showpiece. We had created a fascinating, well-functioning device for use in our school, but it was designed for use with a workbench of unusual quality. None of our students, at that time, had one. The big question became, "Why can't we have all the features of this table—without the bench?" And, of course, the answer became very simple and very realistic: A rigid work-surface, with a pivoting fence. Big capacity. And a structure that could be clamped onto any work surface or onto saw-horses. Why not? The result is shown in working drawings on the following pages so that anybody can build it, clamp it almost anywhere, and hang it on the wall when not in use.

The fence has the T-slot, which allows fine adjustment across the router bit for profile cuts, parts of decorative profiles, and rabbet cuts within the capacity of a ¾-in. straight bit. Moving out of the T-slot and allowing the fence to move away from the bit, you will have dadoing capacity from 0 in. to 20 in. For accurate distance between dado cuts, measure with a steel rule from the bit to the fence, always at 90° to the fence. As the fence is moved farther and farther from the bit, it appears to be a set-up for dadoing triangles. Not so, it's an optical illusion. The purpose of moving the fence to measured positions is to make parallel cross-dado and plough cuts (for shelf ends, dust-separators, drawer bottoms, partitions, etc.). These cuts can be open or blind by completing or not completing the cut.

Tricks to be played with a router in a good table are without end, and we are constantly learning new ones. A vertical pivot guide, for example, has many uses, but most important is in the splining of boards that are not flat but are to be glued up into panels, tabletops, etc. (Most of our students purchase hardwoods pre-dressed to thickness, that were never jointed before going through the planer.) Ordinarily, with today's glues, we do not spline at all. However, splines can be used to force boards that are not flat to work against each other. This, of course, means that the spline cut must run parallel to the surface of the board, usually defining a gentle curve the length of the board. Sometimes the result is an elongated, flattened ogee curve. To make this cut with a dado head on any kind of saw or with a spindle-shaper would result in building in the natural distortion of the board. The cutter performs in a straight line. The line of the board goes its merry way.

By placing the board on edge, against the blunt edge of the vertical guide, the cutter will follow the contour of the board. It is not necessary for the cutter to actually be centered (but near) in the edge of the board, as long as the top of the board (the surface that will be viewed) is placed toward and against the vertical guide. Thus, all spline cuts will match. In making the curve of one board work against another, it is ideal if the curves can oppose each other. This is not always possible—just ideal. By using a ¼-in. straight bit and splines made of exactly ¼-in. material (tempered Masonite or fir plywood), the result will be a perfectly flush surface when the boards are clamped together.

For this splining operation, a hold-in is a necessity. You must have accuracy and control at all times—whether you're moving forward to make the cut, or moving backward to clean out impacted chips. The hold-in need be nothing more complicated than another board, clamped securely to your table edge, pushing its "nose" against the board you are working. When using a fence that is secured at the ends only, it is very important that the fence be supported at the bit. Simply use a board with a squared end, move it to the back of the fence at the bit, and clamp the other end of the board to the table edge. It's not hard to distort even the most rigid fence with hand pressure while feeding material through the cut. After all, we are talking about accuracy (within a couple thousandths of an inch, if you wish), and we are talking about control, which is the basic advantage of the router table in every operation.

This is only the beginning of the story about the many kinds of router tables that can be devised, and their myriad uses. It's this simple: When you buy a router, stay away from the switch-in-handle, and buy two bases. Hang the extra base under any flat surface that will stay flat, and clamp a fence over that surface. Bore a hole for the bit to come up through, and go to work. Or, hang that extra base under a very unusual router table that clamps into a most beautiful workbench.

See the next two pages for diagrams and construction tips for the portable router table.

Wallace M. Kunkel runs the Mr. Sawdust School of Professional Woodworking, Schooley's Mountain, N.J.

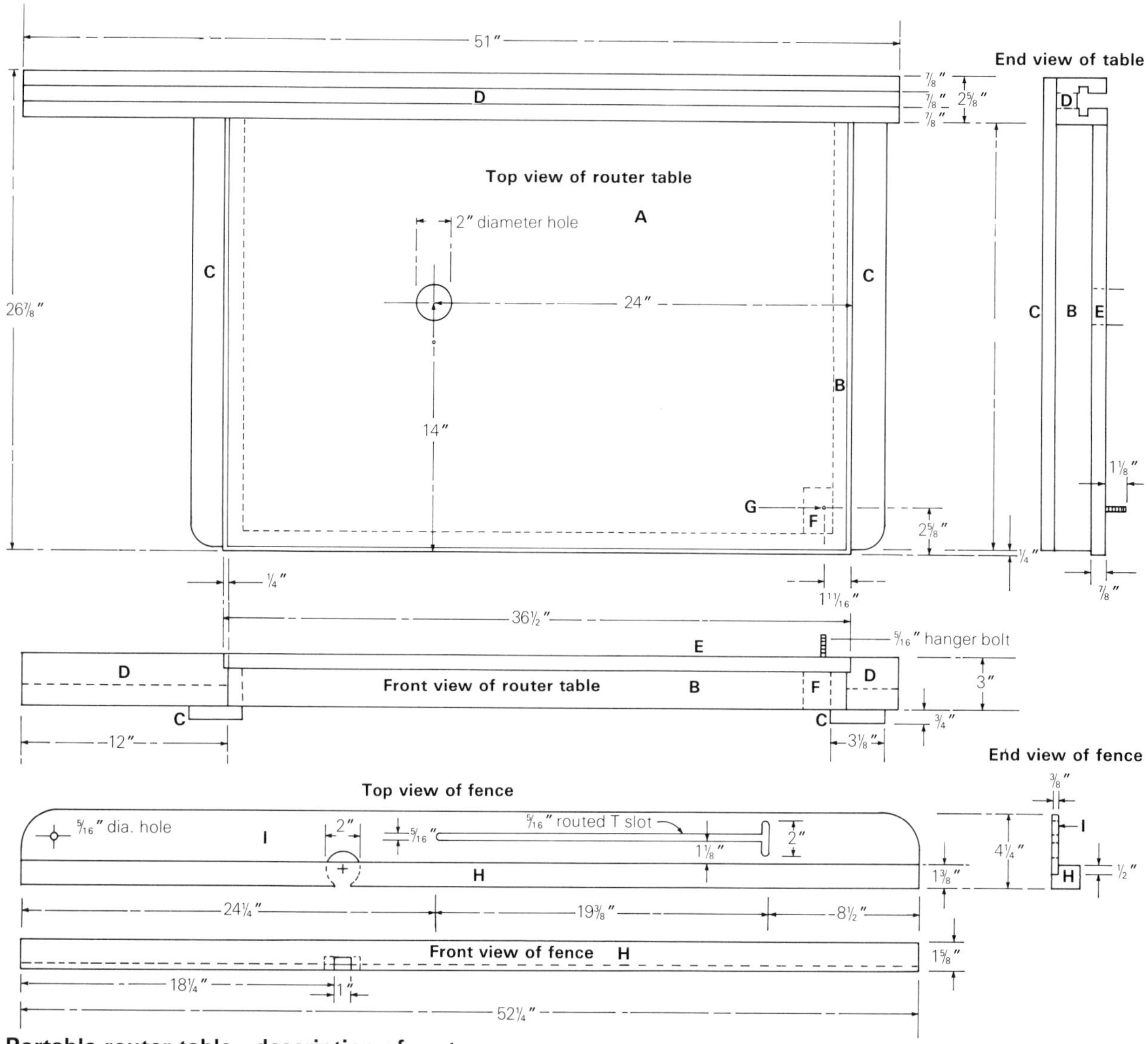

Top view of router table
End view of table
Front view of router table
Top view of fence
End view of fence
Front view of fence
2″ diameter hole
5/16″ hanger bolt
5/16″ dia. hole
5/16″ routed T slot
51″
24″
14″
26 7/8″
36 1/2″
12″
24 1/4″
19 3/8″
8 1/2″
18 1/4″
52 1/4″

Portable router table—description of parts

A 24″ x 36″ x 3/4″ particle board laminated with Formica
B 7/8″ x 2 1/4″ hardwood frame—3 pieces
C 3/4″ x 3 1/8″ x 26 1/2″ hardwood cleat—2 pieces
D 7/8″ x 3″ x 51″ hardwood—2 pieces 7/8″ x 1 1/4″ x 51″—1 piece/Trough
E 1/4″ x 7/8″ hardwood edge trim—3 pieces
F Hardwood corner block for solid support of hanger bolt
G 5/16″ diameter hanger bolt for fence pivot—2 pieces
H 1 3/8″ x 1 5/8″ x 52 1/4″ hardwood fence—1 piece—must be straight
I 3/8″ x 3 1/4″ x 52 1/4″ VC plywood fence base—hole and routed slot must work smoothly with 5/16″ hanger bolt
J 6″ long slide block with 5/16″ hanger bolt—fitted to slide smoothly in trough
K Wing nut and washer to fit 5/16″ hanger bolt—2 of each

Photos: Geoffrey Kunkel

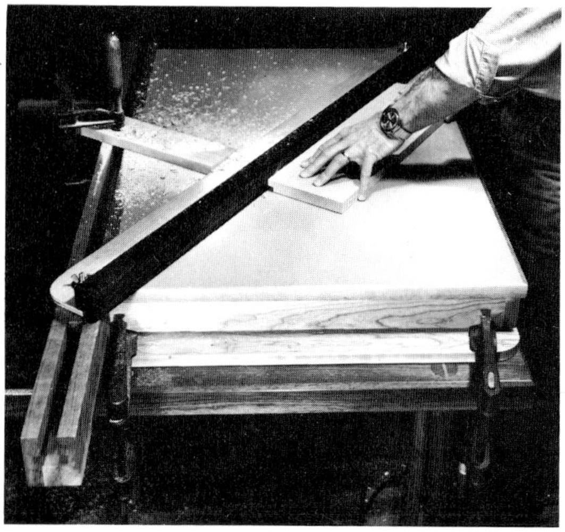

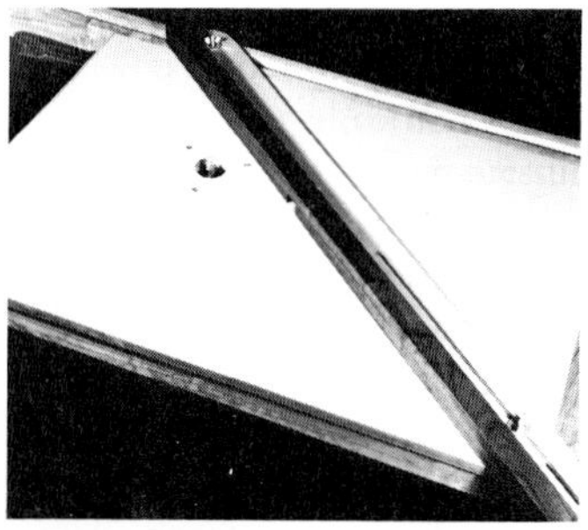

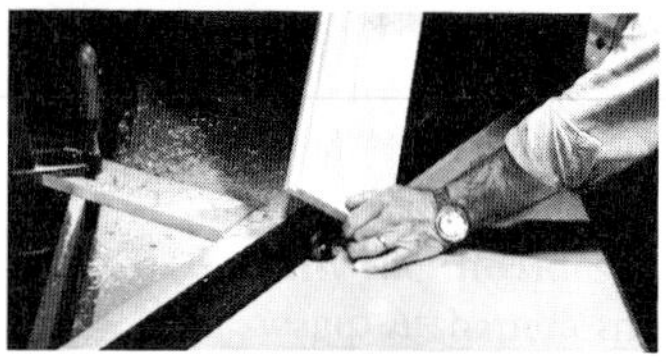

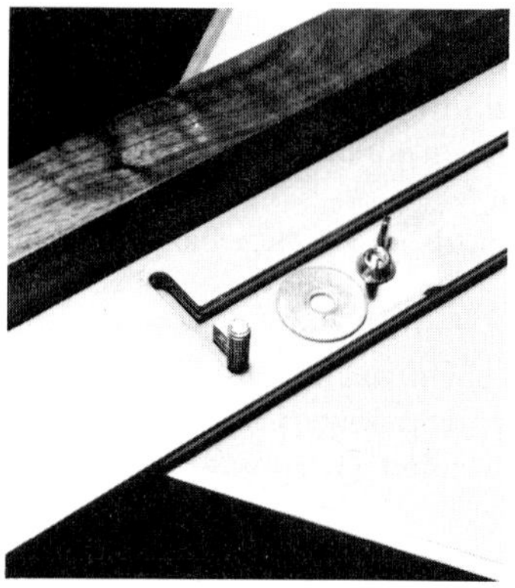

Kunkel's 'sublime' router table. T-slot (above) lets fence move toward or away from the bit, for fine adjustment of profile cuts, parts of decorative profiles or rabbet cuts (left).

Detail of back guide and slide block

Wing nut
K

Washer 1" o.d.

$\frac{5}{16}$" hanger bolt
G

6"

D

$\frac{7}{8}$" $\frac{7}{8}$" $\frac{7}{8}$"

51"

$1\frac{1}{8}$"
$\frac{1}{2}$"
3"

$1\frac{1}{4}$" $\frac{3}{8}$"
$1\frac{3}{8}$"

$1\frac{1}{16}$"
$\frac{1}{2}$"
$\frac{3}{8}$" $\frac{7}{8}$"
$\frac{3}{8}$" $\frac{3}{8}$"

Construction of router table

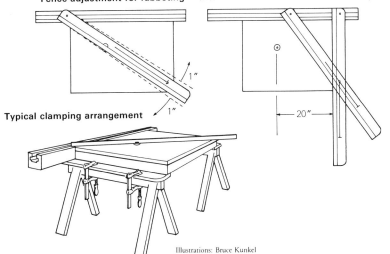

Formica
J
$\frac{3}{4}$" particle board
A
$\frac{7}{8}$" x $2\frac{1}{4}$" hardwood
$\frac{1}{4}$" x $\frac{7}{8}$" hardwood edging
B
F Hardwood corner block
E
C
$\frac{3}{4}$" x $3\frac{1}{8}$" hardwood cleat for clamping

Fence adjustment for rabbeting   **Intermediate and maximum fence adjustment**

1"

1"

20"

Typical clamping arrangement

Illustrations: Bruce Kunkel

Construction Tips

1. Secure frame pieces (B) to underside of particle board (A) *before* laminating with Formica—to cover countersunk screws. Matte-finish, solid-color Formica is best.

2. Flush-trim Formica to (A) with router—all four sides.

3. Back Guide Assembly: Secure slotted piece (D) to back edge of (A)—flush with Formica surface. Then secure $1\frac{1}{4}$" spacer (D) as shown. Then secure remaining slotted piece (D). Stagger screws in each step, countersink and glue.

4. Apply trim pieces (E) with brads and glue.

5. Clamping Cleats (C) must be secured at contact points with screws and glue.

6. Slide Block: Make certain each piece (J) will slide easily in trough before securing together.

7. Fence: (H) must be accurately jointed and dressed. Use 2" Irwin Speedbor bit to bore hole through table (A) from top, and to drill router hole in fence from underside. (Smallest size bit: $1\frac{1}{2}$".)

How to hang router: Remove phenolic disc from router base (leave it off). If your router base has projections that hold templet-guides (Stanley), you will have to rout out the underside of top (A)—$\frac{1}{2}$" deep and slightly larger than diameter of base—to give adequate up-and-down adjustment. If your router base is open (Rockwell, templet-guides are locked into phenolic disc), no rout-out is required. In either case, use phenolic disc for drill-jig. Center over 2" hole in table, drill *from top* through Formica and particleboard. Countersink for bolt heads *very carefully*, not too deep. (Suggestions: Buy an *extra* base. Leave it permanently in place. Avoid switch-in-handle routers.)

Dadoing capacity is from 0 in. to 20 in. when the fence is moved out of the T-slot and away from the bit. Pivot block rides between rails of back guide (at left of photos) and carries fence to desired position.

Top, vertical pivot guide keeps spline cuts parallel to the surface of boards that aren't flat. Flat surface of board should always be placed against the guide, so all the splines match. The hold-in clamped to the table edge pushes against the board being splined for accuracy and control. Above, the finished groove follows the bow of the board.

The Basics of the Bandsaw
Setting up and using this versatile machine

by Tage Frid

The bandsaw is one of the most versatile machines in the shop. It can cut curves, it can rip, crosscut, resaw, and it can cut joints. It can also cut sides of beef with ease, so if you see bits of meat clinging to the wheels in these photographs, it's because that's what I've been doing lately. However, the bandsaw cannot make as smooth a cut as a table saw, because a table saw has a stiffer, thicker blade that stays straighter in the cut. A bandsaw blade must bend around its wheels, so it can also bend in the cut. It is a welded ribbon of steel. Because the two ends are difficult to weld exactly in line and the weld itself produces a raised surface on the blade, the blade pulses, both forward and back and sideways, when moving at high speed. This pulsing makes the cut uneven. Still, because the depth of cut is greater and the blade is narrower, a bandsaw can do things a table saw can't. It's best for cutting curves and for resawing wide stock with minimal waste.

To get the best possible cut on your bandsaw, you first have to choose the right blade and then install it properly. I had a 14-in. bandsaw for many years before getting the 20-in. saw (with a 2-HP motor) I have now. Besides its larger blade-to-column distance (throat) and its greater depth of cut, this larger saw can use a wider blade and run it under greater tension, two important factors in determining how smooth and straight the cut will be. You should always use the widest blade possible for the job. For straight cuts, as in resawing, I use a 1-in. wide blade. For most curve cutting, I use a ⅜-in. wide blade, which will cut to a radius of 1⁷⁄₁₆ in. For tighter curves a narrower blade is necessary; probably three blades (1-in., ⅜-in. and ⅛-in.) will cover most uses.

Another important factor in blade choice is the number and kind of teeth. Bandsaw-blade technology is most developed for metal cutting. There are all sorts of tooth styles and arrangements of tooth set, each one best suited for cutting a particular kind of metal, of a particular thickness, at a particular speed. The choices for wood cutting are not so numerous. For one thing, all wood-cutting bandsaw blades have every tooth set alternately; raker (or unset) teeth do not have an advantage in wood cutting. For a long time wood-cutting bandsaw blades had regular teeth, that is, like a handsaw, they had 0° rake and they were the same size as the gullets between them. This kind of tooth style is fine for cutting in thin stock, but by eliminating every other tooth and increasing the gullet size, chips clear better and the cutting is faster. This is called a skip-tooth blade. With the increased chip clearance, it's possible to put a rake on the teeth, usually 10°, which makes feeding easier, sawing faster. Depending on the

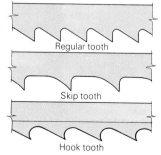

Regular tooth

Skip tooth

Hook tooth

manufacturer, this is called a hook-tooth, claw-tooth, saber-tooth or gore-tooth blade, and it's what most people use now.

The number of teeth per inch is also important for getting the best cut. The thicker the stock, the fewer teeth per inch you should use. Two or three teeth per inch is considered a coarse blade and is best for resawing. Ten or more teeth per inch will cut the best in thin stock. Most of my blades have around five teeth per inch, good for general work; all are high-carbon steel with hardened teeth and flexible backs.

Installing the blade—Some people spend a lot of time installing a blade, going back and forth over the adjustments, really making it more trouble than it has to be. The trick is in doing things in the right order. First unplug the saw, loosen the tension on the upper wheel and back off all the blade guides; this way you can slip the blade easily around the wheels (make sure the teeth are going in the right direction) and concentrate on tensioning and tracking without the guides getting in the way. Tension the blade by turning the tensioning knob that spreads the two bandsaw wheels apart. Most bandsaws have a tensioning gauge that shows the proper tension for each blade width (the wider the blade, the greater the tension). If your saw doesn't have a tensioning gauge, you'll have to develop a feel; some people pluck the blade like a guitar string and seem to know by the sound when the tension is right. Too much tension and the blade can break, too little and it will wander in the cut. When you've tensioned the blade enough to keep it on the wheels, track it. Tracking is done by turning a knob that tilts the axis of the upper wheel, which makes the blade move back and forth on the rubber rim. Rotate the upper wheel with one hand and as the blade coasts, adjust the tracking knob with the other hand until the blade rides in the middle of the rim. Finish tensioning the blade and test-track it again by hand. Now close the doors, plug in the saw, and test at higher speeds by bumping the motor on and off before letting it run continuously. If the blade runs true, you can proceed; if not you have to stop the blade (here's where a foot brake is a time-saver) or let the blade coast to a stop before opening the doors and retracking by hand. Never track the blade or open the door with the blade running at high speed. If the blade slips off or breaks, you want those doors between you and it.

With the blade tensioned and tracked, square the table to the blade; then you can adjust the blade guides. Bandsaws have two sets of blade guides, one below the table and one above. The top set adjusts up and down for different depths of cut. Each set of blade guides consists of a rear thrust bearing and two side supports, which may be ball bearings, hardened-steel blocks or pivoting plates. Ball bearings are best because then can be brought right up in touch with the blade, but they are expensive and clog easily with sawdust. Blocks and plates have to have some clearance, and blocks

Installing a new blade on the bandsaw is easier if you do things in the right order. With all the blade guides backed off, the blade is slipped around the wheels and tensioned. Next the blade is tracked, left, by turning the upper wheel of the bandsaw with one hand while adjusting the tilt of the wheel's axis with the other. Never track the blade with the motor running and the door open. Next adjust the blade guides, first the thrust bearings, upper and lower, then the left-hand side guides. Use a square, right, to make sure you're not pushing the blade out of line, and a piece of paper between the blade guide and the blade for clearance. Then use the same piece of paper, far right, to set the right-hand side guide with the proper clearance.

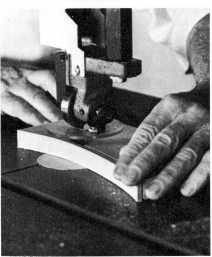
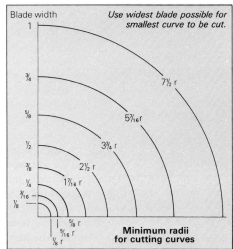

Two basic operations on the bandsaw: Cutting curves, above, should be done with the widest possible blade for the curve; the chart gives the limits of various blade widths. Using too wide a blade will result in heat and stress on the blade as its back rubs in the kerf; this can break or damage the blade. When sawing curves, be sure to keep your hands behind or to the sides of the blade. Resawing, right, is done with the widest blade the saw will handle and an L-shaped fence at the blade. The fence is rounded over where it rides against the planed surface of the board. This way the board can be fed on an angle to compensate for the tendency of most bandsaw blades to lead to one side or the other.

tend to wear at the front and to lose their setting from vibration. I'm happy with the plate side guides that came with my saw because once the plates are mounted, the support from the teeth to the back of the blade is fixed and their sideways position locks down good and tight.

The thrust bearings should be adjusted first. It doesn't matter if you do the upper or lower one first, but both should be set before adjusting any of the side guides. Bring the bearing up so it just touches the back of the blade. As mentioned earlier, a running bandsaw blade tends to pulse, so you'll have to check the adjustment as you turn the wheel by hand. As it runs, the back of the blade should just kiss the thrust bearing. Too close and it can wear the surface of the bearing; too far away and the blade will wander in the cut.

Set the upper and lower left-hand guides next, rather than both upper or both lower. I use a piece of paper (the thickness of a brown grocery bag) between the guide and the blade to gauge the clearance; with ball-bearing guides clearance is not necessary. It's important here that you use a square on the table to make sure you're not bending the blade to the right

with too much pressure from the guides. Besides proper sideways adjustment, you also have to set the guide properly in relation to the front of the blade. It should be just flush with the back of the gullets—too far forward and teeth will wear the guide; too far back and the guide won't provide adequate support. With both left-hand guides set, adjust the two right-hand guides, again using the piece of paper for clearance. Test the way the blade moves through the guides, turning by hand before switching on the machine. Be sure that the weld moves freely through the groove.

Basic bandsaw technique—Probably what you'll be doing most on the bandsaw is cutting curves. The important thing here is to keep your fingers to the side of the blade or behind it—never in front. And, of course, as with all bandsaw cuts, be sure to lower the blade guard to within ½ in. of the top of the stock you're cutting. This guides the blade better and lessens the risk of injury. The most common mistake most people make on the bandsaw is to cut a thick piece and then cut a thinner one without sliding down the guard. While leaning over, concentrating on the line you're cutting, not only are you liable to stick your head into the moving blade, but if the blade breaks, pieces can fly all over like shrapnel. Never use a blade too wide for the radius you are cutting. The stress of the back edge rubbing in the kerf can break the blade. Getting a smooth cut is a matter of evenly feeding and turning the work. Stopping in the middle of a cut can produce an uneven surface, as the blade's vibration widens the kerf. Plan your moves. If a shape will require tight curves or cutting in and backing out the blade, make relatively straight cuts in the waste to remove most of it; then you can concentrate on the contour line without the blade binding. Never force the work into the blade. If the blade doesn't want to follow the line you're cutting, head for the waste side and come back for a closer second cut.

The bandsaw is excellent for cutting circles, with the help of a jig. A jig can also help cut arcs of a circle, which is particularly useful when making forms for curved laminations (photos, page 55, top). The curved ribs of these forms must be identical; because of the bandsaw's depth of cut, you can stack and cut them all at once, thus ensuring uniformity.

The bandsaw is also useful for resawing wide boards. Sometimes I will kerf a wide board along either edge on the table saw, raising the blade between passes, then bring it over to the bandsaw to complete the cut. Bandsawing thus goes faster, and it's easy to keep the thin bandsaw blade in the wider table-saw kerf. But when I have a minimum of material to waste, as with bookmatching figured wood, I will resaw it on the bandsaw alone (last photo on page 54). I use a plywood L-shaped guide at the teeth of the blade, its vertical edge

Straight-line cutting and the bandsaw touch

by Arthur Reed

Although most shops reserve the bandsaw for curves, it's unequalled for cutting straight lines. We have two bandsaws in our shop, a 10¼-in. Inca and a 36-in. American, and together they do most of our sawing. We rip rough stock in thicknesses up to the blade-guide capacity, we resaw for veneer and for matched panels, and we size stock for furniture and cabinets. We even rely on the bandsaw for joinery.

Many woodworkers harbor prejudice against the bandsaw, probably from the frustration of having tried to saw a straight line without being familiar with the balance of forces that allows the machine to work. Perhaps more than any other machine, the bandsaw requires a delicate, learned touch.

One key to success is accurate and careful setting of the guides, so the blade can travel freely through the stock and yet be supported in its travel. Similar coordination is required between blade and rip fence. Bandsaw teeth form a narrow corridor in the stock, a corridor that must pass around the body of the blade without contacting it. Otherwise, the side pressure will twist the blade and make it cut unevenly. Thus the characteristic cutting path of the blade must be determined, and the rip fence must be aligned with it. Since this path is rarely parallel to the sides of the table, we assess the drift of our blades regularly.

True up one face and edge of a piece of 2x4 stock about a foot long. Mark a

pencil line on the face opposite the trued face, parallel to and about 2 in. from the trued edge. Slowly feed the stock, trued face down, into the blade with moderate force and feel for the drift by moving the cut away from and back onto the line. After about 8 in. of feed, you'll find the angle that keeps the saw cutting easily along the line. Turn off the saw, bring up the rip fence and adjust it to hold that angle. The Inca fence allows this adjustment; if yours doesn't, either mark the line on the table and clamp a board fence parallel to it, or make yourself an adjustable fence as shown in the drawing. Finally, take another piece of scrap and rip it along the fence. If the scrap seems either to pull away from the fence or to bind the blade, re-adjust. Otherwise, once set, the drift angle should be constant for the life of the blade, regardless of grain structure, hardness, softness or thickness of the stock cut.

It's also important to develop a technique for feeding the stock into the bandsaw. This determines to a great extent the quality of the cut. Feed should be constant and smooth, though the amount of pressure and sometimes its direction vary; they constitute the "touch," the operator's sense of how the cutting is going. On thicker, harder stock, be aware of the greater work the bandsaw teeth have to do, and feed at a rate the blade can handle. It takes time to develop the correct touch, to learn to back off when certain sounds are heard or when a familiar feeling is replaced by something not quite right. Developing touch is a matter of making mistakes and learning from them. ☐

Arthur Reed operates a custom woodworking shop in Elmira, N.Y.

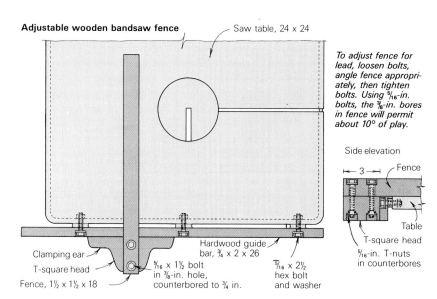

Adjustable wooden bandsaw fence

Saw table, 24 x 24

To adjust fence for lead, loosen bolts, angle fence appropriately, then tighten bolts. Using ⁵⁄₁₆-in. bolts, the ³⁄₈-in. bores in fence will permit about 10° of play.

Side elevation

3

Fence

Table

T-square head

⁵⁄₁₆-in. T-nuts in counterbores

Clamping ear

T-square head

Fence, 1½ x 1½ x 18

⁵⁄₁₆ x 1½ bolt in ³⁄₈-in. hole, counterbored to ¾ in.

Hardwood guide bar, ¾ x 2 x 26

⁵⁄₁₆ x 2½ hex bolt and washer

rounded over, and follow by eye a scribed line. Because of variations in set or sharpness, sometimes through wear, sometimes on new blades, most bandsaw blades will lead to one side or the other. With this L-shaped guide you can shift the angle of feed to follow the lead of the blade. (One of my former students claims proficiency in using no guide at all; he prefers to resaw freehand and thus eliminates the possibility that blade-lead will bind the stock against the fence.)

To resaw with the L-shaped guide, first plane one face and joint one edge of the board. Draw a line on the unjointed edge, parallel to the planed face, and saw with the planed face against the guide and the jointed edge on the table. Push evenly and slowly; don't crowd the blade; let it cut. Keep the feed constant, and keep your hands away from the blade, especially toward the end of the cut; use a push-stick or reach around the blade and pull the board through. Whatever you do, don't push those last couple of inches through with your thumb on the end of the board.

Resawing satisfactorily requires using as wide a blade as possible with two or three teeth per inch for adequate chip clearance. A 1-HP motor is the minimum; 2-HP to 3-HP is best for green wood. Make sure your blade is sharp and properly tensioned, and that the blade guides are adjusted and close to the work. If the cut bellies, it's probably because of inadequate chip clearance. Slow down your feed and/or use a blade with fewer teeth per inch. If you are getting deep striations on the sawn surface, it means one or more of the teeth on that side of the blade are damaged or set wrong. Try holding a carborundum stone flat against that side of the blade while it's running. Keep in mind that even when you get a smooth, flat surface from the saw, there is a good chance the board will cup because moisture content is rarely consistent throughout a board, and resawing exposes new surfaces to the air. You must allow for this and saw your stock thicker than you need. It is also a good idea to put resawn boards aside for a few days before finish-planing and jointing, so they will reach equilibrium with the shop atmosphere. How much stock can you expect to lose in resawing? There's the waste to the kerf, the waste to the jointer (when resawing a number of thin boards from one thick one, it's best to joint the sawn surface of the thick stock after each sawing) and the waste to cupping—figure on losing at least ¼ in. for each sawing.

Bandsaw joinery—There are several joints it makes sense to cut on the bandsaw, especially if there are a large number of them to do. Through dovetails can be cut almost completely on the bandsaw, tilting the table to saw the pins and freehanding the tails after marking them from the pins. Some joints can be done on the bandsaw in conjunction with the table saw. In cutting tenons or lap joints, for instance, the bandsaw can waste the cheeks after the table saw has cut good, clean shoulders. I prefer to make the two cuts on the table saw, but if you don't have a table saw, both shoulders and cheeks can be cut on the bandsaw, as shown in the photos at right.

To saw cheeks on the bandsaw, first mark on the stock the lines for both cheeks and shoulders. Install the widest blade possible and set up a rip fence a distance from the blade equal to the thickness of the cheek waste. Because this is a relatively short cut, it usually isn't necessary to angle the fence to compensate for blade drift (lead). You can set up the fence parallel to the table edge. Next clamp a stop to the fence that will keep the stock from traveling farther into the blade than to

The bandsaw is ideal for cutting circles or arcs of circles when it's equipped with a plywood plate and pivoting trammel to which the stock is pinned. Top, plywood ribs are being cut to identical arcs for use in a bent-lamination form, above.

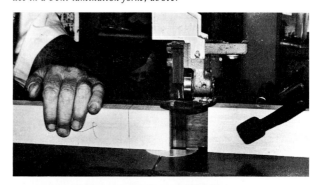

To saw tenon or half-lap cheeks, top, use a wide blade, a fence set to the thickness of the cheek waste and a block behind the blade to stop travel at the shoulder line. To saw the shoulder, above, use the miter gauge; clamp a block to the table for quick and accurate positioning of repetitive cuts.

the line of the shoulder. Hold the stock firmly against the fence and feed it into the blade up to the stop. Saw the cheeks for one side of all the stock you are joining. Don't flip the stock; reset the blade-to-fence distance before cutting the other cheeks to make sure variations in stock thickness do not produce variations in tenon thickness.

If you are also sawing the shoulders on the bandsaw, remove the fence and use the miter gauge. Place one of the pieces of stock against the miter gauge, positioning it so that the blade is in line with the shoulder to be cut. Without moving the stock on the miter-gauge fence, pull the stock and miter gauge back to the front of the table and mark the table where the stock ends. Clamp a stop block to the table at this mark, and you can use it for quick and accurate positioning of each piece to be cut. I don't find it necessary to put a stop block behind the blade to control the depth of the shoulder cut; with the cheeks already sawn it's a simple matter to stop feeding when the waste falls off. □

A bandsaw sawmill
by Lawrence Westlund

I have a 12-in Sears bandsaw and lots of large branches and small tree butts wanting to be sawn into small boards for boxes and the like. I built a free-standing table with a cutout into which my bandsaw table can be positioned and on which slides a carriage, complete with knees and dogs for holding round wood while the carriage is cranked past the blade. The mill for my saw, shown in the photo and drawing, can handle 7-in. diameter logs; dimensions, of course, can be varied for other saws. Most of the work is bolting the stock together to form the table. I did weld the iron for the knees and dogs, though these could be bolted as well. □

Lawrence Westlund is an amateur woodworker in Klamath Falls, Ore.

Frances Westlund

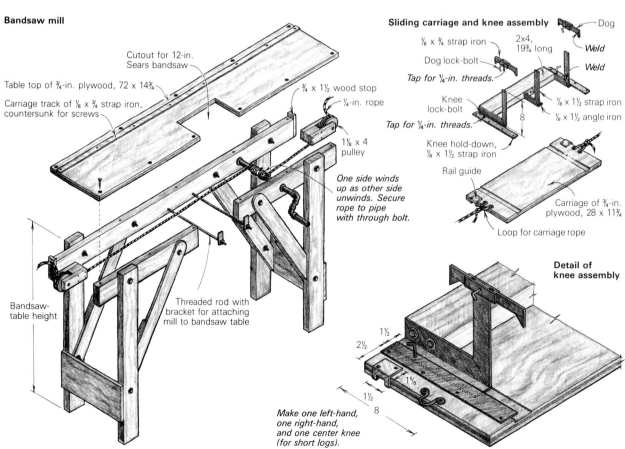

Bandsaw mill

Cutout for 12-in. Sears bandsaw

Table top of ¾-in. plywood, 72 x 14¾

Carriage track of ⅛ x ¾ strap iron, countersunk for screws

¾ x 1½ wood stop

¼-in. rope

1⅛ x 4 pulley

One side winds up as other side unwinds. Secure rope to pipe with through bolt.

Bandsaw-table height

Threaded rod with bracket for attaching mill to bandsaw table

Sliding carriage and knee assembly

⅛ x ¾ strap iron

2x4, 19¾ long

Dog

Weld

Dog lock-bolt

Weld

Tap for ¼-in. threads.

Knee lock-bolt

⅛ x 1½ strap iron

⅛ x 1½ angle iron

Tap for ¼-in. threads.

8

Knee hold-down, ⅛ x 1½ strap iron

Rail guide

Carriage of ¾-in. plywood, 28 x 11¾

Loop for carriage rope

Detail of knee assembly

1½

2½

1⁵⁄₈

1½

8

Make one left-hand, one right-hand, and one center knee (for short logs).

Machining Backwards

Power-fed climb-cutting reduces tearout

by Lew Palmer

Several years ago some friends decided to expand their repertoire of woodworking machinery, so that they could better fill their rapidly increasing orders for oak accessories. On their list of must-haves was a nifty SCM R-9 overarm router, a power-fed affair which they ordered tricked out with all the options. But when they started running their new line of oval mirror frames on it, alas, they suffered a staggering number of ruined pieces, which threatened their anticipated profits.

An anguished call to their machinery supplier brought forth a knowledgeable rep. He took a quick look at their procedures and promptly prescribed the cure: use the power feed to climb-cut, and thereby eliminate almost all machining rejects.

He was right. And the solution to their router problem also worked on their shaper and their more sophisticated machinery to come—and for me. I've found climb-cutting to be one of the most important machining techniques for any profit-minded (thus waste-conscious) woodworker.

Climb-cutting is nothing more than power-feeding (*never* hand-feeding, for that would be terribly dangerous) in the same direction that the knives of your shaper (or whatever) are rotating. This forces each knife to remove only a tiny slice of wood with each cut, which largely eliminates blowouts. The method contrasts with the traditional way cabinetmakers machine wood: feeding against cutter rotation, a technique probably necessitated by hand-feeding, but one that can cause the wood to lift and tear unpredictably.

Climb-cutting, and therefore power-feeding, are indispensable in my shop, where I often have to machine stock to precise dimensions and profiles—stock that's too expensive to replace. I do it on a rather hefty (1500-lb., 1½-in. dia. spindle) SCM TC-120 shaper, equipped with an 8-speed, 3-roller Univer power feed. This attachment offers a relatively slow 2.7-meter-per-minute (about 9-FPM) feed rate which I prefer when shaping unusually deep raised panels. I regard the power feed as essential, even on those rare occasions when I do not

climb-cut. Only a power feed can safely feed material at an optimum, consistent rate, hold it flat and indexed against the table and fence, and shield the operator from blown material.

To me, the only acceptable power feeds are the industrial models you can securely bolt to your shaper table. They weigh in at 150 lb. or so, one reason to operate a more massive shaper. These power feeds consist of a multi-speed 3- or 4-wheel drive unit, a base, and a post-and-arm assembly that allows you to position the feed variously. They retail from industrial woodworking ma-

Normal cutting vs. climb-cutting

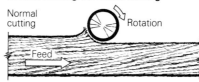

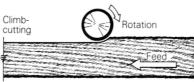

Feeding against cutter rotation allows feeding by hand, but the cutter tends to lift and tear out the wood. Climb-cutting virtually eliminates tearout, but necessitates using a power feed, or else the cutter will grab the stock.

Substituting for the standard two-part shaper fence, Palmer's one-piece fence, used in conjunction with the Univer power feed, makes for safe, precise shaping.

chinery suppliers for $1100 to $1500, with the more expensive ones offering more speeds and feed wheels. For maximum versatility, instead of hard-wiring the feed to a box, you can attach a plug to one end of the cord and plug it into a receptacle on the side of the shaper. Then you can easily transfer it to another machine, such as a tablesaw.

These feeds, for the most part, are limited to working linear stock. One technique I've found advantageous for jointing, profiling and dimensioning a large amount of stock is to feed material against a one-piece auxiliary fence, instead of or in addition to the standard two-part shaper fence (photo, below left). A piece of straight phenolic plastic, steel, or even Baltic birch plywood will suffice. My fence, for example, is ½-in. thick steel plate, 6 in. by 84 in., slotted to allow for bolting to the shaper table on the operator's side of the spindle. I position the feed so that the first and second infeed wheels straddle the spindle, and I tilt the feed toward the auxiliary fence, so that the stock is held tight.

The auxiliary fence has two shortcomings. When you need to profile extremely narrow or thin stock, the feed wheels can't grab it properly. In such situations, I use a thinner fence (¼ in. or so), or I rabbet the side of a Baltic birch fence, which creates a flat running surface and raises the stock above the face of the fence. For wide stock that won't fit between the auxiliary fence and the spindle, a dimension dictated by the size of the shaper table, I revert to the regular shaper fence, which straddles the spindle.

While climb-cutting linear stock has eliminated up to 20% of the waste and machining hassles I once suffered, the technique's real advantage is with curved stock, where some part of the material must necessarily be machined against the grain, as with my neighbors' oval picture frames. Power-feeding curved stock requires more sophisticated equipment than I have, such as the R-9 overarm router, but for those shops moving into such production, cutting backwards may be a big step forward. □

Lew Palmer has a cabinet shop in Carmichael, Calif. Photo by the author.

Q & A

How to buy a thickness planer?

As shop tools go, the purchase of a thickness planer represents a major investment, and selecting one that best satisfies your needs can be compared to buying a car. The same questions arise: what make, model and price range? The 12-in. to 15-in. planers are usually chosen by the hobbyist or small-shop operator, since 12 inches is about as wide as most lumber these days, and glued-up panels are usually 24 inches or wider. This seems to rule out the 18-in. and 20-in. machines: price jumps dramatically as width increases.

Small planers fall into two basic groups. One consists of scaled-down models of planers designed for industry, and is represented by the machines of Powermatic, Rockwell (Delta), General and Poitras. The second group consists of planers designed from the start for smaller shops, often according to quite different principles. This group includes such highly engineered machines as the Inca and Makita, Williams & Hussey's open-sided planer-molder, and the Foley-Belsaw line of planers and combination machines.

Determining which factors ought to govern a purchase is a matter of how the planer will be used. *Fine Woodworking* magazine's Consulting Editor Lelon Traylor, of the school of manufacturing technology at the University of Southern Illinois, explains:

"After width, feed speed is a key specification. For home-shop, nonproduction use, one slow feed speed is fine. Figured woods must be planed at a slow feed rate or the surface will be splintered and torn. But in school shops and cabinet shops a faster feed is necessary because time is money. Thus a machine with variable speeds meets a variety of planing conditions. The diameter of the cutterhead is also important, larger being better, as is accessibility for sharpening and maintenance. On some machines, the cutterhead lifts right out for quick changing, while others have attachments for sharpening the knives in place. Another important feature not found on all small planers is powered lower feed rollers, which help prevent the lumber from hanging up.

"It's difficult to acquire direct experience with a wide variety of planers. Yet when shopping one must be sure of getting value. Planers made for industry are not the same as toasters made for retail—manufacturers who make shoddy or impractical goods do not stay in business long. So, when evaluating a planer, I would look first at performance factors—size, feed, cutter style and cutterhead diameter, horsepower, table length. Most likely, I would end up with two comparable machines. I would then compare weights, giving preference to the heavier. Finally, I would want to know whether I was getting value, so I would figure the price per pound. You would not buy a machine on this basis alone, but it is a useful rule of thumb."

Machine builders and users often disagree on which material, aluminum alloy or cast iron, is best for tables, trunnions and housings. Traylor insists upon cast iron. Says he, "Two critical requirements in machine design are no deflection under load and resistance to vibration. For me these translate into mass, and the way to get mass is to design and build with cast iron. Cast iron is heavy, it damps vibration, threads cut in it won't strip, and a machine made of it won't wobble around the room. Aluminum components are light, threads strip, and machines made of it will vibrate and wobble around. Some aluminum machines are well engineered and balanced, and some aluminum alloys are very strong. But wood is a variable material; cutting it exerts unpredictable forces, and you need the mass of cast iron."

The opposite point of view is championed by Garretson W. Chinn, president of Garrett Wade Co., importers of the Swiss-made Inca woodworking machines. Says Chinn: "Historically, it's true that thick sections were needed for machine castings and fittings because the only material available was cast iron, which gave the weight needed to damp vibrations from rotating parts that were not dynamically balanced. However, as structural steels and aluminums were developed, it became possible to build lighter components utilizing ribbed sections with rigidity equal to heavy iron castings. While sheer weight is a time-honored way to achieve rigidity and strength, today the same ends can be achieved by more scientific means. Still, much woodworking-machine design continues to be founded more on tradition than on accurate analysis of machine stresses based on working loads. It's not just weight but performance that counts."

Belsaw planer

What about the Belsaw 12-in. planer? Since it's in the low end of the price range, I'd appreciate an opinion.
—Bill Martin, Mesa, Ariz.

The Belsaw is a no-frills machine. It is designed without the pressure bar that normally presses down on the stock between the cutterhead and the outfeed roller. The chipbreaker appears to be more of a chip deflector—a chipbreaker is supposed to press down on the lumber right up close to the knives, preventing splintering and also holding the stock against the table. The table feed rate is 12 FPM, although a pulley change permits a faster speed. The feed rolls, like those on the Makita, are rubber covered and are guaranteed for a year. The amateur should get several years from a set of rollers.

The basic Belsaw 912 weighs 300 lb. and costs $688 (1979). Considering price, construction and versatility, it should fit the needs of many hobbyists and small-shop operators. To compare it with the Rockwell, however, is like comparing a pickup truck to a Cadillac. The design approach is different, for a different market. But you can get your money's worth with either. Belsaw also offers a machine that planes, rips and molds in one operation. —Lelon Traylor

Planer won't feed

I recently purchased a Powermatic Model 160 thickness planer and am not happy with the way it stops feeding after the wood leaves the infeed roller. The boards must be pulled by hand to plane the last several inches. No amount of adjusting the pressure bar or the outfeed roller seems to help.
—John Ellenz, Topton, Kans.

If feeding stops after the stock leaves the infeed roll, one of two problems (maybe both) exist. Either the table rolls are too low (they should be .007 in. above the surface for finish planing), or the pressure bar is too low. More than likely it's the pressure bar.

Turn the two pressure bar adjusting bolts clockwise several turns. Start the machine and feed a 3-ft. 2x4 into the planer on the extreme left-hand side of the table. When the stock contacts the pressure bar, it will stop. If your machine is equipped with a shaving hood, you can make the next adjustment with the motor running. If not, you must shut the power off before you try to adjust the pressure bar. Turn both pressure bar adjustment bolts counter-clockwise in ¼-turn increments. Then with the machine running, apply gradual pressure to the end of the stock. When the pressure bar is just at the cutting arc of the knives, the stock will free up and feed smoothly. Now raise the table by one turn of the wheel and repeat the operation, feeding from the right side of the machine. Don't raise the pressure bar beyond the cutting arc of the knives, or you'll get snipe.
—Jim Ramsey, Powermatic-Houdaille Inc.

Changing feed rates

...My 12-in. Powermatic had a feed rate of about 21 feet per minute and produced a quite decent surface. However, a slower feed rate ought to yield an even better surface, so I decided to see what could be done. It turns out to be fairly simple and cheap to reduce the feed rate by 20%, to about 17 FPM. This required replacing a 2½-in. sheave on the gear side of the cutterhead with a 2-in. sheave. The operation does not change the position of the cutterhead relative to the table, so there is no problem of cutterhead realignment. The 2½-in. sheave could probably also be replaced with a 3-in. if one wanted to increase the feed rate to about 25 FPM. I prefer the slower speed now that I have it. A friend who owns a 16-in. Powermatic, with variable feed, eventually set it for the slowest rate and has not changed it since.... —Ernest C. Tsivoglou, Atlanta, Ga.

This type of modification is possible on most planers, and is commonly done, using machine pulleys or chain-drive sprocket wheels sold by industrial hardware dealers.

Williams & Hussey

...The best bet for a hobby-shop operation may be the Williams & Hussey planer, which can be bought for about a third of the price of the more elaborate machines, provided one forgoes power feed.... —John Black, Camarillo, Calif.

For small work it does a good job. Difficulties arise on boards with considerable variation in thickness. The board will probably hang up, requiring you to change the thickness setting and start over. To surface a board that is wider than the cutterhead, you are in the same situation as running a 12-in. plank over a 6-in. jointer. It is difficult to get the two cuts to match. This is providing the grain run-out even permits surfacing from either end. —Lelon Traylor

Fixing snipe

Could you explain why a thickness planer tends to dip its cut in the first few inches, and if there is a way of preventing this? —Ken Corbett, Proctor, Vt.

If the lower feed rolls of a planer are set higher than normal, uneven cutting (called snipe) occurs on both ends of the board. As the lumber passes over the infeed roll, the chipbreaker pushes the wood down against the bed of the planer. After passing under the cutterhead it comes in contact with the pressure bar, which also holds it down, but as it comes to the outfeed roll it must climb up and over the roll, which thereby raises the board into the cutterhead. As the board passes out of the planer it drops off the bottom infeed roll, causing uneven cutting. The fix is to adjust the relationship of the rollers to the table. Roughsawn and uneven lumber requires a higher setting on the lower rolls than finish planing—for finish planing, try ⅟₃₂ in. or less for roll height above the bed. —Lelon Traylor

Back-bevel reduces tear-out

I've found that it's possible to virtually eliminate chip-out with any planer or jointer by back-beveling the face of the cutting knives to give a smaller cutting angle. With the hard maple that I use, there is no "right" direction to feed a board, as grain direction will usually change several times in its length....Slow feed and shallow cuts help, but don't eliminate the problem. Back-beveling does, and makes it possible to feed boards from either end. An additional benefit is that the knives stay sharp much longer.

Cutting angle is the amount of forward tilt given the knives by the manufacturer when milling the knife slots in the cutterhead. This angle is measured from a line drawn down the flat face of the knife to a line connecting the knife tip and the center of the cutterhead (see diagram). Notice that the cutting angle has nothing to do with the angle of the sharpening bevel. Most manufacturers seem to make their planers and jointers for working softwoods, by building in cutting angles of 30° to 40°. At this angle the knives tend to slide under the chip and lift it up. This works great on softwoods but hardwoods need cutting angles in the range of 5° to 20°, to give more of a scraping action and less of a slicing and lifting action.

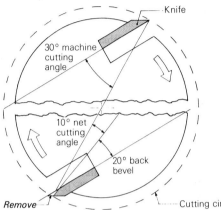

To reduce the cutting angle it is necessary only to grind a second bevel (called a back-bevel) on the flat faces of the knives. In this way it is possible to reduce the cutting angle to nothing at all, and even to make it negative. The angle of the back-bevel is determined by the relationship between the cutting angle built into the machine and the net cutting angle you want to end up with. I've seen planers with net cutting angles as low as 5°, though I prefer 10° for both my planer and jointer, as this does an acceptable job on softwoods and a superb job on hardwoods. When I sent the knives out for sharpening I included a drawing, with all the angles I wanted clearly marked. One grinding shop refused the job, saying it wouldn't work. But it does. Everything I plane, from curly maple to walnut burl, comes through just fine.

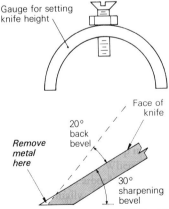

I also had a lot of trouble setting the knife height, until I made the C-shaped gauge shown above. Its two legs are placed on the head and the screw is locked at the right height, so it can be used as a feeler gauge to test the height of both ends of all the knives. Cheaper machines are liable to have out-of-round heads, however, in which case you'll have to purchase a machinist's dial indicator. —Brian Burns, Palo Alto, Calif.

Repairing Bandsaw Blades
And how to make up your own from bulk rolls

You don't need welding equipment to braze narrow bandsaw blades. A propane torch can generate enough heat, and silver solder is strong enough for a good joint. Any small shop can deal with the nuisance of a broken blade by repairing it on the spot. And if bandsawing is a daily operation in your shop, you can save money by buying blades in bulk rolls. This also lets you choose from a variety of widths and teeth, some of which aren't generally available in made-up blades. One commercial supplier, DoAll (256 N. Laurel, Des Plaines, Ill. 60016), sells a skip-tooth, ¼-in. blade in 100-ft. rolls. Cut and soldered, each blade ends up costing about $3, and the entire process takes little longer than sharpening and honing a dull tool.

Bandsaw blades break for a variety of reasons. Sometimes a sharp, new blade will snap when you trap it by trying to saw too tight a curve, or when you skew the work. You can repair this type of break successfully, but fixing other kinds of breaks may be a waste of time. A dull blade, for instance, will break if it's pushed too hard, but repairing it won't be worthwhile unless you can sharpen it too (see facing page). Older blades, even ones that are still sharp, sometimes break because they've gotten brittle through work-hardening, having been flexed over the saw's wheels a few times too many. These blades aren't worth fixing either, because it's likely that they'll soon break in another spot.

You can probably buy silver solder and a compatible flux at the local hardware store, but be sure that it's about 45% silver with a melting point near 1100°F, or it will bead up on the blade without flowing. You'll need to make a holding jig (figure 2) from angle iron or scrap metal to position the ends of the blade while you solder it. The jig can be tucked away when you're not using it, then clamped in your bench vise when you need it.

Soldering metal is akin to gluing wood: success depends more on the fit of the parts than on the strength of the bonding material. Attempting to bridge an open joint with solder won't work. For this reason, the scarf joint (figure 1) should be a perfect fit and carefully aligned. First heat the blade ends red with the torch, then cool them slowly to soften the steel. The surfaces of the scarf should be at least three times as long as the blade is thick. The ends to be joined can be shaped on a bench grinder—either freehand or with a simple guide block—or they can be filed. One trick that ensures a matching joint is to lay one blade end over the other and bevel them both at the same time. The operation is easier than putting a bevel on a chisel, so use whatever method suits you.

Metal, like wood, must be clean for a good joint. Some low-temperature solders are hollow, and contain acid for cleaning the metal, making soldering a one-step operation. But high-temperature silver solders require a separate flux that is formulated to work with a particular solder's alloy and melting temperature. Flux performs several functions: when heated, it chemically cleans the metal, helps the solder flow and speeds heat conduction. Vapors from flux are very irritating, and some solders give off toxic fumes, so provide ventilation. Apply the flux to the scarf surfaces before you heat the joint. You can trap a flattened piece of cold solder in the scarf, or you can preheat the blade and drip solder onto it. If you drip the solder, it is not enough merely to melt it—you must get the blade itself hot enough to cause the solder to flow thinly over the metal and into the scarf.

As in gluing wood, the joint should be held tight while the solder sets. One jig, left, has a built-in adjustable screw support. Immediately after the initial soldering, you press down on the scarf with a screwdriver tip and reheat the joint until the solder flows. As an alternative that does without the screw, you can design the jig so you can grip the joint with a pair of pliers to clamp it and cool the molten solder. A traditional method requires brazing tongs (similar to blacksmiths' tongs). Set up the scarf with flux and cold solder, then grab

(continued on page 62)

Fig. 1: Scarf joint

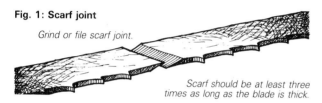

Grind or file scarf joint.

Scarf should be at least three times as long as the blade is thick.

Fig. 2: Blade-holding jigs

Polette's jig

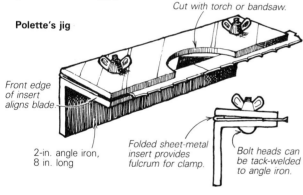

Cut with torch or bandsaw.

Front edge of insert aligns blade.

2-in. angle iron, 8 in. long

Folded sheet-metal insert provides fulcrum for clamp.

Bolt heads can be tack-welded to angle iron.

Adams' jig

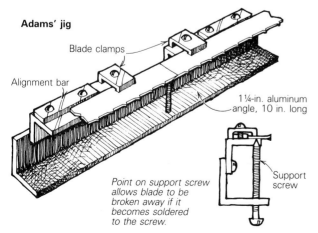

Blade clamps

Alignment bar

1¼-in. aluminum angle, 10 in. long

Point on support screw allows blade to be broken away if it becomes soldered to the screw.

Support screw

Bandsaw-blade sharpening jig

by Robert Meadow

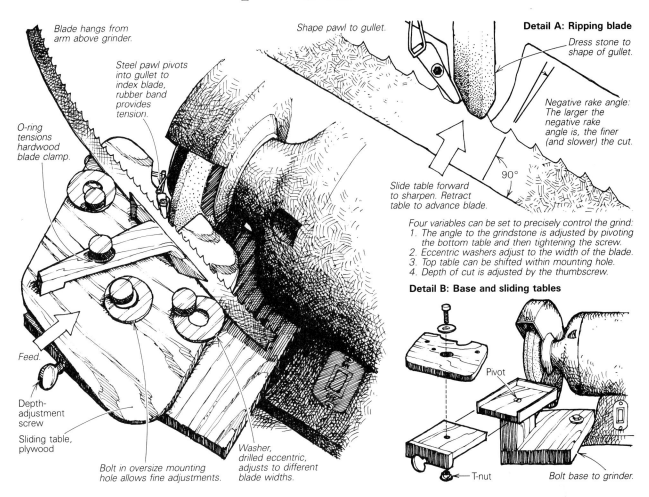

Blade hangs from arm above grinder.

Steel pawl pivots into gullet to index blade, rubber band provides tension.

Shape pawl to gullet.

Detail A: Ripping blade

Dress stone to shape of gullet.

Negative rake angle: The larger the negative rake angle is, the finer (and slower) the cut.

90°

O-ring tensions hardwood blade clamp.

Slide table forward to sharpen. Retract table to advance blade.

Four variables can be set to precisely control the grind:
1. The angle to the grindstone is adjusted by pivoting the bottom table and then tightening the screw.
2. Eccentric washers adjust to the width of the blade.
3. Top table can be shifted within mounting hole.
4. Depth of cut is adjusted by the thumbscrew.

Detail B: Base and sliding tables

Pivot

Feed.

Depth-adjustment screw

Sliding table, plywood

Washer, drilled eccentric, adjusts to different blade widths.

Bolt in oversize mounting hole allows fine adjustments.

T-nut

Bolt base to grinder.

Factory-fresh bandsaw blades leave a lot to be desired if you want to resaw slices thin enough for veneer or for instruments such as the lutes I build. The teeth are usually uneven, and they are sharpened to points like a crosscut or a combination blade, not square across like a ripping blade, which is the best shape for resawing. I built a sharpening rig that attaches to a standard bench grinder, adjusts to blades of various widths, and sharpens blades for ripping, with a slight negative rake and square-faced teeth. This not only improves a new blade, it greatly prolongs its life—the blade can be resharpened many times. I can adjust the mechanism and sharpen a 6-ft. blade in about 10 minutes. It will then cut slices that come off the flitch looking like they've already been sanded with 40-grit paper.

The setup is made from scrap and a few pieces of hardware. No doubt you can adapt a similar design for a dollar or two. The only real expense is the Nor-bide dressing stick used to shape the stone to match the gullets of the blade. That cost me $27.

The rig almost builds itself. First, attach the flat plywood base to your grinder. Next, choose your favorite blade, turn it inside out, and use the Norbide stick to true the grindstone to the shape of one of its gullets, or use the gullet shape shown in the drawing. Then, with the grinder turned off, line up the blade so that the stone fits the gullet—this will show you the height of the post, the angle at which the blade should be clamped and the angle at which the sliding table will have to move. The outside washers on the sliding table act as cams. They can be adjusted to different-width blades, and can also be used to change the sharpening angle slightly. Fine adjustments can be made by loosening the central bolt and shifting the upper layer of the sliding table. At the back of the sliding table, a thumbscrew controls the depth of cut.

The steel pawl, tensioned by a rubber band, indexes the blade. It pivots and clicks into each successive gullet as you slide the blade into position to sharpen the next tooth. When you reach the weld in the blade, you can just grind that tooth shorter freehand if the spacing is uneven. If you have a variety of blades with different-size teeth, you'll find it best to have interchangeable grindstones and pawls to fit.

I'm delighted with the results this gadget produces and I'm sorry I didn't make it years ago. It has had only one drawback so far: A friend of mine had been complaining that his 14-in. Rockwell bandsaw was too underpowered to resaw 12-in. stock. I made him an offer for the saw, then made the mistake of sharpening a blade for him. He promptly cancelled the sale. □

Robert Meadow runs The Luthierie, an instrument-making and woodworking school in Saugerties, N.Y.

the joint with the red-hot tongs. This activates the flux, melts the solder and clamps the joint all in one step. You can even get away with not clamping by taking advantage of the springiness of the blade. Align the scarf joint in the holder, then bend the ends of the blade until the joint is tight.

If you heat and cool the metal too quickly, it will be brittle. Manufacturers—who weld blades with an intense shot of electricity—reheat the joint at a lower voltage so it will cool slowly. But if the joint cools too slowly, the metal around the joint will be too soft. Conditions will vary depending on your torch, your solder, how you clamp and the speed at which you work. It's best to make a few practice repairs. Try to bend each joint. If the metal is too hard, it will snap. The remedy is to cool the joint more slowly. The blacksmiths'

tongs do this automatically, but cold pliers will probably leave the blade brittle. In this case, heating the joint with the torch until it turns the same blue color as the rest of the blade will temper it to the correct degree of spring. If the metal is too soft, it won't have any spring, and will bend easily. In this case, cool the joint more quickly.

After the solder has set, file away any excess from the sides and back of the blade—only the solder in the joint itself contributes to the strength of the bond. □

This article was compiled from information contributed by three woodworkers: Wash Adams, from Richardson, Tex.; Doug Polette, a professor at Montana State University in Bozeman; and John Leeke, of Sanford, Maine.

Japanese Resaws
Two small machines with big blades

by Rich Preiss

Resawing is a superb technique for getting the most out of your wood. You can slice thick planks to near their finished size and thereby lessen the amount of lumber that gets chewed up by the surface planer. After planing, resawn planks can be bookmatched to reveal attractive figure. Yet in many shops, resawing is difficult work. Large industrial bandsaws that do this task effortlessly are expensive and bulky; the smaller machines that shine at fine scrollwork bog down when you feed wide, thick stock into them. Two highly specialized bandsaws from Makita and Hitachi, two of Japan's best-known tool manufacturers, might resolve this dilemma.

These machines, which are scaled-down versions of the industrial bandmills that convert heavy logs to lumber, have been on the American market for three years now. Equipped with wide, coarse blades and geared motors, they are designed specifically for resawing. I borrowed one of each machine—a Makita 2116 and a Hitachi B600A—and tested them in my shop. I tried cutting all kinds of stock, from hard rosewood to softer oak and walnut. I used the machines for both resawing and ripping, and found that they did these tasks quickly and accurately.

The Makita costs about $1,300; the Hitachi, about $1,650 (figures vary, so shop around)—relatively high prices for bandsaws of this size, but a fraction of what you would pay for an industrial bandsaw that will resaw as well. I resawed boards up to 12 in. wide, dimensioned heavy timber and ripped boards to finished widths. I even resawed my own 1/16-in. thick veneer from wide boards, a job I wouldn't attempt with a standard bandsaw. This veneer was practically ready to use straight from the saw, requiring very little subsequent planing.

When I uncrated the saws, I was surprised at their small dimensions. Unlike other bandsaws that have base cabinets to elevate the table to a standard 40-in. working height, these resaws are designed for use at 29 in. to 30 in. This looked

odd to me at first, until I realized that it means you don't have to hoist large timbers or heavy boards to chest height, balancing them precariously during the cut. Of course, you still have the option of blocking the resaw to any height, but I found that I soon got more comfortable working over the material instead of behind it.

A second unusual feature of these machines is the seemingly small size of the motors. But these high-speed motors run the saws' drive wheels through a geared transmission and pulley arrangement that gives enough torque for this kind of work. The 2-HP Makita motor, with its greater RPM, makes for a smoother cut, but will lag sooner than the slower, 3-HP Hitachi. If you rely on these saws continuously, or for extensive resawing of maximum-width boards, larger motors can readily be adapted to the universal mounting plates on these saws. Both seem built heavily enough to take more power, especially the Hitachi.

The real eye-opener on both machines is the width of the blade—2⅜ in. on the Makita and 2⅞ in. on the Hitachi. The blades have swage-cut teeth tipped with Stellite, an alloy harder than steel but softer than carbide. The tips are fused to a thin blade body, resulting in a highly tensionable blade that cuts a narrow kerf. At $48 for the Makita and $70 for the Hitachi, these blades are expensive. But they run cool and should last a while. You can resharpen them once or twice by hand with a file, but when they get really dull, you'll have to take them to a sharpening shop equipped to grind Stellite.

The guides on both saws are conventional friction-type blocks made of Bakelite. They are as wide as the blade, and about ⅜ in. thick, with the middle section relieved so that the blade will run cooler. Both have thrust bearings behind the blade, but the Hitachi's bearings run in line with rather than at right angles to the blade axis—an unusual arrangement I'd never seen before, but one that seemed to work fine.

I preferred the Makita's blade-adjustment mechanism, es-

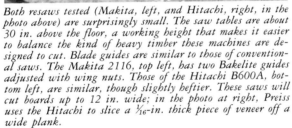

Both resaws tested (Makita, left, and Hitachi, right, in the photo above) are surprisingly small. The saw tables are about 30 in. above the floor, a working height that makes it easier to balance the kind of heavy timber these machines are designed to cut. Blade guides are similar to those of conventional saws. The Makita 2116, top left, has two Bakelite guides adjusted with wing nuts. Those of the Hitachi B600A, bottom left, are similar, though slightly heftier. These saws will cut boards up to 12 in. wide; in the photo at right, Preiss uses the Hitachi to slice a 1/16-in. thick piece of veneer off a wide plank.

pecially the tracking control, which stays put without having to tighten an additional locknut, as on the Hitachi. The upper guides and thrust bearing on the Makita saw are fixed to a solid block, and are simpler to adjust than the Hitachi's, whose base tends to tilt when loosened.

I found quite a few other differences between these two machines. The wheel shafts and bearings on the Hitachi saw are about 50% larger than on the Makita. And like most industrial machines, the Hitachi has adjustable gibs on the upper blade-tensioning ways, enabling fine adjustment for future wear. The Makita lacks this feature, but I'm not sure it makes much difference to the average user anyway; nevertheless, it's a nice touch that's better to have than not. The Hitachi frame is made of fabricated steel, but is about 40 lb. heavier than the cast-iron Makita. The weight difference has little bearing on performance, though—either saw is stable enough to do what's expected of it.

Both saws are equipped with fences whose length ends at the front edge of the blade. The Makita's fence cleverly swings clear of the table, and it includes a vernier fine-adjustment control, two features that speed the work when you have to set up the saw several times a day. The stubbier Hitachi fence, however, locks more firmly and deflects less noticeably under feed pressure. In addition, it has a coarser rack-and-pinion adjustment that won't clog and bind when filled

with sawdust, a problem that made the Makita fence annoying to work with. The Hitachi also has a spring-steel holddown that I found handy for holding boards against the fence. The Hitachi has another feature I liked: a manual brake that quickly stops the blade for safety and for speeding adjustments.

After working with these saws for more than a month, I can only conclude that, for me, they aren't an essential basic machine like a tablesaw or a jointer. I don't do enough resawing or timber-sizing to justify a machine devoted to just that one purpose. Since I tested these saws, Hitachi has redesigned its blade guides to accommodate narrower blades, and one Makita dealer has devised a kit to do the same thing, but I haven't tested either. For my money, these saws are best kept to resawing, leaving scrollwork for the lighter—and usually less expensive—saws designed for that job. If I did have the need for one of these saws, I'd pick the Hitachi, despite its higher price. This machine's heavier, more sophisticated construction and greater power make it more akin to the kind of industrial-quality machinery we would all buy if we could afford it. □

Rich Preiss supervises the architectural woodworking shop at the University of North Carolina at Charlotte.

The Jointer
How to adjust, sharpen and use this basic machine

by Tage Frid

1

After the circular table saw, I feel that the jointer and the thickness planer are the most important big machines in a woodshop, especially for a person who wants to make a living from woodworking. These two machines are a big investment but will pay for themselves over the years. An old out-dated jointer and thickness planer can sometimes be bought quite inexpensively and will usually do as good a job as a new machine. Don't buy an old jointer with a square head—it's too dangerous. The smallest jointer I would buy

would be a 6-in. model (an 8-in. one is preferable), with a 1-HP motor. The smallest thickness planer I'd buy is a 12-in. one with a 2-HP motor.

A jointer is a machine that planes, joints or surfaces a board, ending up with one side perfectly flat (1). The table in the front of the rotating knives is called the infeed table, and the one in the back is the outfeed table. The difference in height between the infeed and outfeed is the thickness of wood planed off with each pass.

On a jointer with a round cutter-

head, I would never run a piece shorter than 10 in. Jointers with square cutter-heads have a larger opening. These aren't made anymore, but if you buy a used one it might be of this type. I would never run anything shorter than 15 in. on such a jointer. When jointing the face of a board, use a good push-stick. Never run end grain over the jointer—it is too dangerous. End grain is very hard and often shatters rather than cutting. Don't pass the edges of plywood over a jointer either—the glue will put nicks in the blade.

---

1. Setting jointer knives — Knives on a jointer should be parallel to the outfeed table and all at the same height. Use a straight stick to set the jointer knives. *First unplug the machine.* Then make a pencil mark on the stick at the beginning of the outfeed table (**A**), while the cutterhead is below the table.

(**B**) Then move the cutterhead forward (carrying the stick with it) and (**C**) make a second mark, again at the beginning of the outfeed table (**D**).

Now move the stick to the opposite end of the knife and repeat the procedure. If the stick moves the same amount, the knife is parallel to the outfeed table. If it does not, loosen the nuts that hold the knife in place and correct before retightening. When that knife is parallel, be sure to tighten all the nuts. Move to the next knife and set it in the same way, using the same stick and the same two markings (so the height of the second blade is the same as the first). Continue until all the knives are aligned. Be sure all the knives are secured before you start the machine. Raise the outfeed table so it is level with the knives.

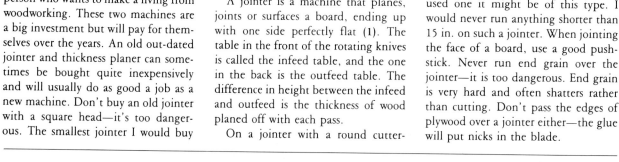

A

B

C

D

---

2. Sharpening the knives — An easy way to sharpen the jointer knives without removing them is to use a router. Remove the plastic plate from the base of the router and screw on a piece of ¾-in. plywood. (See **A**, page 65, top. The two grooves in the bottom of the plywood have nothing at all to do with the sharpening process—I used a scrap piece of plywood.) Place a medium-grit grind-stone in the router.

You must be able to control the position of the knives so they will all be ground the same amount. To do this, drill two holes in the center of the infeed table (**B**). The first

hole, closer to the knives, is about 1½ in. from the opening for the cutterhead. The second hole is directly behind the first, about 3 in. from the edge of the opening. Thread the first hole to receive a ³⁄₁₆-in. or ¼-in. screw. Then cut a thin but stiff piece of sheet aluminum or steel about 7 in. long. Drill a hole in the center of the metal strip about 2½ in. from the end of the piece on the side closer to the cutterhead. Be sure the screw fits snugly into the hole. Then drill a second hole in the strip corresponding to the second hole in the table. The exact measurements may vary; the important thing is

that the metal strip keep all the knives in the same position.

Fasten the metal strip to the infeed table and (**C**) insert a steel pin into the second hole (I use the end of a nail set). Push the cutterhead tight up against the metal strip. Then lower the infeed table until the bevel of the knives is parallel with the outfeed table (**D**). Secure the cutterhead by inserting wooden wedges at both outside ends of the knife head.

Set the router on the outfeed table with the piece of plywood resting on the table. Set the depth of the grindstone so that it just touches the bevel of the blade. Be sure you are wearing proper face and eye protection. Start the router and (E) carefully move it back and forth over the blade until the stone stops cutting. Be sure to keep the plywood piece flat on the table.

When the first knife is ground, remove the wooden wedges and the tapered steel pin. Swing the metal strip out of the way and move the cutterhead so that the next knife is on top. Reposition the metal strip, insert the steel pin and wedge the cutterhead again. Continue sharpening until all the knives are ground. Do not change the height of either the infeed or outfeed tables, or of the grindstone in the router.

The knives are sharp when a small burr appears on the back of each knife along its whole length. It is not necessary to remove this burr. If you want to make the knives a little sharper, you can hone each one by hand with a honing stone. I usually don't

bother with this step at all.

If the knives still are not sharp after one grinding, repeat the process. They can be sharpened this way about five times before you will have to reposition them farther out. After each sharpening you have to raise the outfeed table to the same height as the knives.

B

C

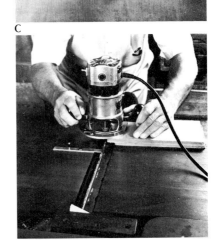

A

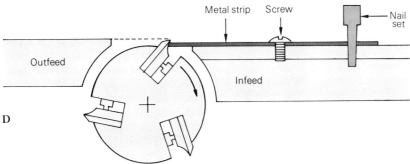

Metal strip — Screw — Nail set — Outfeed — Infeed

D

E

3. Operating the jointer — The infeed table controls how much of a cut is to be taken off the boards. In a soft wood, I would never take off more than 1/16 in. in one pass. In extremely hard wood or a wood with unusual grain pattern (like curly maple), I would take much less at each pass.

Before you pass wood over the jointer, look at the edge of the board to see which way the grain runs. Running the board so that the cutting action goes with the grain produces the smoothest edge (A). However,

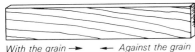

With the grain → ← Against the grain

A

the grain sometimes reverses direction in the middle of the piece and you cannot avoid roughing up some of the wood. Either handplane the board or take the roughness out later by scraping and sanding after milling is complete.

When using the jointer for a board that is slightly bowed, either take the same amount off of each end first or start jointing in the middle to correct the bowing on one face. Here (B) I took it off each end. When one face is roughly straightened out, feed the wood in again with the straight face down. When approximately five to six inches have passed over the knives, push the wood down on the outfeed table and ease up the pressure over the infeed table (C). Because the board is perfectly flat after pass-

ing over the knives, putting pressure only on the outfeed table keeps the board flat and straight. Otherwise, if the board is twisted and all the pressure is on the infeed table, the board will continue to be twisted and the twist will get jointed into the piece so that very shortly you will have a piece of uneven thickness that follows the twist.

Once one face is flat, you can joint the edge. First put a square at the end of the infeed table (D) and check that the fence is square. Then (E) joint the edge, keeping the face of the board tight against the fence. When matching edges are jointed, check to see how they fit. If they do not fit tightly for their entire length, joint the boards again. Note: The safeguard has been removed for clarity of the photograph.

If the joint is convex, of course the boards have to be jointed again. To correct a convex

C

D

B

E

edge (F), flatten the curve by running the center of the board over the jointer. Then take one full pass. Whenever you joint an edge for a glue joint, pass the board over the jointer slowly so that the surface gets very smooth. If this burnishes the surface, the knives need resharpening.

When you are jointing boards to be edge-glued, joint each board with the opposite face against the fence. If the fence is slightly off square, the next board will be off square the opposite way and the two will fit together, gluing up straight. But the two faces of the board must be parallel, to use this technique. That is, the board should have been put through a thickness planer.

To demonstrate this point, the fence was set well off square. (G) Note how the edge of the board slopes down under the square. Even if the two edges are not square, but the opposite faces of the board are run against the fence, the two boards will still glue up straight (H).

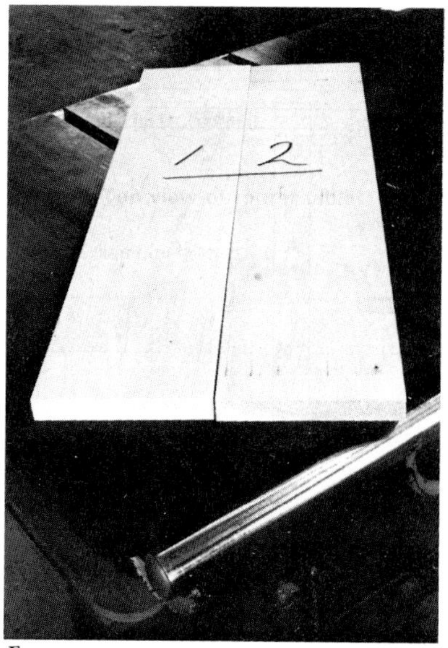

F

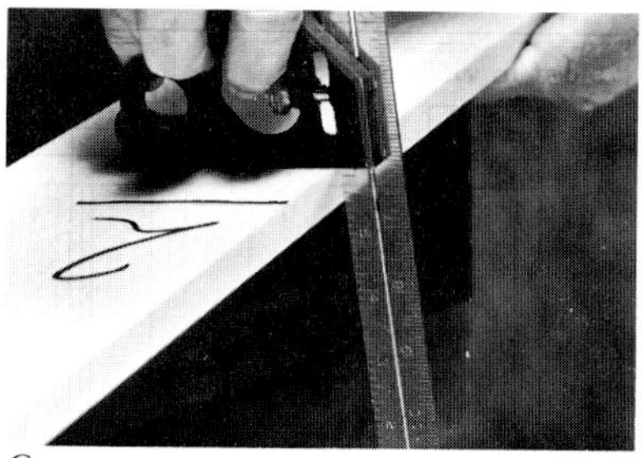

G

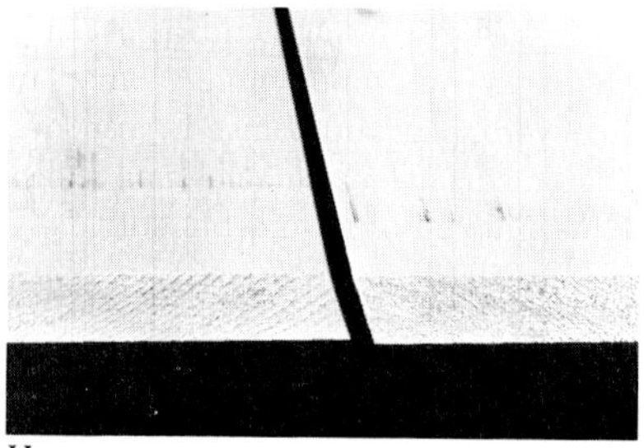

H

4. Thicknessing with the jointer — If a thickness planer is not available, the jointer can be used. First you must make a jig to fit the jointer that can take different widths of board. The photo (A) shows the jig apart and upside-down. You use it by cutting a rabbet all along both edges of the board, at the thickness you want. The rabbets ride on the jig while the board goes over the jointer and this way keep the board the same thickness from end to end (B).

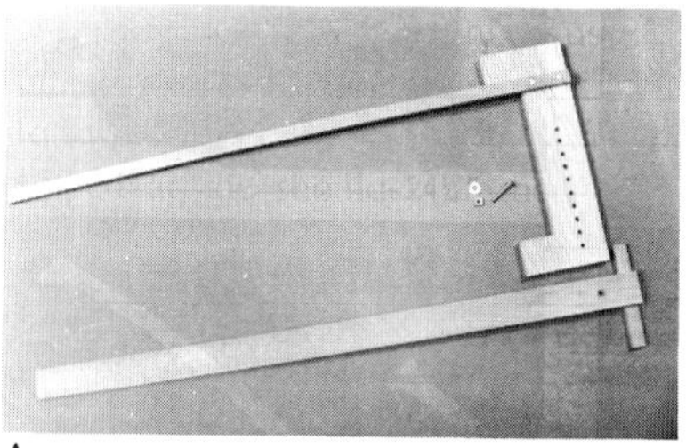

A

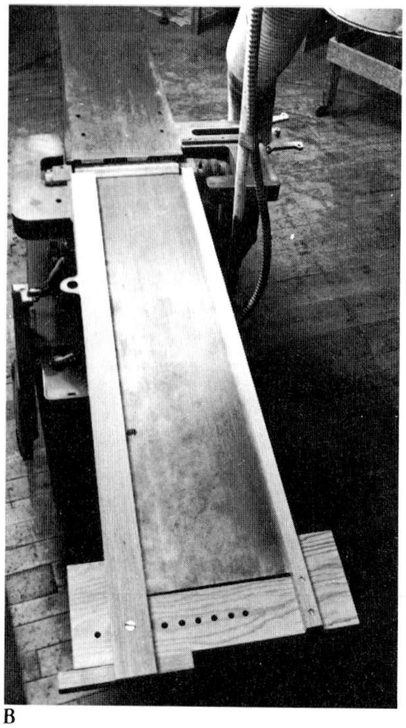

B

The jig shown in the drawing (C) is made to fit my 8-in. jointer. The long 1¾-in. piece is made like a *T*-square and is movable so it can be adjusted to the width of the board, either by making a slot for a bolt in the ¾-in. plywood back piece, which holds the jig in position, or by drilling several holes through which a bolt can go. I feel the holes are safer because even if the bolt is not tightened down properly the *T*-square piece cannot slide.

The *T*-square has to be exactly 90° to the plywood back piece. The long ¾-in. piece, which is fastened to the back piece, is slightly off 90° toward the inside of the jig. This way the two long pieces will fit tightly into the rabbets cut along the board. If used right, this jig is safe. For an extra precau-

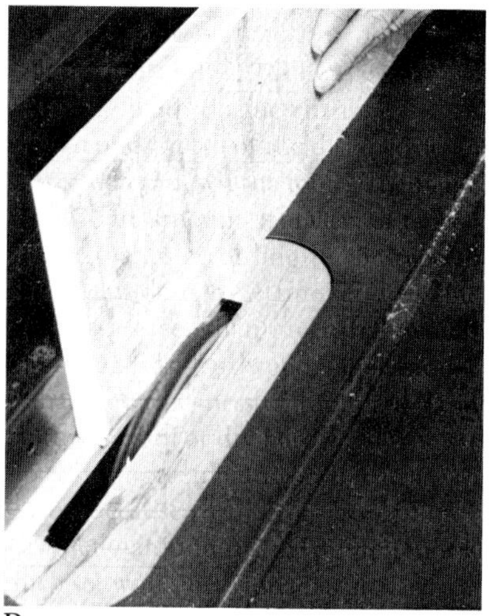

D

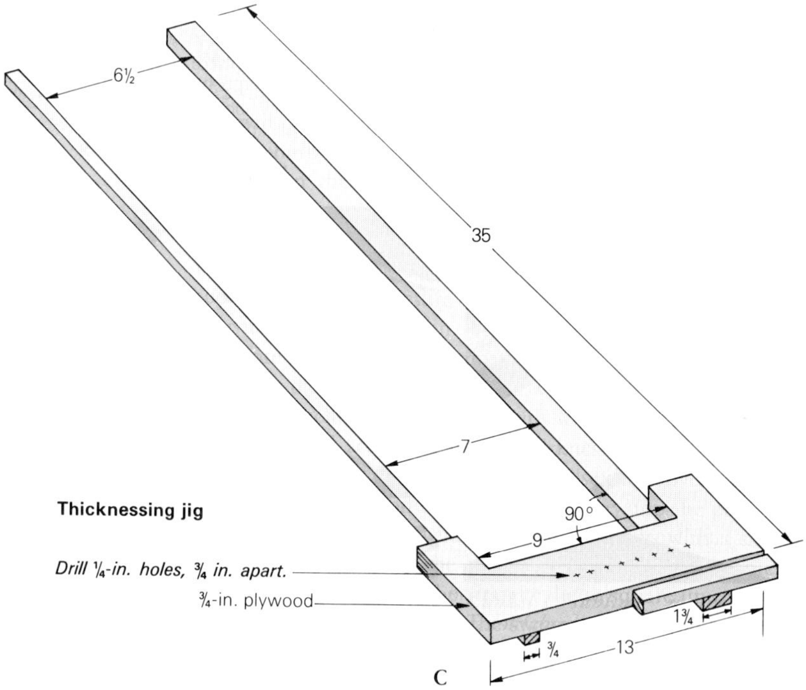

Thicknessing jig
6½
35
7
90°
9
Drill ¼-in. holes, ¾ in. apart.
¾-in. plywood
1¾
¾
13

C

tion, secure the plywood back piece to the infeed table, either with bolts or clamps.

To use the jig, joint one side of the board flat and also one edge, then cut the board to width. Using either an electric router with a fence or a dado head on the table saw (D), run the rabbet on both edges of the board. Set the rip fence to the exact finished thickness you want and raise the dado head at least ½ in. above the saw table. Now lower the infeed table, but make sure the tops of the two long pieces of the jig are still higher than the outfeed table. You gauge how much to adjust the tables by how much wood you have to remove (E). Run the board over the jointer (F) and gradually lower the infeed table until the top faces of

the two long pieces of the jig end up level with the outfeed table (G). Remember that the rabbet should still be at least ⅟₁₆ in. deep for the final cut, so the board will be able to ride securely in the jig. Now the board is flat and the faces parallel. If you made the rabbet a tiny bit fat at the start, you can still joint a finishing cut without the jig, without throwing it out of parallel. □

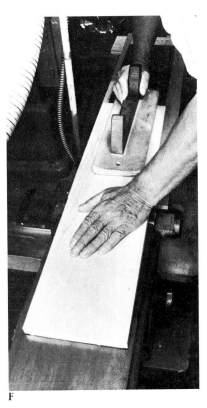

E

F

G

This article is adapted from Tage Frid Teaches Woodworking, Book 1—Joinery *(The Taunton Press, PO Box 355, Newtown, Conn. 06470). Tage Frid is professor emeritus of woodworking and furniture design at Rhode Island School of Design.*

Q & A

Setting jointer table—*I am having difficulty setting the outfeed table of my 8-in. jointer at the proper height in relation to the knives. I try to set it in exactly the same plane as the top of the cutting arc, but very seldom do I get a perfectly straight edge, especially on long boards. What am I doing wrong?* —*Larry Green, Bethel, Conn.*
To joint a perfectly straight edge on a long board requires more than a properly adjusted machine; it demands correct technique as well. You're right about the outfeed table being the same height as the knives at the top of their cut, but this adjustment can be tricky, and the slightest variation will produce a difference in the jointed surface. If the outfeed table is lower than the knives, you'll get a concave surface (a sprung joint); if the outfeed table is higher than the knives, the opposite will happen. And, even if the outfeed table is set exactly at the height of the knives, you'll get a sprung joint if the table, not locked firmly in its ways, angles down slightly from the cutterhead. In fact, one way to produce a sprung joint is to loosen the lock screw that bears against the gibs. This lets the outfeed table droop. Also, putting the proper pressure on the gibs is necessary to get a good cut.

To set the outfeed table in the right relation to the knives, get a freshly jointed board, lay it on the outfeed table and rotate the cutterhead so the knives make contact with it. If they lift the board from the table, even slightly, raise the table until the knives make tangential contact only. If you still do not get a straight edge, determine whether it is concave or convex, and raise or lower the table minutely to compensate.

When jointing long, heavy stock, you should support the work at the outfeed end with a roller that's precisely the same height as the outfeed table. While feeding the stock, concentrate downward pressure over the outfeed table, just behind the cutterhead. Too much pressure on the work as it passes over the infeed table can produce a convex edge.

. . .The solution given for Larry Green's problem takes time to set up. Instead, set the outfeed tables at their closest, get an 18-in. piece of jointed ¾-in. board and take a light cut on one edge for about 1 in. Using a soft-lead pencil, shade this 1-in. area. Reverse the board and joint its entire length. If the pencil marks wipe off completely, raise the outfeed table a few thousandths of an inch. If the marks are not wiped off at all, lower the table. When the jointer is correctly adjusted, the knives should remove all but a trace of the marks.
—*Floyd R. Vertil, Stockton, Calif.*

. . .This happened to me. . .the outfeed table was warped, partly because I had left a grinder clamped to the end of the table for several days. A good machine shop can take a light cut on both tables with a milling machine and bring them into the same plane again. The finish need not be as smooth as the original. —*John Wood, Tyler, Tex.*

Setting jointer knives—*How far should jointer knives protrude from the cutterhead? How far can they be ground down before they have to be replaced (i.e., how far can they be jacked up in the cutterhead groove before there isn't enough contact to hold them safely)?*
—*Floyd W. Foess, Federal Way, Wash.*
BILL RAMSEY REPLIES: Rockwell uses the Underwriters Laboratory standard: jointer knives should protrude ⅛ in. beyond the cylindrical cutterhead. Any more and they can hit the edges of the feed tables. We use a dial gauge to set them accurately at the factory; a square placed on the jointer outfeed table works as well, but it's slower. Replace jointer knives when the full face of the lock-bars won't bear against the side of the knife; knives that narrow have insufficient surface area to hold them safely in place. [Bill Ramsey is plant manager at Rockwell (now Delta) Power Tool's Tupelo, Miss., plant.]

Shop-Testing Five Jointer-Planers

Combination machines solve some problems, have drawbacks too

by James A. Rome

After the machine saws, a jointer and a thickness planer are likely to be the woodshop's most-needed stationary tools. It would be delightful to own a big, cast-iron jointer with an 18-in. planer to match, but, even ignoring the cost, most of us just don't have the room. Faced with this problem a year ago, I went on a mail-order shopping trip for a jointer-planer: a machine that would combine both functions into one compact unit.

I discovered that at least six companies build such machines, based on two design schemes. European and American manufacturers have preferred the over-under design in which a single cutterhead does both jointing and planing. The Japanese favor a side-by-side design—really just a medium-size jointer fastened to the side of a thickness planer—with two separate cutterheads running on a common shaft. The difference between the two basic designs is more than mere appearances. Although you can make a side-by-side go from planing to jointing by walking a step or two, its jointer head is only half as wide as its planer. The over-under machines can joint stock the same width as they can plane, but changing operations requires manipulation of tables and guards.

Lacking a useful way to compare one machine to another, I bought a Makita 2030 side-by-side, which I used happily for

a year, until an unfortunate accident (see box, page 74) prompted me to replace it with the other Japanese combination, the Hitachi. When I offered to write about my experience with these two machines, *Fine Woodworking* arranged for me to test three more as well. In order of price, the test machines were the American-made Belsaw ($700), the Austrian Emco ($1,000), the Makita ($1,350), the Hitachi ($1,500) and the Swiss Inca ($1,500). I did not test another American-made machine, the $2,104 cast-iron Parks model #11, because it's available only on special order (Parks Woodworking Machine Co., 1517 Knowlton St., Cincinnati, Ohio 45223).

Before getting down to specifics, let's review the basic functions of jointers and thickness planers. The jointer can start from a roughsawn surface and make it into a face side or edge: flat and smooth, free of twist, cup or warp. Once the cut has been started, the jointer is self-jigging in that it determines where it is going by referring to where it has just been. The thickness planer, on the other hand, power-feeds wood between its bed and cutterhead, and thus it requires one smooth, flat surface in order to create a true surface on the other side of the board. Many people, lacking a wide jointer, prepare both sides of a board by repeated passes through the planer. While this procedure will make both sides smooth

The Belsaw model 684, left, is one of two fabricated steel combination machines tested by the author. For conversion from a jointer to a planer, the hinged infeed and outfeed tables flip sideways, as shown in the photo above. The planer's maximum width of cut is 8⅜ in., the narrowest of all the machines tested. The guard leaves part of the cutterhead exposed during jointer operation, right, and because it's hinged on, rather than to one side of the table, it reduces the jointer's effective cutting width by nearly 2 in.

and parallel to one another, it won't remove all of the warp.

Setting up the machines was straightforward, no thanks to the instruction manuals, which were universally terrible. I went about my analysis with the needs of a serious but non-professional woodworker in mind, using these tools in the course of three months of small-project woodworking. I checked the jointer and planer tables for flatness, and measured the noise level generated by each machine. I paid particular attention to how each machine's knives could be removed and replaced, since precise knife adjustment is crucial to accurate planing and jointing (all five machines have two-knife cutterheads). To find out how the combinations would handle various woods, I planed oak, redwood, and goncalo alves, a hard tropical wood with interlocked grain.

The Belsaw 684 combination evolved from the company's popular 12-in. surface planer, the price of which has been kept low by the use of fabricated steel instead of cast iron. Unfortunately, in this case, cost-cutting has yielded a bulky, heavy tool (198 lb.) whose jointer is seriously flawed.

To convert the Belsaw from jointing to planing, you loosen a couple of catches and flip the tables sideways, so that the cutterhead shroud can pivot up from below, where it is stored when the machine is a jointer. A microswitch blocks motor operation unless the guard is installed, a safety feature the other two over-under machines lack.

As a planer, the Belsaw works reasonably well, given the 1-HP motor. Its feed rate of 28 ft./min. is brisk enough as long as you don't take too deep a cut in a single pass, in which case it stalls. The 8⅜-in. maximum width of the planer is inadequate for most cabinet work, and because the Belsaw lacks a depth feeler gauge, I found it hard to tell just when the knives start to bite. When I tried the dowel-cutting knife that Belsaw sent, the motor balked and blew my 20-amp circuit breaker. The other molding knives worked better.

Belsaw makes no attempt at sawdust control. Dust is dumped on the planer outfeed table, or under the jointer where it gets into everything, including the chain-and-sprocket depth-setting mechanism. To keep chips from jamming the works, you have to clean them out frequently by opening up the hinged side shrouds. There's also no anti-kickback device, but the machine's skinny rubber feed rollers probably grip the wood well enough to prevent it being shot out the back. None of the over-unders I tested has bed rollers, an omission that doesn't seem to hurt planing performance if you keep the tables waxed.

I found the Belsaw jointer almost unusable and somewhat unsafe. The fence, which tilts but doesn't slide, is inadequately supported and will deflect ½ in. horizontally, somewhat less vertically. The hinged tables are unsupported on the fence side. Press down, they give, ruining the flatness of the cut. Also, the jointer guard pivots on the infeed table rather than to one side of it, reducing the cutting width from 8⅜ in. to 6⅝ in. Worse yet, in use, the guard leaves a dangerously large triangle of cutterhead exposed.

Belsaw's knife-setting system seems elegant, but is difficult to use. Each knife fits into a dovetailed slot in the cutterhead where two bolts bear against the back edge of the knife, raising or lowering the knife to the desired height, which you measure with a plunger gauge that straddles the knife slot. I could adjust knife height easily enough, but when I tightened the locking wedge, the knives crept up. I had to loosen the

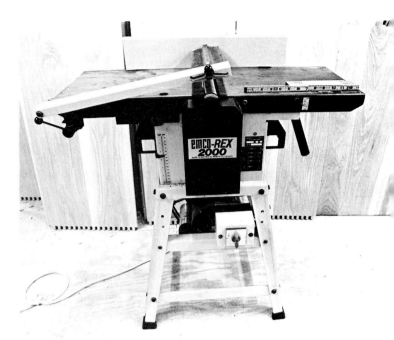

The Emco-Rex 2000, the basic power unit of a versatile multipurpose machine, has the overarm jointer guard common to European stationary tools. It detaches for planer conversion.

wedge and start over with the knives low so that snugging the bolts pushed them to the correct height.

The Emco-Rex 2000 is made by the same folks who make Unimat lathes, the Emco-Maier Company. Strikingly painted in orange and black, the 2000 is the basic unit of a multipurpose machine. You can add a tablesaw, a slot mortiser and a shaper. The Emco is made of fabricated steel, but is smaller than the Belsaw and, at 143 lb., is also lighter.

To convert the machine from a jointer to a planer, you remove the jointer outfeed table by turning a couple of bolted catch hooks a half turn. A plastic guard placed over the cutterhead is wedged in place by moving the jointer depth control, which is a lever instead of the usual knob or handwheel. The guard also acts as a duct which funnels shavings into an adapter that can be connected to your shop vacuum.

The Emco's steel feed rollers are deeply serrated and feed positively, but when I tried to plane off a light cut, they left noticeable marks in the surface, requiring another pass at a deeper setting to remove. Since the feed rollers aren't adjustable, this is a real drawback, because on hard woods such as birch or maple, you sometimes have to take a shallow cut to get a good surface. If the rollers lose their grip on the stock, anti-kickback pawls keep it from exiting violently.

To adjust the knives, you raise them with a screwdriver and push down with a block of wood. When the knives are correctly positioned, you tighten bolts to fix them in place. To measure knife projection, you place a plastic gauge across the jointer mouth and then hand-rotate the cutterhead. The knives are right when they just grab the gauge at the top of their arc, scooting it a marked distance. On my machine, the sheet-steel tables weren't flat, so the short gauge was useless. I had to make a longer one out of wood. Even then, knife-setting was a tedious trial-and-error affair.

The planing performance of the Emco was good, although leisurely, at a feed rate of 16.4 ft./min. With its 2½-HP induction motor, the Emco has plenty of power and never stalled, even when pushed hard. At the slow feed rate, thicknessing 100 bd. ft. of 4/4 lumber will likely take the better part of a day, and boards wider than the 10³/₁₆-in. maximum will have to be ripped down.

The Emco jointer guard consists of a sheet-metal stamping held above the cutterhead by an adjustable arm. For edge-jointing, it slides away from the fence; for face-jointing, you shove the board under the guard, an operation requiring you to lift your hands (or, better yet, push blocks) as you pass the guard. This little shuffle leaves an unjointed bump in the board, which the planer must skim off. I ignored the temptation to work without the guard: 10 in. of exposed cutterhead is too scary.

Because its tables are supported on both edges, the Emco jointer is more accurate than the Belsaw, but still too short for truing long stock. Anyone accustomed to an expensive jointer will find the movable, tiltable fence flimsy, yet it's solid enough, and would be quite good if you bolted a wide board to the fence to lengthen and stiffen it.

The Inca 343-190 jointer tables, bed and frame are made of pressure-cast aluminum, generously ribbed for strength and bending resistance, resulting in a tool that's very rigid, yet, at 114 lb., the lightest of the group. The jointer-planer I tested is an improved version of the old model 510, which has been discontinued. The Inca's jointer tables are a usable 42½ in. long, and it will plane and joint boards 10¼ in. wide.

The Inca has an unusual feature for a planer in this price range: a two-speed feed (11.5 ft./min., 16.5 ft./min., and

Inca's combination is the only one of five tested that sports two feed rates, which are controlled by the lever above the motor. The flap screwed to the jointer fence covers the cutterhead when the fence is moved forward.

neutral) which can be changed by a shift lever while the wood is being planed. When I wanted to shift speeds, however, I always found myself standing on the side of the machine opposite the lever. Anyway, even at its high speed, the Inca is a slowpoke. I would have been glad to trade the speed changer for a decent depth feeler gauge, which the Inca lacks.

The Inca does a beautiful job of planing, especially if you take thin cuts, which you can do because the knurled feed rollers don't mar the wood the way the Emco's do. On the goncalo alves, the Inca tore out less than did the other planers, perhaps because its cutterhead knives are supported right out to their tips, thus limiting chatter. The Inca was outstanding at planing very thin pieces of wood (less than ⅛ in.). The standard 1½-HP motor is too small, however, and prone to stall. Garrett Wade, the Inca distributor, says a 2-HP (220V) motor is a no-cost option. I'd recommend it.

The Inca converts from planer to jointer similarly to the Emco. Also, like the Emco's, the Inca's jointer guard gets in the way. When face-jointing, wide boards chatter unless you press downward fairly near the cutterhead. I found this awkward to do. The jointer fence is one piece of solid, heavy aluminum supported on a ribbed pedestal a third of the way down the infeed table. This arrangement isn't rigid enough, and though it's stiffest where you apply pressure when edge-jointing, it deflects more than I like at the outfeed end. I was able to rig my shop vacuum to collect the planer's shavings, but couldn't do the same for the jointer—it dumps them on the planer table. A new plastic hood developed by Inca supposedly solves this problem.

Of all the machines tested, the Inca's knife-adjustment system is the most accurate. Each knife has two slots into which the head of an Allen bolt fits. Turning these bolts raises or lowers the knife. This system is handy if you have knives that are low at the center, as mine were. I raised both ends about 0.005 in. until the center was at the correct height, snugged the center locking bolts, then lowered each end to the correct height. To measure knife height, Inca supplies a very nice $80 dial indicator with an aluminum base, although I got just as close using the Emco method and a flat, straight piece of wood.

The Makita 2030 is one of a half-dozen stationary woodworking tools sold by Makita in the United States. Solidly constructed, it shows how the Japanese are using cast iron much the way Inca uses aluminum: relatively thin castings with plenty of stiffening ribs. You can also buy the machine with a 14-in. non-tilting circular ripsaw mounted alongside the planer (model LM3001). If you already own a radial-arm saw instead of a tablesaw, such a combination might be ideal. The Makita will plane boards up to 12 in. wide and joint to 6⅛ in. wide.

The Makita arrives ready to run (ditto the Hitachi), but the two columns upon which the machine is supported elevate it only 20 in. above the floor—uncomfortably low for my 6-ft. frame. I bolted the machine to a 2x4 stand on locking casters, raising the jointer table to about 35 in. above the floor. I included casters on the stand so that I could roll the 276-lb. machine around in my cramped shop.

Most Japanese stationary machines, including the Makita and Hitachi combinations, are powered by universal motors, not induction motors. Universal motors, which also drive routers, are small and light, but must whine up to high

(continued on page 72)

Learning how to read the grain

by R. Bruce Hoadley

Before feeding a board into a surface planer or hand-planing it, it's important to read the board's grain, or you risk tearout. There are many routines for doing this. Most woodworkers simply examine the edge of a board to determine the inclination of the cell structure. But close scrutiny may sometimes be too time-consuming, as when feeding a large quantity into a jointer or a surface planer, or when you simply cannot see any useful detail because the lumber has roughsawn edges. Even-grained and fine-textured woods such as basswood pose similar problems.

One helpful gimmick when planing flatsawn boards is to use the board's U-shaped or V-shaped surface figure to determine grain inclination. As shown in figure 1, on the pith side of a board (the heart, or inside, of the tree), the tips of the Vs point with the grain, so you would hand-plane in that direction. On the bark side, the Vs point against the grain. My memory crutch goes like this:

Pith* side, *Plane* with the *Points* (of Vs) *Bark* side, *Backwards

The rule works on boards with any visible V-shaped markings. After a while it becomes automatic. You instinctively glance at the end when you pick up a board; if you are working a pith side, you subconsciously hand-plane with the points, and so on.

Of course, with wood it's not always that simple. For example, you may have a board with Vs going in both directions. Let's assume you have a board that has a bark side surface with the appearance shown in figure 2. The "bark side, backwards" rule of thumb helps you recognize zones of the board, so you would hand-plane zones A and C from left to right, as shown, but zone B from right to left. If you keep in mind that the knives of jointers and planers actually cut in the opposite direction to the direction of feed, reading the Vs would also help you decide to send the board into a planer left-end-first. You can anticipate good results over most of the board (zones A and C), but with possible trouble where the cutterhead would be working against the grain (zone B). Knowing where the troubles will occur, you can take lighter cuts, slow the rate

of feed, or use alternatives (such as abrasive planers or sharp hand-tools) to minimize filling and sanding later.

Complete Vs are handy, but they're not always present. Consider the boards shown in figure 3, where the points of the Vs are gone and only their sloping sides are present. The drawing shows which way the Vs pointed in the wider board from which each strip was removed. Careful inspection reveals that within each growth ring the latewood edge indicates which way the Vs point. This is difficult to determine with even-

grained woods (such as birch or maple), but with uneven-grained woods (such as spruce, hemlock, fir, oak or butternut) it will be as easy as looking at the V-direction. Another way to state the rule is: On the pith side, within each growth ring, plane from early to late; on the bark side, backwards.

Every board came from a tree stem—the growth-ring figure can help you to interpret the inclination of the grain. If you learn to read it and work with it, you will have fewer surprises, and better surfaces in your finished work. □

Bruce Hoadley is professor of wood technology at the University of Massachusetts at Amherst, and the author of Understanding Wood, A Craftsman's Guide to Wood Technology *(The Taunton Press).*

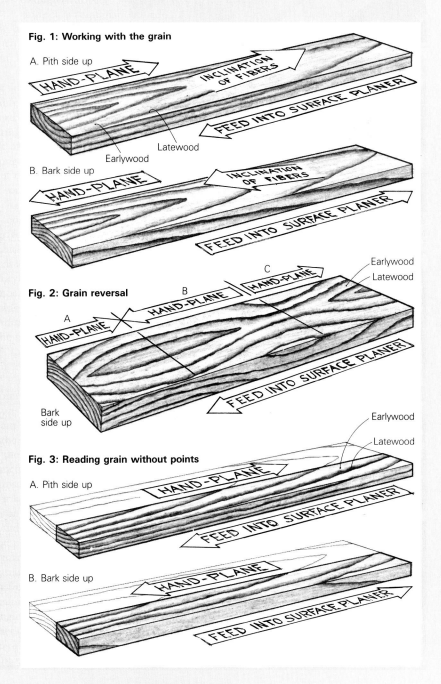

Fig. 1: Working with the grain

A. Pith side up

Latewood
Earlywood

B. Bark side up

Fig. 2: Grain reversal

Earlywood
Latewood

Bark side up

Fig. 3: Reading grain without points

Earlywood
Latewood

A. Pith side up

B. Bark side up

Four unpowered bed rollers support boards fed through the Makita 2030. While you walk around the machine, stock can be temporarily shelved on two return rollers on top of the planer.

When the Makita fence is advanced over the cutterhead, the knives are left dangerously exposed as stock is fed.

speeds to develop their rated power. As a result, they are dangerously noisy (ear protection is a must) and, lacking torque, they bog down under load. The Makita's 2-HP motor is fine for most jointing and for planing narrow stock. It chokes when you try to plane more than $\frac{1}{32}$ in. off a wide board in a single pass. Set aside some time if you're going to mill a stack of lumber. And figure on cleaning up a mess—the planer tosses the chips onto the emerging board, the jointer leaves them on the floor. I liked the Makita's four adjustable bed rollers, especially the two outboard rollers which prop up long boards, preventing them from being sniped—gouged too deeply—as they emerge from the machine. Two return rollers atop the machine offer a handy perch on which to rest the board while you walk to the infeed end for another pass.

As a thicknesser, the Makita has great gauges. A plunger-type feeler gauge above the planer infeed table will tell you how much you're planing off a board before you feed it, and a nearby placard tells how much of a cut you can take for a given width without bogging the motor. The thickness indicator, also a plunger, is calibrated in eighths, reads easily, and can be set as a stop for repeated cuts to the same thickness. The jointer gauge (like all the others) is rudimentary at best.

After struggling with the short jointer tables on the over-under machines, I found it surprisingly easy to accurately edge-joint a long board on the Makita's 59-in. tables. The tradeoff, of course, is a 6⅛-in. cutterhead that's not very useful for facing wide, warped stock prior to planing. Supported at two points, the fence is rigid (although mine was warped), it's movable and it tilts. It has one glaring problem, though. If it's moved forward, the cutterhead is exposed on the back side. None of the other machines tested has this hazard.

Setting knives in the Makita is touchy. Instead of fitting into slots, the knives are sprung against a squarish cutterhead by steel clips and held fast by bolted-on, half-round covers. To adjust the knives, you stick a screwdriver through slots in the blade covers and pry up on the bottom edge of the knife. Two small wooden blocks, which span the jointer mouth or rest on machined surfaces above the planer cutterhead, push the knives to the correct level. Compared to the Inca, this is a crude arrangement, and it takes lots of trial and error to get right. The Makita does have one saving grace: the cutterhead has an external wheel, so you can rotate it by hand, with a pin to lock it at top dead center.

The Hitachi F-1000A, at 320 lb., is the heaviest machine I tested, and its four steel support columns make it sturdier than the Makita. Its planer and jointer capacity and running gear are similar to the Makita's, but the Hitachi lacks the outboard bed rollers, an annoying shortcoming which I was able to remedy by mounting my own outfeed roller on a plywood outrigger.

Though Hitachi claims 3 HP for the howling little motor that powers this machine, I couldn't detect any advantage over the Makita's claimed 2 HP. As planers, they perform equally, though the Hitachi is better at chip-handling. Planer chips are ducted through an oblong chute that exhausts out the side of the machine. Chips from the jointer are similarly ducted downward. I fashioned wooden plugs to fit into these ports, then drilled the plugs to accept the hose from my shop vacuum. Now I can run the machine all day long without making a mess, although I do have to stop fairly frequently to empty the vacuum.

Hitachi's knife-setting method is quite elegant and nearly as accurate as Inca's. Like the Makita, the knives are fastened to a squarish cutterhead by bolted-on plates. A detent pin on the handwheel locks the cutterhead at top dead center. The knives are spring-loaded, so you just pop them in place and push them down to height with a couple of magnetic clamps. They stay put while you tighten the locking bolts.

The Hitachi's cast-iron jointer fence is the best of all the machines I tested. It's heavy and easy to adjust, and it stays where you put it. I felt safer using the F-1000A, as well. It's festooned with bright yellow warning stickers, and has little

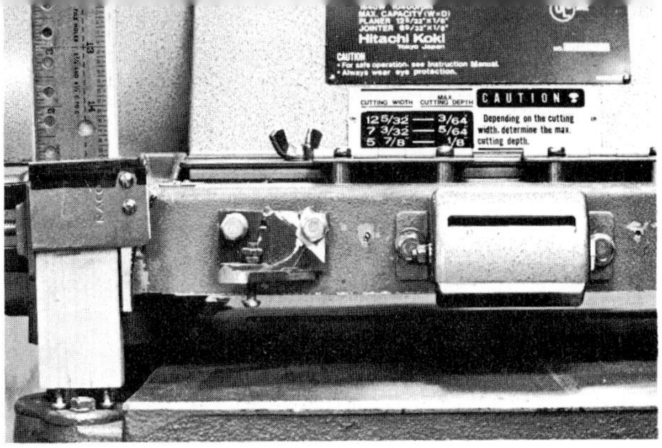

niceties such as a metal cover over the cutterhead handwheel and a little metal flap that guards the exposed knives when the jointer fence is pulled forward. For storage in a tiny shop, the jointer has one other clever feature: its 63-in. jointer tables unlock and pivot downward about a foot from each end.

The Hitachi I bought has terrible gauges. The thickness gauge is calibrated in twelfths of an inch, and there's ¼ in. of parallax-producing space between the pointer and the scale. I cobbled up my own replacement out of a broken corner clamp and a metal rule. Originally, my machine had no feeler gauge at all, so I fashioned a crude version of the Makita gauge using the rest of the corner clamp and a stove bolt. Hitachi has since designed a gauge, and it's a beauty. It not only tells you where the blades will begin to cut, but how deep the cut will be. If you own an F-1000A without this, Hitachi's service manager, Keith Drake (4487-F Park Dr., Norcross, Ga. 30093), will supply one for free.

The Hitachi F-1000A has two bed rollers but no outboard rollers. Rome mounted his own outfeed roller on a plywood outrigger. With standard table extensions, the Hitachi has 63-in. tables, the longest of the tools tested. Before Hitachi supplied him with a new, well-designed feeler gauge, Rome made his own from a stove-bolt plunger mounted in a broken corner clamp, above.

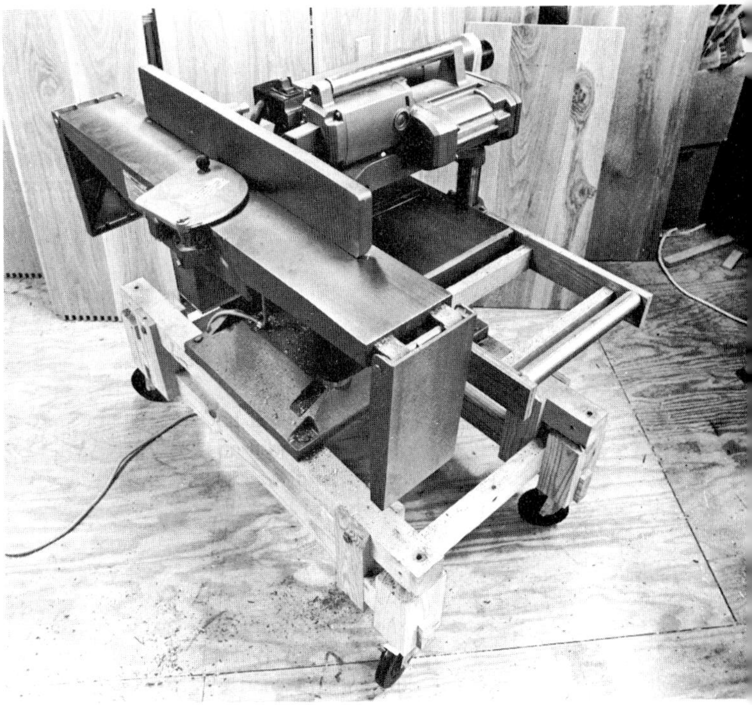

Which to choose? In picking a jointer-planer, I'd take several things into consideration. First, how wide a jointer do you need and how long must its tables be? The over-unders have wider jointers which are perfect for flattening one side of a wide, cupped board in order to give the planer a true surface to work from. Because the tables are so short, though, you'll have a hard time truing the face or edges of a long board. The side-by-sides have longer tables but narrower cutterheads, thus wide boards must be ripped before face-jointing and then glued back up to width. If you have to follow this routine, the wider side-by-side planers will be preferable for cleaning up your glued stock. Weight and size should be considered too. A small, light machine can be more easily pushed aside when it's not needed, but tends to move about when you're shoving big pieces through the planer.

I had a couple of friends try these machines, and all of us agreed that as planers they stack up about equally. But we found the over-unders compromised as jointers, especially the Belsaw, because of their shape: they're so wide that you have to lean over them, feeding the stock at arm's length. A wide

Comparison of Specifications

	Belsaw 684 (USA)	Emco-Rex 2000 (Austria)	Inca 343-190 (Switzerland)	Makita 2030 (Japan)	Hitachi F-1000A (Japan)
Price	$700	$1,000	$1,500	$1,350	$1,500
Watts input	1800	1920	1580	1400	1640
Advertised horsepower	1	2 1/2	1 1/2	2	3
Revolutions/minute	6,000	6,000	6,000	7,000	10,400
Feed rate (feet/minute)	28	16.4	11.5, 16.5	27.8	31.2
Cuts/inch	36.0	61.0	86.0, 61.0	41.9	55.6
Planer					
Blade width (inches)	8 3/8	10 3/16	10 1/4	12	12 5/32
Maximum thickness (inches)	4 1/2	5 7/8	6 5/16	6 1/4	6 5/8
Minimum thickness (inches)	1/4	1/8	1/8	1/4	3/16
Table dimensions (inches)	8 1/16 x 28 1/2	9 3/4 x 17 3/4	10 1/4 x 15 3/4	11 3/4 x 23 1/2	11 7/8 x 24 1/8
Jointer					
Blade width (inches)	8 3/8 (6 5/8 usable)	10 3/16	10 1/4	6 1/8	6 9/32
Table size (inches)	9 3/8 x 35 5/8	12 3/8 x 33 3/4	11 x 42 1/2	6 1/8 x 59	6 3/8 x 39 1/2* *63 with extensions
Weight (pounds)	198	143	114	276	320
Return rollers	0	0	0	2	1
Bed rollers	0	0	0	4	2
Sound level (dB)†	91	85	85	97	98

† Measured at ear level with a Radio Shack sound level meter, "A" weighting, no wood being cut. A difference of 3 dB *doubles* the apparent noise level.

jointer is nice, but what good is it if it's too short to true a long board? Then there's the matter of switching from one function to the other. Aside from the nuisance, you can't use both jointer and planer simultaneously. This can force you to use more inefficient sequencing while truing your wood.

I was disappointed with the Belsaw. Its low price isn't much of a value if half of the combination doesn't work. The people at Belsaw were helpful and happy to talk to me on their toll-free number, but goodwill can't offset a badly designed machine. Unless you are severely constrained by money, I can't recommend the Belsaw 684. On a tight budget, I'd consider Belsaw's model 804 planer-molder, about $550, and a separate jointer.

The Emco-Rex 2000 is probably the better budget choice. It gets the job done, but it requires more care and skill to get good results than do the more expensive machines. Its sheet-steel construction gives me doubts about its durability.

The Makita is a worthy machine which I liked better than the Belsaw or Emco. Yet it suffers in comparison with the Hitachi. The $150 lower price tag hardly offsets its draw-backs. Makita's lack of customer service (see box, below) persuades me to take my future business elsewhere.

My difficulty is in choosing between the Hitachi and the Inca, machines that have obviously been designed according to different philosophies. Both are well designed and well made, though one is light and elegant, the other heavy and sturdy. I favor the Hitachi's side-by-side design, but I admire the Inca for its compactness and engineering finesse. I think the Inca would be best for the craftsman who does careful, low-volume work and who doesn't often need to straighten long boards. I'm glad I bought the Hitachi, however. Apart from face-jointing wide boards, it can do all that the others can, with considerably more ease. It was the only machine on which the fence and tables were perfectly flat and straight. It's built like a tank, and the people who sell it are knowledgeable and helpful. For me, that's a winning combination. □

James Rome, a part-time woodworker, is a plasma physicist for the U.S. fusion energy program in Oak Ridge, Tenn. Photos by the author. All prices are 1980 estimates.

Don't answer the phone while adjusting jointer knives

I was installing the knives in my Makita 2030 jointer-planer when the phone rang. When I finished the call, I went back and turned on the machine, forgetting that I hadn't tightened the bolts. As the knives whirred up to speed, a horrible screeching noise ensued, followed by a shower of shrapnel. The jointer guard deflected most of the metal shards and I wasn't hurt.

After I regained my composure, I realized what I had done wrong. It was a cheap lesson in how *not* to set jointer knives. Valuable as the experience was, I learned even more when I tried to fix the thing.

Just taking it apart was a chore. The jointer tables are attached to the planer by hardened-steel drift pins. Driven into blind holes, these pins seem designed more for fast factory assembly than for easy removal. Hours of tugging finally opened up a gap large enough to insert a hacksaw blade into. Several blades later, I cut through the pins and separated the tables.

There followed another struggle to remove the jointer head from its press-fit into a bearing cup in the outfeed table. While doing this, I realized that if the drive belt connecting the motor to the shafts ever breaks, the jointer head will probably have to be removed to replace it. In principle, it might be possible to slide apart the coupled pulleys that connect the planer and jointer shafts, but in practice, forget it.

I had to decide whether to fix the tables or to buy new ones. This decision was surprisingly difficult. Although Makita stocks parts at various locations throughout the country, each distribution center has different prices and tells a different story. Makita in Atlanta was willing to sell me a new outfeed table for about $400. Makita in New Jersey claimed that they had a sale on an old-style outfeed table and the price was

Rome's knife-setting accident tore chunks from both infeed and outfeed tables. Here they are reinstalled, after being built up by nickel welding and flat grinding.

$30. Makita in Atlanta said there was only one style of outfeed table. Makita in New Jersey said the sale was over.

I decided to repair the machine. It cost me $50 to get the cast-iron tables welded back together with nickel. It cost another $50 to have the tops of the tables ground flat. The nickel was hard enough to ruin several carbide tools. I had to belt-sand down the bottoms of the welds facing the jointer head.

Reassembling the 2030 was relatively straightforward. My struggles, however, were not over. Without the jointer blades, the machine ran smoothly up to speed. But when I installed the knives, it vibrated severely enough to walk across the floor of my shop. I weighed the blades and their cover plates, and found them to be perfectly balanced. I bought a new planer head (another $70) and readjusted the drive pulleys. The machine was still unbalanced.

In disgust, I sold it, as a planer only, to a friend. He found the problem. When I ordered a new spring-steel blade holder, Makita had sent me two of them stuck together. This raised the blade and its heavy cover about $\frac{1}{16}$ in., causing the out-of-balance condition.

My misadventures with the Makita explain why I am now the owner of a Hitachi F-1000A.   —*J.A.R.*

EDITOR'S NOTE: To sort out customers' technical problems, Makita has added a national service manager to its staff. Write to 12930 E. Alondra, Cerritos, Calif. 90701, or call (213) 926-8775.

Combination Machines
What they do, where to get them

Although most woodworkers set up shop with a painstakingly accumulated collection of new and used machinery, a carefully chosen combination machine might be better. Price and quality aside, space constraints can necessitate having one machine that performs the functions of several. When electricity first came to the cabinet shop, the result was a profusion of cutters and blades run by a series of jackshafts growing out from a single, enormous motor. American woodworkers soon found single-function machines, each with its own motor, to be more efficient and flexible. As a result, the combination machine became almost exclusively a hobbyist's machine. The one design that succeeded, now made by Shopsmith and Super Shop, is basically a lathe whose headstock incorporates a variable-speed mechanism and a quill feed. A table attached on top converts the lathe into a table saw, disc sander or horizontal borer. With the lathe ways swung up vertical, it's a drill press. Accessories can be mounted, taking power from the headstock, to add a band saw, jigsaw, jointer and (in the case of the Super Shop) a milling machine.

The situation is different in Europe, where limited space has forced cabinetmakers to stay with the combination idea, and the machinery industry has continued to refine it. Several European firms make lightweight combination machines for the hobby market. Austria's Emco-lux, for example, makes a machine that in its upright position is a band saw and in horizontal position, a table saw. The most common design, however, uses a stationary motor mounted under the main table to power a circular saw (whose arbor usually does not tilt), a jointer and a thickness planer. In some versions a spindle emerges from the side with a compound-action table for horizontal boring and slot mortising. In others the motor belts to a vertical shaft for spindle shaping. Machines of this design range from the 110-lb. Lurem Compact to the 2,910-lb. Steton #1, available with 20-in.-wide cast-iron planer/jointer beds. None of these machines has infinite variable speeds; multiple speeds are provided by step pulleys. They do have in common with the Shopsmith and Super Shop the advantage that the main table and some of its fences and jigging facilities can be used in the operation of more than one mode.

The specifications given on pages 76 to 79, compiled in 1980 from the manufacturers' literature, are only for machines made or distributed in the United States.

The Shopsmith: Comments and adaptations

In 1980 *Fine Woodworking* magazine asked its readers to comment on combination machines they had used. All of the many letters received were about the Shopsmith, which has been made and sold in this country for more than three decades. Most of the Shopsmith owners are happy (one called it "the engineering marvel of the century"). Their most common complaint was that the saw table is too high and too small. Changing modes seems no problem for most owners, or at least they tolerate the nuisance in exchange for the space-saving advantages. Some bought their Shopsmiths for hobby use and continued to rely on them when their hobbies became full-time businesses. But most have found it inadequate for professional work—too small, too light and underpowered. Excerpts from the reader comments follow.

The basic Shopsmith, purchased in 1948, has been the mainstay of my hobby. I've added the jointer and the band saw and they have proved sturdy, accurate and easy to adjust. . . . Separate tools would have been more convenient, but compactness and convertibility have been a necessity. I have increased the large capacity of the lathe by turning hardwood billets and fitting them into the tubular ways. . . . The Shopsmith does not lend itself to being fit with a dust collection system. If anyone has licked this problem, I would love to learn the secret. —*David E. Price, Baltimore, Md.*

In terms of innovative design features, manufacturing quality and service, I doubt Shopsmith can be beaten. The two drawbacks I have found are lack of power for some operations and table rigidity. It is not a machine for heavy-duty work. —*J. Robert Icard, Winston-Salem, N.C.*

Here is a tip for Shopsmith Mark V owners. I was pleased to find it a highly versatile and a generally well-built machine. However, the amount of side-to-side play seemed somewhat excessive, particularly during drilling and turning. It appeared to be due to the fact that the spindle is supported by a single ball bearing at the front of the quill. I took the quill and spindle to an experienced tool-and-die maker at a local machine shop, who confirmed the feasibility of adding a bearing to the rear of the quill (see sketch).

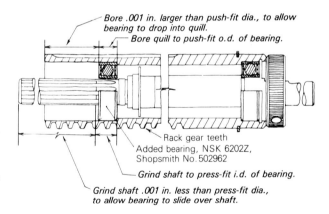

Bore .001 in. larger than push-fit dia., to allow bearing to drop into quill.

Bore quill to push-fit o.d. of bearing.

Rack gear teeth
Added bearing, NSK 6202Z, Shopsmith No. 502962

Grind shaft to press-fit i.d. of bearing.

Grind shaft .001 in. less than press-fit dia., to allow bearing to slide over shaft.

The splined outside diameter of the shaft was ground to permit press-fitting the new bearing onto the shaft (minimal grinding is required; thus the depth of the spline teeth is not significantly altered). The quill was then chucked in the lathe and bored to accept the outside diameter of the bearing as a push-fit. (This bore must be deep enough to permit full retraction of the quill into the machine without interference between the bearing and the face of the splined drive inside the machine.) The bore and outside diameter of the shaft were slightly relieved to facilitate assembly of the components. This modification has eliminated the spindle's side-to-side play and has also greatly reduced the amount of chatter encountered in faceplate lathe work. Total cost of this modification was less than $20, including the machining and purchase of a new bearing. —*James E. Harriss, Dubuque, Iowa*

My Mark V experienced the same side-to-side play in the quill as James Harriss' did. Instead of using an NSK 6202Z bearing (0.5906-in. bore) as he did, I used an NDH 499502H (0.6250-in. bore), so there was no need to grind the splines. To get a press fit of the bearing, the shaft must be either lightly and evenly dimpled or else knurled-and-turned to press-fit diameter between the end of the splines and the shoulder. The stock bearing used in front of the quill (SKF 466041) will also work but it is 0.003 in. larger in the outside diameter than the NDH bearing.

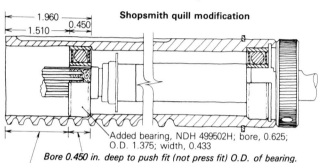

Shopsmith quill modification

Added bearing, NDH 499502H; bore, 0.625; O.D. 1.375; width, 0.433

Bore 0.450 in. deep to push fit (not press fit) O.D. of bearing.
Bore 1.510 in. deep to 0.001 in. larger than push fit, so bearing will drop into quill.

I was misled, though, by Harriss' estimate of less than $20. I neglected to get an estimate; my after-the-fact investigations provided estimates from reasonable to astronomical.
—*Steve Aga, Glendale, Ariz.*

Being able to "borrow" the machine settings from one mode to the next is good. For example, you can replace the table-saw blade with a chuck and drill at the right angle to the cut just made—helpful in doweling miter joints. But changing modes is a nuisance. The change can be completed as fast as the manufacturer states but the machine settings cannot. Many settings must be duplicated with fences, arbors and tables.
—*Robert L. Koch, Tarkio, Mo.*

It makes the finest possible disc sander, a very handy and versatile drill press, an excellent horizontal boring machine, a rather shaky lathe and an undersized and underpowered table saw.
—*Evan Burkhart, Bethlehem, Pa.*

It is not a tool for the naive. For instance, the table-saw setup requires five separate locking operations. This unusual attention to setup detail is necessary for safe operation.

For the price of a new Shopsmith I have managed to purchase used, over the last 2½ years, a 10-in. table saw, a 6-in. jointer, a 36-in. lathe, a heavy-duty shaper (all Rockwell/Delta) and a lever-crossfeed horizontal end mill. I've kept my Shopsmith, though, because it is easily moved about the shop and even fits into the back of my Volvo station wagon, making it convenient to use on the job site.
—*W. Hugh Vance, Galveston, Tex.*

I would not attempt to saw a 4x8 plywood panel as they frequently illustrate. I tried and thought it dangerous....If I had more room, instead of buying separate machines I would probably use my accessories (I have a full set) on separate stands with separate drives.

Spending several hours on careful adjustments pays off handsomely. The alloy nuts and bolts hold firmly and rarely need readjustment. Limitations are few. When using universal arbors, the blade locknut interferes with the trunnion support bar for a 45° cut; thus limiting one to Shopsmith blades, or limiting the depth of cut. Likewise, inability to tilt the saw table to the left is somewhat annoying. Incidentally the small table is not a limitation to me since I've learned to reverse the miter gauge in cutting wide boards and use the runner on large panels. All in all, my Shopsmith has performed dependably for 27 years.
—*J. W. Pochomis, Harbeson, Del.*

Variable speed and quill feed, plus ability to use the rip fence and miter gauge in every mode, offer endless possibilities.
—*Billy Hill, Orange Park, Fla.*

Lurem 210 — *France*

42 in. by 36 in. by 34 in. on steel-rolling stand. 1½-HP single-phase or 2 HP 3-phase motor; 3 speeds. Five modes, plus tenoning carriage; 600 lb.; $3500. ($5.83/lb.).

Thickness planer: Max. width, 8 in.; max. thickness, 6½ in. Two knives, 6,000 RPM. Auto-feed, 22 FPM. Cast iron table, 17⅛ in. by 8¼ in.

Jointer: Max. width, 8 in. Cast iron table, 47⅛ in. long.

Table saw: 10-in. blade, 4,300 RPM. Aluminum table, 13 in. by 34 in.

Horizontal borer/mortiser: ½-in. chuck, 3,000/6,000 RPM. Single-lever-adjust table feed and cross travel.

Spindle shaper: 1-in., ¾-in. or ⅝-in. spindle can be oriented vertically, horizontally or tilted; 3,000/6,000 RPM.

Also available: Lurem 260, which is the same as the 210, except it has a 10-in. planer/jointer, a cast iron saw table and a larger and/or second motor available. It weighs 800 lb. and costs $4,700.

Distributors: Same as for Compact, p. 78.

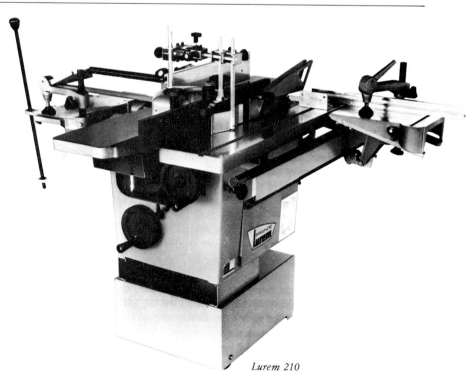

Lurem 210

Pinheiro UIR 350 *Portugal*

76 in. by 72 in. by 56 in., cast-iron tables, enclosed steel base. Two motors, each 3 HP *or 4* HP. *Five modes, plus tenoning carriage; 1,763 lb.; $4,750. ($2.69/lb.).*

Thickness planer: Max. width, 14 in.; max. thickness, 6 in. Three knives, 5,000 RPM. Auto-feed, 33 FPM.

Jointer: Max. width, 14 in.; table, 72 in. long, lever adjust.

Table saw: 12-in. blade, 5,000 RPM. Runs off planer/jointer motor. Table, 33⅝ in. by 19¼ in., tilts to 30° and is raised and lowered by handwheel for depth of cut. Crosscut carriage with hold-down.

Horizontal borer/mortiser: ¾-in. chuck, 5,000 RPM. Table, 18⅜ in. by 8⅞ in., with hold-down. Handwheel-adjusted height, lever-operated travel. Knife-grinding fixture, standard.

Spindle-shaper: 1³⁄₁₆-in. spindle, 6,000 RPM. Uses table-saw table, fences and tenoning carriage.

Distributor: Henry Weigand Corp., Box 831, Claremont, N.H. 03743.

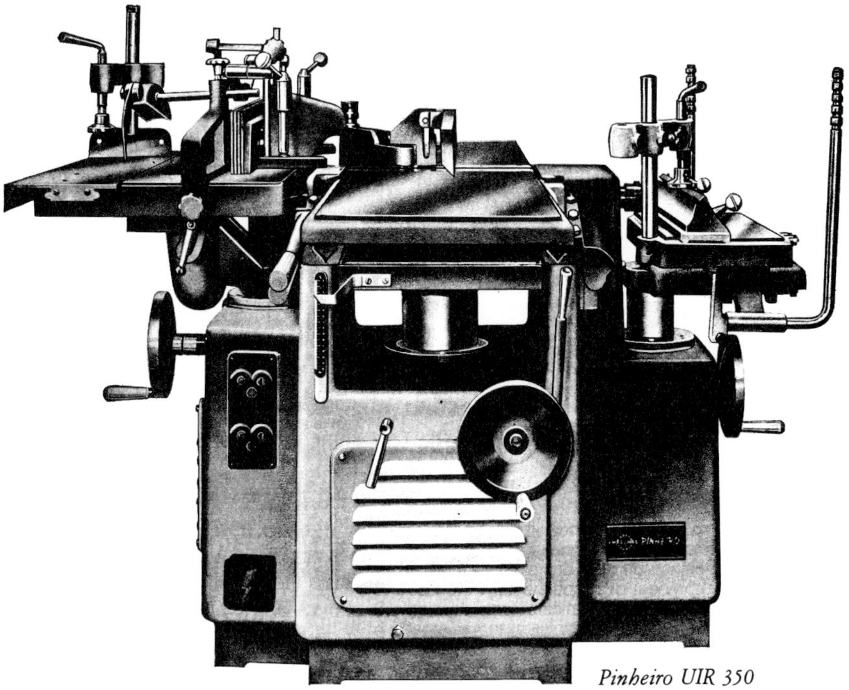

Pinheiro UIR 350

Steton #1 *Italy*

84⅝ in. by 82 in. by 40 in.; cast-iron tables and enclosed steel stand. Two motors, 3½ HP *and 3½/4½* HP. *Five modes, with tenoning carriage; 2,535 lb.; $5,500. ($2.17/lb.).*

Thickness planer: Max. width 16 in.; max. thickness, 8 in. Three knives, 3,100 RPM. Auto-feed 20/40 FPM.

Jointer: Max. width 16 in. Table, 84⅝ in. long.

Table saw: 12-in. blade, 3,100 RPM. Arbor is raised and lowered for depth of cut, but does not tilt (nor does table).

Horizontal borer/mortiser: ¾-in. chuck, 3,100 RPM. Table, 20 in. by 10⅜ in. Knife-grinding fixture, standard.

Spindle shaper 1⅜-in. diameter, 1,400/2,800 RPM.

Also available: Model with 20-in. planer/jointer (2,910 lb., $5,800).

Steton #5 *Italy*

*64¾ in. by 34 in. by 37⅞ in.; cast iron tables and enclosed steel base. 2-*HP *motor, 5,000* RPM. *Three modes; 1,014 lb.; $3,500. ($3.45/lb.).*

Thickness planer: Max. width, 10 in.; max. thickness, 8 in. Three knives. Auto-feed, 23 FPM.

Jointer: Max. width, 10 in. Table, 62 in. long.

Horizontal borer/mortiser: ⅝-in. chuck. Table, 15¼ in. by 7⅝ in. Knife-grinding fixture, standard.

Also available: 12-in. planer/jointer (1,080 lb., $3,800), larger sizes up to 20 in.

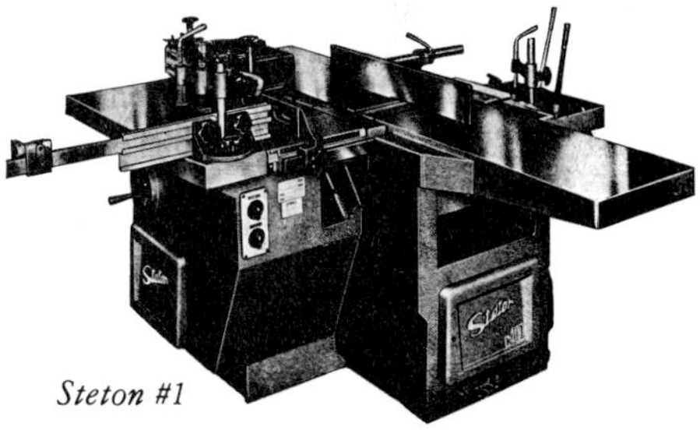

Steton #1

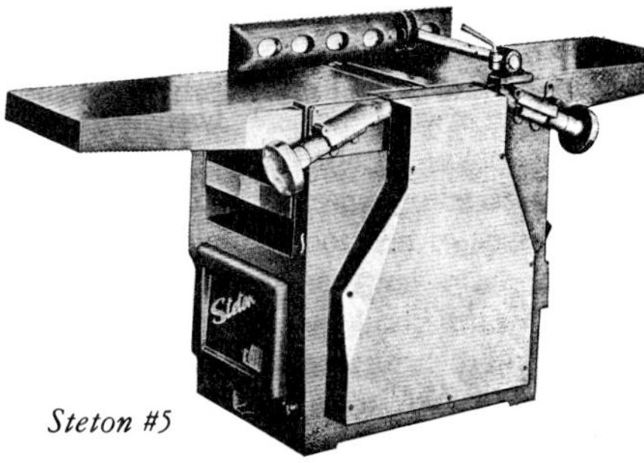

Steton #5

Steton #8 *Italy*

60¼ in. by 30¾ in. by 39⅜ in.; cast-iron tables and enclosed steel base. Two motors, 4 HP *and 4⅕* HP *(two speeds). Two modes, with tenoning carriage; 1,642 lb.; $2,350. ($1.43/lb.).*

Table saw: 16-in. blade. Arbor is raised and lowered for depth of cut but does not tilt (nor does table). Table, 48 in. by 21¼ in. Sliding crosscut table, 55⅝ in. by 22 in.

Spindle shaper: 1⅜ in. spindle, 3,200/6,400 RPM.

Distributor: (for all Steton models) Henry Weigand Corp., Box 831, Claremont, N.H. 03743.

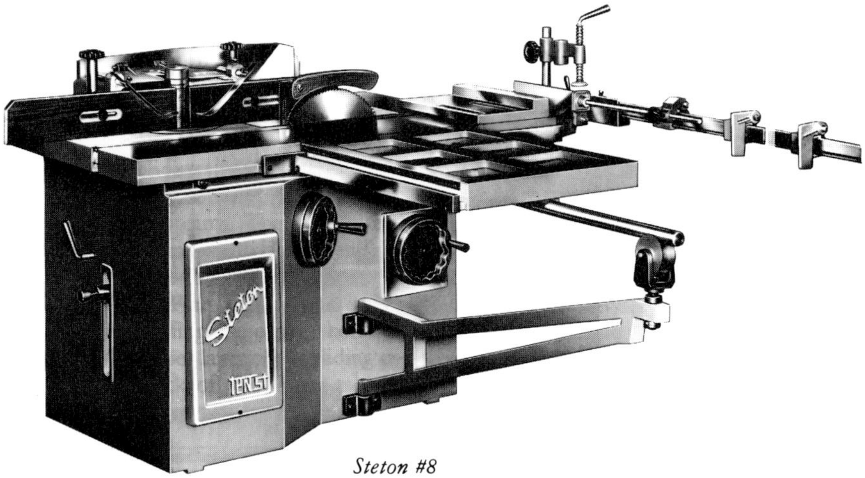

Steton #8

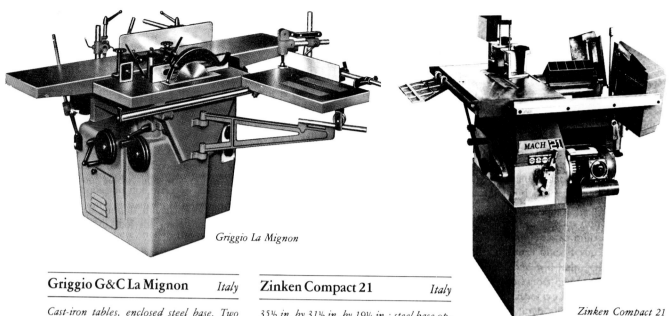

Griggio La Mignon

Zinken Compact 21

Griggio G&C La Mignon   *Italy*

Cast-iron tables, enclosed steel base. Two motors, each 2½ HP. Five modes, with tenoning carriage; 1,403 lb.; $5,000. ($3.56/lb.).

Thickness planer: Max. width, 12 in.; max. thickness, 8 in.; Three knives, 4,500 RPM. Automatic feed, 23 FPM.

Jointer: Max. width, 12 in.; table, 64⅞ in. long.

Table saw: 10-in. blade, 3,800 RPM. Arbor is raised and lowered for depth of cut, but does not tilt (nor does table). Table, 26 by 12 in. Crosscut table with hold-down.

Horizontal borer/mortiser: ¾-in. chuck, 3,800 RPM. Table, 16 in. by 8 in., with hold-down.

Spindle shaper: 1³⁄₁₆-in. spindle, 4,800 RPM (3,500/7,000 RPM available). Uses table-saw table, fences and tenoning carriage.

Also available: Models with 10-in. planer/jointer ($3,350) and with 14-in. planer/jointer ($6,000).

Distributor: Henry Weigand Corp., Box 831, Claremont, N.H. 03743.

Zinken Compact 21   *Italy*

35½ in. by 31½ in. by 19¼ in.; steel base optional. Cast-aluminum body, cast-iron tables, covered with stainless steel. 1½-HP single or three-phase motor, three speeds through belted pulleys; lever changeover. Five modes, plus tenoning carriage; 220 lb.; $1,750. ($7.95/lb.).

Thickness planer: Max. width, 8¼ in.; max. thickness, 4⅜ in. Three knives, 4,600 RPM. Auto-feed, 23 FPM.

Jointer: Max. width, 8½ in. Table, 27½ in. long.

Table saw: 8-in. blade, 3,500 RPM. Table, 27½ in. by 17¾ in., tilts 45°. Crosscut table with cam-action hold-down.

Horizontal borer/mortiser: ⅝-in. chuck, 4,600 5PM. Table with cam-action hold-down moves 4 in. (depth) by 5 in. (cross feed).

Spindle shaper: 1-in. spindle, 8,000 RPM.

Accessories: Sliding crosscut table, 19⅛ in. by 9⅞ in., for use also with shaper ($230).

Distributor: Henry Weigand Corp., Box 831, Claremont, N.H. 03743.

Lurem Compact   *France*

40 in. by 30 in. by 20 in. (plus wood stand). 1¼-HP motor, 3 speeds through belted pulleys. Five modes, plus tenoning carriage; 110 lb.; $2,800. ($25.45/lb.).

Thickness planer: Max. width, 6 in.; max. thickness, 3½ in. Two knives, 7,000 RPM. Auto-feed, 18 FPM.

Jointer: Max. width, 6 in. Cast-iron tables, 33½ in. long.

Table saw: 8-in. blade, 5,700 RPM. Aluminum table, 18⅞ in. by 18⅞ in. Lever-adjust blade height. Tilting arbor on lever-locked trunnion. Sliding crosscut carriage with work hold-down.

Horizontal borer/mortiser: ½-in. chuck, 3,500/7,000 RPM. Handwheel-adjust table height; single-lever-adjust table feed and cross-travel; cam-action hold-down.

Spindle shaper: 1-in. ¾-in. or ⅝-in. spindle can be oriented vertically, horizontally, or tilted; 5,700 RPM.

Accessories: Sanding disc, sanding drum, knife grinder, table-saw extension bars.

Distributors: E.W. Gunderson, 726 S. Keeneway Dr., Medford, Ore. 97501; Henry Weigand, Corp., Box 831, Claremont, N.H. 03743; International Woodworking Equipment Corp., 11665 Coley River Circle, Fountain Valley, Calif. 92708.

Machine modes	Thickness planer	Jointer	Table saw	Horizontal borer	Slot mortiser	Spindle shaper	Lathe	Drill press	Disc sander	Band saw	Jigsaw	Overarm router	Belt sander	Milling machine
Emcostar	☐	☐	■	☐		☐		■		■		■		
Emcostar Super			■	☐		☐		☐						
Griggio	■	■	■	■	■	■								
Lurem Compact	■	■	■	■	■	■		☐						
Lurem 210	■	■	■	■	■	■								
Pinheiro UIR 350	■	■	■	■	■	■								
Shopsmith		☐	■	■			■	■	■	☐	☐		☐	
Steton #1	■	■	■	■	■	■								
Steton #5	■	■	■											
Steton #8			■											
Super Shop	☐	☐	■	■		■	■	■	■		☐	■		☐
Zinken Compact	■	■	■	■	■	■								

■ Standard ☐ Accessory

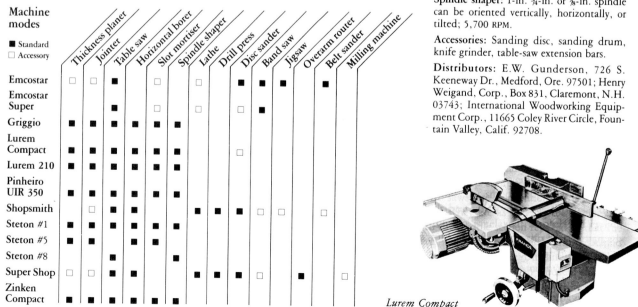

Lurem Compact

Emcostar
Austria

28 in. by 23 in. by 26 in. (31 in. high in band-saw mode). Aluminum tables, plastic housings. ½/¾-HP motor, 1,500/3,000 RPM. Five modes; 97 lb.; $995. ($10.26/lb).

Table saw: 8-in. blade. The table, 14⅞ in. by 12 in., is raised and lowered to adjust depth of cut and tilts on trunnions.

Band saw: 5⅝-in. throat; 4¾ in. depth of cut; max. ⅝-in. blade. Table, 10 in. by 8 in.

Jigsaw/fretsaw: ½-in. stroke; uses table-saw table.

Disc sander: 6⅞-in. dia. Table, 7 in. by 9 in.

Belt sander: 31⅞ in. long by 1½ in. wide; 21/42 FPM.

Accessories: Jointer/planer: max. width 8 in.; max. thickness, 2¼ in.; table, 26¾ in. long; auto-feed, 12 FPM ($895). Lathe, 19¾ in. between centers; 9-in. swing ($130). Mortiser, ½-in. chuck; table, 6 in. by 16 in., 4-in. travel ($230).

Also available: Emcostar Super, fewer modes, but larger: ¾/1⅒ HP motor; 10-in. table-saw blade with 21⅜-in. by 15¾-in. table, and 8⅛-in. band saw with 13⅞ in. by 10⅝-in. table (136 lb.; $1,395).

Distributor: Emco-lux, 2050 Fairwood Ave., Columbus, Ohio 43207.

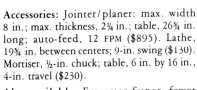

Emcostar

Super Shop
U.S.A.

69 in. by 24 in. by 41¾ in., 81 in. in drill-press mode. Cast aluminum and steel. Aluminum stand includes four drawers. 1½-HP motor, 30 RPM to 7,200 RPM variable speed in 3 ranges. Six modes; 500 lb.; $2,495. ($4.99/lb.).

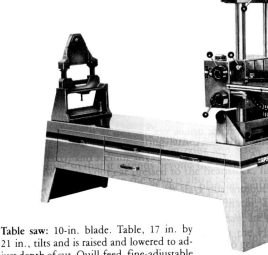

Super Shop

Table saw: 10-in. blade. Table, 17 in. by 21 in., tilts and is raised and lowered to adjust depth of cut. Quill-feed, fine-adjustable sawblade.

Lathe: 34 in. between centers; 17-in. swing over tubular-steel ways.

Drill press: ⅝-in. chuck; 17 in. from spindle to column; max. 31 in. from table to spindle; 5-in. quill travel, ⅝-in. chuck. Uses tilting saw table with rip fence and miter gauge for jigging.

Horizontal borer: Same as drill press, except stock may be of unlimited length.

Disc sander: 12-in. diameter. Quill feed.

Overarm shaper/router: R-8 taper chuck handles 1/16-in. to ¾-in. bits.

Accessories: Metal lathe equipment (6-in., 4-jaw chuck; 6-in., 3-jaw chuck; power feed; compound tool rest) $319; vertical milling equipment; 6-in. jointer; molding machine; 12-in. planer; 15-in. band saw.

Distributor: Fox Industries, Inc., 11000 Hampshire Ave., S. Bloomington, Minn. 55438.

Shopsmith
U.S.A.

71 in. by 19 in. by 41½ in., 76¼ in. high as drill press; on steel stand with casters, 2 HP motor, 700 RPM to 5,200 RPM variable speed through Reeves drive system. Five modes; 195 lb.; $995. ($5.10/lb).

Table saw: 10-in. blade. Table, 18⅜ in. by 14 in., tilts and is raised and lowered on rack and pinion to adjust depth of cut. Quill-feed, fine-adjustable sawblade.

Lathe: 34 in. between centers; 16½-in. swing over tubular-steel ways. Tool rest has rack-and-pinion height adjustment.

Drill press: ½-in. chuck; 16½ in. from spindle to column; max. 26 in. from table to spindle; 4¼-in. quill travel. Uses tilting saw table with rip fence and miter gauge for jigging.

Horizontal borer: Same as drill press, except stock may be of unlimited length.

Disc sander: 12-in. diameter. Quill feed.

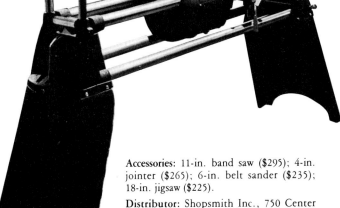

Accessories: 11-in. band saw ($295); 4-in. jointer ($265); 6-in. belt sander ($235); 18-in. jigsaw ($225).

Distributor: Shopsmith Inc., 750 Center Dr., Vandalia, Ohio 45377.

Shopsmith

Super-Surfacers
Fixed-knife planers slice the wood paper-thin

by Paul Bertorelli

At all of the woodworking machinery shows in recent years, knots of incredulous people have gathered around small Japanese surfacing machines that can peel off a perfect shaving as long and as wide as the board they plane. Called super-surfacers, the machines are fixed-knife planers fitted with a powered belt that propels the wood under the knife, cutting like an enormous, inverted hand plane. They leave such a glass-smooth finish on the workpiece that it's hard to decide which is more interesting, that shimmering planed surface or the shaving. Evidently the onlookers haven't solved this dilemma either, because relatively few of these machines have been sold in this country.

This marketing flop seems curious. The Japanese have always had a knack for making products that Americans will buy by the shipload, but they couldn't seem to give away super-surfacers, despite the trade show demonstrations, which left little doubt that the machines work. So why haven't more been sold? Are they too expensive? Do they not perform as advertised? Or have these companies simply reached the outer boundaries of what sometimes seems like an insatiable American appetite for the latest gadget?

Hoping to answer these questions, we borrowed two super-surfacers and tested them in our shop for four months last summer. Later, I queried Hitachi and Makita executives to learn about the origin of these fascinating tools.

It turns out that the super-surfacers were developed for Japanese house carpenters, who must cut and fit heavy beams and plane them to a mirror finish before hanging them. Powered fixed-knife planers were first made 20 years ago, though the operating principle goes back at least a century to a traditional tool that made thin shavings for use as wrapping paper. This device, similar to the Western cooper's plane, consisted of a 1-ft. wide plane iron with the edge projecting up through a heavy table. Wood was pushed over the blade by means of a pivoting arm that gave the operator the considerable leverage needed to shove the chunk over the knife to make a shaving.

In a tradition-bound industry like Japanese carpentry, super-surfacers were slow to catch on. But demand has become brisk enough to support at least four manufacturers—Hitachi alone makes 5,000 super-surfacers a year—and sophisticated surfacers now find use in production shops and factories, where they do what sanding machines do in the West. The Japanese firm that holds the early patents on powered fixed-knife planers, Marunaka International, even makes auxiliary knife sets which cut simple chamfers, rounds and rabbets. And Marunaka is reportedly experimenting with fixed-knife shapers and molders.

Super-surfacers do not replace conventional rotary-head planers. In fact, a good rotary planer is needed in conjunction with a fixed-knife machine, since the latter works only when it starts with flat stock of uniform thickness.

In the United States, these machines remain a curiosity—dealers estimate that fewer than 250 of them are in use. I contacted a few woodworkers who have them and found that the machines seem to do the job they're designed for.

Eric Anderson, of Cape Neddick, Maine, who makes furniture and kitchen cabinets, bought a Hitachi super-surfacer last summer. "Before I got it," Anderson told me, "I basically did what everyone else does—I used a belt sander." Now, said Anderson, he routinely feeds rotary-planed stock and cut-to-size cabinet parts through the super-surfacer. He gets a far better finish in a fraction of the time.

One California woodworker I was told about couldn't care less about the shiny surface—it's the shavings he wants. He lined up four super-surfacers end to end in his shop, feeds incense cedar through, and then bags up the shavings to sell as closet odorizers.

Not all buyers like their super-surfacers. Clarence Gross, of Lima, Ohio, bought a rotary planer and a super-surfacer last spring, planning to use both for planing rough lumber. The super-surfacer disappointed him: "Oh, it would do it all right, but after a while I just kept using the other planer...took too many passes to plane rough stock," Gross said. Intrigued by such experiences, I was anxious to try these machines for myself.

Using the surfacers—I have to admit I was skeptical when we first decided to borrow and test two super-surfacers. I had seen the ads and read the sales hype, but I had no idea what I would actually want to do with these two machines parked in the middle of the shop. They seemed like expensive gimmicks to me, albeit well-engineered ones.

I didn't doubt that they could plane softwood nicely, but what about hardwood? Once they were set up (Makita's LP 2501 and Hitachi's FA-700), I scoured the shop for the nastiest wood I could find: bird's-eye maple, crotch walnut and a piece of rowed-grain padauk.

The first thing that struck me was how forcefully the surfacer's heavy rubber belt grabs the stock out of your hand and shoots it past the knife. The board clatters right off the outfeed roller table, the shaving whooshes off the knife. I was amazed to find that the surfacers planed the walnut and maple nearly perfectly and did a respectable job on the padauk. After four months of testing and casual use of the machines for three woodworking projects, I can see lots of uses for these things, though at $2,500 for the Hitachi and $2,700 for the Makita—plus $600 to $1,500 for the essential sharpener (all prices 1982 estimates)—I can't, as an amateur, afford one.

As I worked with these tools, I realized that in principle a super-surfacer works exactly like a hand plane. For an iron, it has a massive $5/16$-in. thick knife, 10 in. long, $2\frac{1}{2}$ in. wide and tipped with high-speed steel. A similar secondary knife mounts atop the cutting knife to serve as a chipbreaker. In

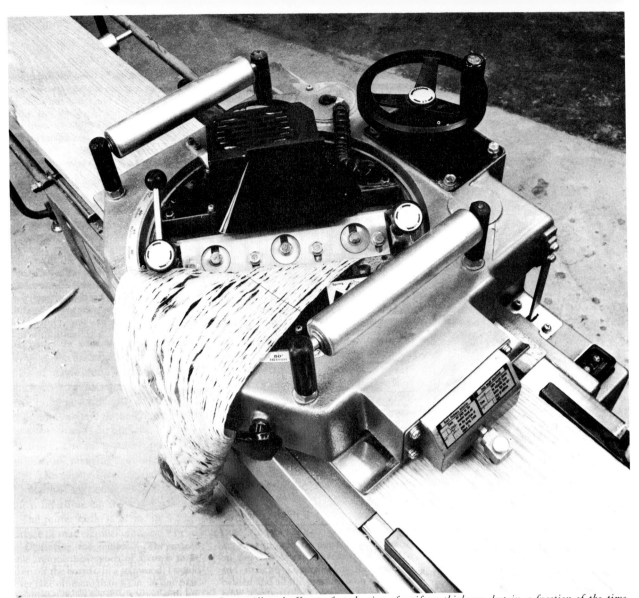

Like a well-tuned hand plane, a super-surfacer will peel off a perfect shaving of uniform thickness—but in a fraction of the time. This photo shows the Hitachi's knife set to about a 20° skew angle; the curled shaving is about 0.002 in. thick.

both machines, the knife assembly is bolted to a heavy cast-iron fixture which rides above the feed belt on adjustable columns. As with hand planes, super-surfacers require sharp knives and proper adjustment of both cutting depth and mouth opening. You adjust the mouths of these machines by moving a plate in the cutterhead and locking it down with bolts. In both softwoods and hardwoods, taking shavings about 0.002 in. thick leaves the best surface. Thicker shavings are possible, particularly in softwoods, but thicknesses over 0.008 in. or so draw protesting clanks from the feed mechanism, or else the board jams against the knife. The knives are bedded at a 35° angle—close to that of Japanese planes but shallower than the 40° to 45° of Western planes. You can vary the cut's angle of attack, from 0° (that is, the knife's edge at 90° to the length of the work) for soft, straight-grained woods, to 60° for harder, refractory woods. The effect is the same as skewing a hand plane in these woods.

I found one thing puzzling about both machines, however. Instruction sheets, though virtually incomprehensible, recommend higher angles of attack for softer woods than for hard. This made no sense—I skew a plane to ease the cut only in hard, tough woods. Toshio Odate, author of *Japanese Woodworking Tools: Their Tradition, Spirit and Use*, told me that

to get the best surface on softwoods, the iron in a hand plane should bed at about 30°. Hardwoods, Odate said, plane best with an iron bedded close to 40°.

Odate went on to contend that when you rotate the turntable on a super-surfacer from 0° to, say, 45°, you lengthen the cutting bevel where it strikes the wood, effectively lowering the bed angle. To illustrate his point, Odate whittled a mock plane iron out of a scrap of wood. When he sliced one corner off at 45°, the compound angle formed where this cut intersected the cutting bevel was indeed less than the original bevel angle. A little trigonometry showed that skewing the knife's turntable to a 60° angle of attack produces an effective bed angle of 19°, about half the bed angle when the knife meets the stock head-on, at 0°. This effect applies to hand planes as well: when you skew the angle of attack, you are effectively working with a lower-angle plane, although the effect isn't significant at skew angles less than 40°. In addition, the bevel of a skewed plane slices somewhat sideways into the wood fibers, instead of encountering them head-on, thus reducing the likelihood of tearout. This allows the machine to plane hardwoods, although Odate says it would work better if it had a higher or an adjustable bed angle. As presently designed, the machines are best suited for soft-

The Hitachi (above left) and Makita (right) super-surfacers are both overhead, fixed-knife planers designed for finish-planing large, dimensioned timber. Both will plane wood up to 10 in. wide and 7¼ in. thick in a single pass. Width capacity drops to a 5-in. maximum when knives are skewed to 60°. Fixed-knife planing exerts enormous forces on the machine, and its knife, as the photo at right shows, is far heavier than any found in a hand plane. Knife and chip-breaker are made of ⁵⁄₁₆-in. thick steel. As with a hand plane, the high-speed steel-tipped knife must be sharpened frequently to get the best surface quality.

woods, even though American woodworkers are more likely to want to plane hardwoods.

Though they are identical in basic design, the Hitachi is generally sturdier and more sophisticated, and the one I'd pick if I were to buy. Its two spring-loaded, depth-adjustment knobs are easier to set than the Makita's pair of fine-thread bolts. The Hitachi has a pair of gauges for installing the knife correctly; the Makita has no such aids. Decoding the manuals takes real creative thinking—they're both awful.

We had no special sharpening equipment for our tests, but I wish we did. Ernie Conover, of Conover Woodcraft Specialties in Parkman, Ohio, who sells the Hitachi machine, recommends buying one of the two motorized grinders made especially for sharpening surfacer knives. The cheaper of the two grinders costs $600, but I think this extra expense should be considered part of the machine's price. You need razor-sharp edges and precise bevel angles to get the most out of a super-surfacer. Conover's method is to hollow-grind a 30° bevel on the grinder's 60-grit, 7-in. diameter wheel. Then he hones a 32° microbevel with a 600-grit, waterstone wheel. Between the coarse and fine wheels, Conover knocks off the wire edge with a hand slip-stone. Sharpening by hand is possible but difficult. I couldn't get good results.

I found it difficult, too, to measure knife durability. When planing poplar with a fresh knife, I got flawless surfaces through maybe 200 linear ft. Then surface quality dropped noticeably for about that much more work, before it was time to resharpen. A dull knife is most troublesome when you try to plane against the grain, which you must do somewhere along most boards. If you want to surface boards wider than the machine's 10-in. maximum, you can feed half of the width

one way, turn the board end-for-end and feed the other half. Increasing the angle of attack reduces fuzziness and tearout, but it also reduces the effective cutting width of the machine.

Dirt, Conover told me, is the knife's worst enemy. Wood must be clean and butt ends should be sawn off, or at least cleaned, and their leading edges should be chamfered before they are fed into the machine. Boards that have been sanded shouldn't be surfaced; abrasive particles could be embedded in the wood.

Having these machines around was fun, and I found that compared with sanding equipment of equivalent capacity they're cheaper and capable of a far better surface. So why haven't more woodworkers bought them? It's tempting to argue that the technology is just too alien to the American way of doing things; we sand, whereas the Japanese plane. I think the real reason, though, is simpler: the makers of fixed-knife planers haven't explained well enough what they'll do. These planers do have a place in shops where lots of flat stock has to be smoothly finished. If they are ever marketed sensibly for just that purpose, I'll bet you'll see a lot more of them. □

Paul Bertorelli is editor of Fine Woodworking *magazine. Fixed-knife planers are available in the United States from these Japanese companies: Hitachi Power Tools U.S.A. Ltd., 4487-F Park Dr., Norcross, Ga. 30093; Makita U.S.A. Inc., 16 World's Fair Dr., Somerset, N.J. 08873; Southwest Machinery Co., 9507 Santa Fe Springs Rd., Santa Fe Springs, Calif. 98670 (Marunaka International); and also from Shinko Machinery Works, Inc., No. 740 Matsutomi-Kamigumi, Shizuoka City, Japan (Grand Super Surfacer).*

The Pin Router
Basic setups for this versatile machine

by Dennis R. Wilson

Typical industrial-capacity pin routers consist of a spindle chuck and motor, suspended from an adjustable column and arm or a cast-iron frame. Photo: Ekstrom Carlson.

The overarm router is basically a shaper with the cutting tool above the table. Not only can it shape and mold the outside edge of stock, but it can plunge-cut, groove, bore and excavate for inlay. The overarm router can also cut mortises, tenons and rabbets. It is especially valuable as a production machine for making identical parts, using jigs and templates.

The basic machine (right) consists of a C-shaped frame, a top-mounted spindle chuck and motor, and a movable table that can be raised and lowered by a treadle. Located directly beneath the centerline of the cutter spindle is a vertically adjustable guide pin. This is what gives the pin router its versatility as well as its name.

Modes of operation—There are six basic ways to operate the pin router. The first is freehand. This is similar to using a portable router freehand, except that you move the stock instead of the router, and there is the advantage of being able to see the work. Also, the table-elevating mechanism makes starting and stopping cuts within the perimeters of the stock easier.

The second mode uses a straight fence for straight-line shaping. Adjustable factory fences are satisfactory, or you can make your own from a dense hardwood or cabinet-grade plywood. If the fence is divided into two sections, the entire surface of the stock can be routed by offsetting the outfeed fence by the amount of stock being removed. This is similar to jointing. For shaping less than the whole edge, use a single fence and set it up as follows: Bring the table up so the cutter just touches the top of the fence, and align the fence with the deepest contour of the cutter. Then, with the router running, raise the table so the cutter plunges into the fence until you reach the depth of cut you desire. This will give the stock full

EDITOR'S NOTE: Manufacturers of pin routers include Ekstrom Carlson, 1400 Railroad Ave., Rockford, Ill. 61110; Rockwell (Delta), 400 N. Lexington Ave., Pittsburgh, Pa. 15208; Porter, 520 Plymouth NE, Grand Rapids, Mich. 49505; Onsrud, 2100 S. Laramie Ave., Chicago, Ill. 60650; and Wesflex, Box 5227, Westport, Conn. 06880. They are also often found at used-machinery dealers or tool auctions for companies going out of business. Three ideas for fashioning your own pin router appear on page 85.

support as it is being routed. The fence should be cut open behind the cutter for chip clearance. Chips that are carried through to jam between the cutter and the work will dent the surface and show up as blotches in finishing. Evacuating the chips with a vacuum helps.

The third mode is shaping with the workpiece pressed against a pilot on the cutting tool. The workpiece can be straight or any irregular shape. This method works best with ball-bearing pilots, since solid pilots often score and burn the wood. In order to start the cut safely, a pivot block of hardwood with about a ¼-in. diameter tip can be clamped to the table about 1 in. from the cutter.

In mode four, the stock is pressed against the guide pin. This method, as method three, requires that a part of the stock edge is not cut, and the final shape of the piece must be finished smoothly before shaping the edge. The diameter of the guide pin and the height of the table determine the depth of cut. Stock can be routed straight or curved, and you can rout inside or outside edges, but use a starting block.

Mode five is basically the same as mode four, except the workpiece is set on top of a pattern or jig. The pattern is

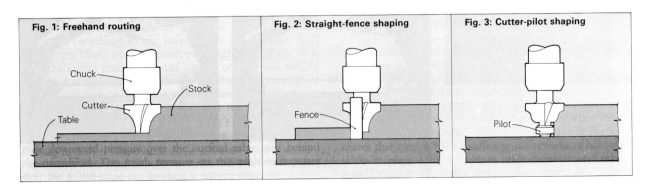

Fig. 1: Freehand routing	Fig. 2: Straight-fence shaping	Fig. 3: Cutter-pilot shaping
Chuck / Stock / Cutter / Table	Fence	Pilot

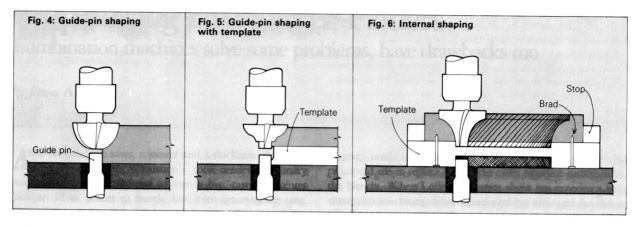

Fig. 4: Guide-pin shaping

Guide pin

Fig. 5: Guide-pin shaping with template

Template

Fig. 6: Internal shaping

Template

Brad

Stop

pushed against the guide pin, and thus the entire edge of the workpiece can be shaped. The workpiece can be held in place by screws, double-sided tape, brads or stop blocks. Normally the pattern is exactly the same size as the routed workpiece, but the pattern can sometimes be offset.

Mode six is for internal shaping, scroll cutting and flat-relief carving. The workpiece is fastened to a template whose underside has been routed out to follow the guide pin. The amount of stock removed is determined by the diameter of the pin, the diameter of the cutter, the size of the cutout and the height of the table. As in any shaping operation using guide pins or shaper collars, the precise shape of the cutout depends upon the pin radius and the cutter radius.

Mode six is good for routing multiple recesses for inlays. Place the inlay upside down on the template bottom and scribe a line around the inlay. Rout or cut this recess out precisely to the scribed line; the accuracy of the inlay fit depends on the accuracy of the recess in the template. Locate the workpiece on the top of the template. By using a ¼-in. diameter guide pin and a ¼-in. diameter straight end mill or router bit, the cutter will exactly duplicate the template recess.

Modes five and six are normally used where duplicates are being made or where the piece being routed would otherwise be difficult to handle safely. In production runs, quick-release clamps, such as the lever type made by the De-Sta-Co Div. of Dover Corp. (346 Midland Ave., Detroit, Mich. 48302), can be used to hold the workpiece down. You might also choose to add handles or grips to add better control when routing. When you make your templates, be sure to use a material that is warp-free and hard enough to withstand pressure against the guide pin. For example, hard maple, plywood, tempered Masonite and aluminum work well. Use the highest

possible degree of accuracy in making your template, since any imperfection in the guide edge of the form will be duplicated in the workpiece. To further guard against mishap, wax both the template and the router table for smoother travel.

In all routing and shaping operations, safety and efficiency come first. Make sure no cutouts in the edge to be routed are smaller than the guide-pin diameter, and take care where abrupt changes in edge direction could catch and throw the workpiece. Either allow extra length for the workpiece or add a small starter block which can be cut off later. Shape profiles that require considerable stock removal with multiple passes, taking a light cut in each. Check the security of guides and clamps before turning on the router.

Cutters—Standard ¼-in. shank diameter router bits can be used as well as ¼-in. to ½-in. shank diameter end mills (two flutes provide the best chip removal and the cleanest cut). Special shaper arbors with collars can also be used. Some heavy-duty machines (including Ekstrom Carlson and Onsrud) can be fit with a rosette chuck which takes flat steel cutters (available from Woodworkers Tool Works, 222 S. Jefferson St., Chicago, Ill. 60606). The chuck has a ⅛-in. slot and an allen screw to lock in the cutter—a single knife made from an oil-hardening tool-steel blank with a cutting area 1½ in. to 3 in. wide and 1¼ in. high (photo below left). It is different from the cutter used on a standard shaper spindle though many of the grinding techniques and uses are the same. The important advantage of the rosette chuck is that the cutter is positioned only ¹⁄₁₆ in. off the diameter of the spindle, so the profile of the routed piece will differ little from that of the cutter. These cutters are ground to shape on both ends, but one end is relieved, so only the opposite end does the cutting.

The typical spindle speeds used in routing are 10,000 RPM or 20,000 RPM. My pin router is set up for 10,500 RPM because I use cutters up to 3 in. in diameter; I prefer the rosette chuck and blades that I have ground. With end mills or standard router bits less than 1¼ in. in diameter, 20,000 RPM could be used. Shaper collars used on the router should not run faster than 10,000 RPM and should be designed for overarm routers.

The methods illustrated here could be used on vertical milling machines, drill presses or on homemade rigs with a router. However, you should not use a rosette chuck here, since the router and drill press are not designed for the radial thrust loads these operations place on the equipment. □

Rosette chuck and T-blank, ground on both sides, but relieved so there is only one cutting edge.

Dennis Wilson

Dennis Wilson, of Wynne, Ark., is a mechanical engineer who also operates his own woodworking business.

Homemade overhead and pin routers

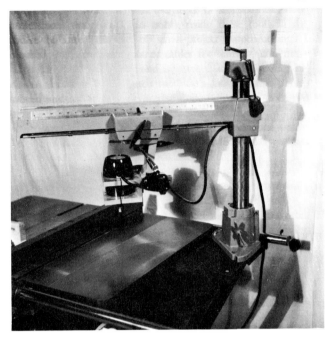

This home-brewed overhead router (left), made by Larry Churchill of Mayville, Wis., is not actually a pin router in that it doesn't have a guide pin, though it could. Instead, Churchill uses the fence and miter gauge of his table saw to guide the work. It was these features, the flat table and the need to save space that brought his table saw together with his router and the transport mechanism of a radial-arm saw. (HIT Distributors, 2867 Long Beach Rd., Oceanside, N.Y. 11572 has adapters that fit together most routers and radial-arm saws; Shopsmith, 750 Center Dr., Vandalia, Ohio 45377, has a router arm for converting a router into an overarm router.) Churchill's setup allows the router to be moved in relation to the work—for plunge cuts, straight-line routing, routing arcs and routing freehand without a router base to obscure the work. For this design, Churchill recommends a saw mechanism with the elevation crank overhead. Mount the base plate so the router moves parallel to the table. To rout arcs, remove the saw-arm miter stops. In designing the router bracket (Churchill used aluminum), make sure the bit will reach the table when the arm is lowered all the way. Photo: Larry Churchill.

When Laszlo Gigacz, of Jordan, N.Y., needed a pin router, he added to his router table an oak arm to position a steel shaft with stop collar directly over the router chuck (right). The upside-down pin router has advantages: The router is more rigid when mounted to a table rather than to an arm, and you can see the pin as it follows the template. If you have a router table already, this method couldn't be easier. The arm swings out of the way when you want your router table back. Photo: Staff.

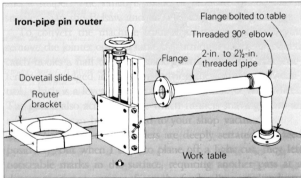

Iron-pipe pin router

Flange bolted to table

Threaded 90° elbow

2-in. to 2½-in. threaded pipe

Flange

Dovetail slide

Router bracket

Work table

Doug Wahl's pin router is basically 2½-in. black pipe and fittings. Wahl, of Washingtonville, N.Y., is a supervisor in a metal-working house. He machined the inside diameter of the T for a slip fit of the horizontal pipe, and welded the plate on top for tapping in the two bolts that secure the pipe. He machined the router bracket too, though Stanley sells brackets for their routers, and there's always the alternative of making a bracket from hardwood. The pin in the table is a socket-head cap screw with its head machined to the diameter of the router bit. It's secured through the top of the table by a nut and washer. The router can be elevated in fixed increments by substituting pipes of different lengths for the column. Fine adjustment is accomplished by means of the spiral groove in the router body (it's a Stanley R2-L, discontinued in 1951) and a key in the bracket, just like the adjusting arrangement between the router and its portable base. For routers that are not spirally grooved, Wahl suggests attaching the router bracket to a dovetail slide with crank screw (fashionable in hardwood or available in steel from Setco Industries, 5890 Hillside Ave., Cincinnati, Ohio 45233). The drawing above shows this alternative in a design simpler than the one in the photograph. It calls for standard pipe fittings and does not require welding. Photo: Doug Wahl.

Air-Powered Tools
What's available and where to get it

by Lyle Laske

Stationary compressor with horizontal air receiver.

In the past 15 years, quite a few independent furniture-makers, sculptors and college woodworking shops have adopted pneumatic (air-driven) tools. They have done so for the same reasons these tools dominate the furniture industry: few moving parts and therefore low maintenance, light-weight handpieces (compared to electric tools) and therefore reduced fatigue and fewer mistakes, and safety. Yet pneumatic tools are largely unknown in general woodworking. They have not entered the consumer market, mainly because of the high initial cost of a suitable compressor.

In a pneumatic system, air compressed by machine flows under pressure through a pipe or hose to activate the tool. Most tools rotate by the force of compressed air against a vaned rotor. Some reciprocate, by means of a valve-and-piston arrangement. Because they have no heavy, copper wire armatures, pneumatic tools are light and compact. They do not overheat, and they can be repeatedly stalled in the work without damage. They start quickly, have variable-speed control, and stop immediately when caught or dropped—all important for safety. Also, there is no danger from electric shock or sparks. Slip-ring couplers permit quick changes from one tool to another at the work station. And since the tools are useless without an air supply, pilferage from school shops and studios is almost eliminated.

There are pneumatic equivalents for nearly every electrically powered tool, from sanders to saws, drills, grinders and routers. Furthermore, there are some pneumatic tools with no electrical equivalent, in particular, the rolling-pin contour sander, power adze and jackhammer-style carving gouge. These three, along with big, high-speed cutting burrs (ball mills) powered by heavy-duty grinders, are tremendously valuable to sculptors and carvers who work with green logs and large stacked forms. They save hours of gouge-tapping, filing and hand-sanding.

Besides the tools shown and described in this article, industry uses a large variety of special-purpose routers and laminate trimmers, which could be most useful in general woodworking and small production shops. There is also a huge variety of pneumatic clamping and positioning machinery, for gluing sub-assemblies and for holding parts in position on the assembly line.

Another factor to consider in evaluating pneumatic tools is the finishing room—the same compressor will of course run spray equipment. If you do convert, don't ignore pneumatic staplers and nailers. Although industry uses them to put the furniture together, they are more suitable for making packing crates, thus saving time for more creative work.

Although these tools are designed and manufactured for industry, there is nothing to stop an individual or a small

Lyle Laske, a sculptor, teaches art at Moorhead State University in Moorhead, Minn.

woodworking enterprise from converting to air power—the suppliers can be tracked down. I've surveyed the industry in the course of preparing this article. The accompanying charts and lists should provide enough clues to find what you need in your particular situation. The prices of the tools listed may seem high when compared to electrical tools made for the consumer market. This is because industrial tools are manufactured to withstand long hours of constant, daily use. And it must be noted that using electricity to compress air is less efficient than using it to power a tool directly.

Compressors The important factor in designing a pneumatic system is air flow, measured by the pressure of the air delivered, and by the volume of air delivered in a given time. Air pressure is measured in pounds per square inch (psi); most pneumatic tools operate at 90 psi. Flow rate is measured in cubic feet per minute (cfm). Air consumption varies from tool to tool and is also affected by pipe and hose diameter. Most tools demand between 20 cfm and 50 cfm. It is essential to match the compressor to the tools to be used.

From the multitude of compressors on the market, there is basically only one type suitable for furniture-makers, sculptors and school shops: the positive-displacement, reciprocating (cylinder piston) unit type. Industry classifies unit-type compressors as those driven by ¼-hp motors to 25-hp motors, which at 90 psi deliver air volumes ranging from less than one cfm up to 90 cfm. Single-acting or single-stage pistons produce pressure when moving in one direction, and double-acting or two-stage pistons generate pressure when moving in both directions. The reciprocating compressors discussed in this article are all cooled by air and powered by an electric motor.

A large-capacity compressor is always attached to an air receiver or storage tank, which absorbs the pulses of air produced by the piston and provides a constant flow. It also acts as a reservoir to handle air demands that may for a short time exceed the capacity of the compressor. The reservoir of air reduces the operating time of the compressor, thus decreasing wear and maintenance. With a suitable air receiver, a 5-hp to 10-hp compressor ($1,200 to $4,000) will be more than adequate for a small shop. A larger compressor, up to 25 hp, will be necessary when more than one or two people are likely to be working at once. (All prices are 1978 estimates.)

The air receiver is usually a cylindrical tank, and the compressor motor is usually mounted on top of it. Receivers may be purchased with either horizontal or vertical stationary mountings, or may be mounted horizontally on wheels.

Operating costs can be reduced if the compressor is located in a clean, cool, well-lit room, large enough to accommodate machine servicing. If the compressor must be in a dusty studio/shop, an outside filtered-air intake protected from rain and debris is recommended. The sound of a large compressor can be reduced by a baffle wall or walls. Mounting the compressor/receiver on special rubber pads reduces vibration stress and noise.

Small, portable reciprocating unit compressors in the 1/10-hp to 3/4-hp range without receivers are called diaphragm compressors. The air is compressed by a durable membrane that flexes back and forth to force air through the hose. This type of compressor is usually used for spraying paint, although a 1/3-hp model that produces 2.5 cfm at 40 psi is sufficient to power a dental handpiece or a small grinder.

Reports of exploding air receivers are rare, but the potential is as real as the possibility of shock with electricity. The American Society for Mechanical Engineers (ASME) has safety standards for compressors used in schools and in places of business and general public assembly. In most states, compressors located in the public sector are inspected annually for safety. In Minnesota this inspection is done by the state boiler inspector or by an insurance inspector.

The single most important safety factor is the lifting lever safety valve, which opens before air pressure in the receiver can reach a dangerous level. This safety valve usually has an attached finger ring to pull for inspection.

Smaller single-stage compressors (frequently portable) for farm and residential use need not comply with ASME standards because they are not in constant use. These compressors are well suited to the needs of many woodworkers. However, some of these compressors are equipped with a preset safety valve, which can corrode and become inoperable. The preset valve should be replaced with a lifting lever safety valve.

Portable compressors manufactured for consumer use do not have large cfm capacities. As an economy measure, two consumer compressors might be hooked together with a tee to deliver a cfm flow rate comparable to a heavy-duty stationary compressor. Two consumer compressors cost about two-thirds as much as a heavy-duty industrial compressor. But for extensive use, the heavy-duty compressor will be more durable, thus more economical. Good used compressors can be found at liquidation sales, such as the closing of an auto service station. Ask to see the safety inspector's certificate and look for signs of deterioration. Check the seams and the junction of the legs (vibration stress) to the cylinder for cracks and corrosion. Be sure the lifting lever safety valve works.

Moisture control

When air is compressed it becomes hot, and with the increase in temperature comes a proportional increase in the amount of water vapor the air can hold. This water vapor condenses in the receiver or in the main air line

	Free Air Delivered (cfm)	Receiver Size (gal.)	Price Range (1978) Compressor only	Mounted After-Cooler
hp				
1/2	1.5 - 2.9*	7 1/2 - 8	$120 - $155	
3/4	1.8* 3.5	30	$200 - $900	
1	4.2* 3.1 - 6.4	30 - 60	$250 - $1,100	$300 - $400
1 1/2	5.8 - 6.2* 4.3 - 7.1	30 - 80	$300 - $1,300	$300 - $400
2	5.0 - 7.0* 4.2 - 9.1	60 - 80	$400 - $1,695	$300 - $400
3	4.0* 9.6 - 14.7	60 - 120	$400 - $1,810	$300 - $400
5	17.2 - 20.2	60 - 120	$1,540 - $2,400	$300 - $400
7 1/2	26.8 - 33.6	80 - 120	$2,000 - $3,500	$500 - $600
10	34.0 - 37.4	80 - 120	$3,000 - $4,000	$600
15	52.7 - 60	120 - 240	$4,000 - $5,500	$600
20	71.0	120 - 240	$4,500 - $6,000	$600
25	90	240	$5,000 - $6,500	$600

Table title: Compressors

* Some consumer models rate cfm at 40 psi. At 90 psi, cfm is less.

Manufacturers of Air Compressors and Dryers

Binks Manufacturing
9205 W. Belmont Ave.
Franklin Park, IL 60131
(1/8-30 hp)

Campbell-Hausfeld
100 Production Drive
Harrison, OH 45030
(1/10-30 hp)

Curtis Toledo
1905 Kienlen Ave.
St. Louis, MO 63133
(1/2-125 hp)

The DeVilbiss Co.
P.O. Box 913
Toledo, OH 43692
(1-25 hp), dryers

Dresser Ind., Inc.
N. Main & Russell Rd.
Sidney, OH 45365
(1-300 hp)

Emglo Prod. Corp.
Route 403 South
Johnstown, PA 15905
(1/2-25 hp)

Fliteway Sales, Inc.
Box 39
Horicon, WI 53032
(1/2-30 hp)

Gardner-Denver Co.
1800 S. Gardner Expwy.
Quincy, IL 62301
(1/2-500 hp)

Ingersoll-Rand
Box 636
Woodcliff Lake
NJ 07675
(1/2-4,000 hp)

Kellogg-American, Inc.
565 Cedar Way
Oakmont, Pa 15139
(3/4-200 hp)

Montgomery Ward
(1/2 and 3/4 hp)

Quincy Compressor
Colt Industries
217 Maine Street
Quincy, IL 62301
(1/3-300 hp)

Richland Industries
1140 Sextonville Road
Richland Center
WI 53581
(1/2-5 hp)

Sanborn Mfg. Co.
118 W. Rock Street
P.O. Box 129
Springfield, MN 56087
(3 and 5 hp)

Schramm Inc.
800 E. Virginia Ave.
West Chester, PA 19380
(1/3-200 hp)

Sears, Roebuck & Co.
(1/2-5 hp)

Superior Pneumatic
Box 9667
Cleveland, OH 44101
(3/4-3 hp)

Thomas Ind., Inc.
1419 Illinois Ave.
Sheboygan, WI 53081
(1/4-5 hp)

Dental laboratory handpiece, at 25,000 rpm, does the same job as the more common flexible-shaft grinder but is less tiring to control. A slightly larger tool, the industrial pencil grinder, runs at 50,000 rpm. Users of flexible-shaft tools know that small high-speed steel burrs aren't very durable. Dental supply firms sell carbide burrs, which last much longer, for about $3 each.

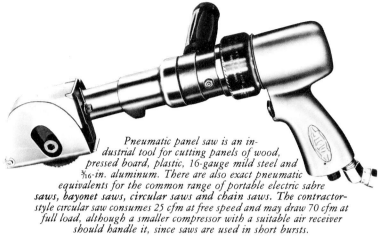

Pneumatic panel saw is an industrial tool for cutting panels of wood, pressed board, plastic, 16-gauge mild steel and ³⁄₁₆-in. aluminum. There are also exact pneumatic equivalents for the common range of portable electric sabre saws, bayonet saws, circular saws and chain saws. The contractor-style circular saw consumes 25 cfm at free speed and may draw 70 cfm at full load, although a smaller compressor with a suitable air receiver should handle it, since saws are used in short bursts.

The pneumatic carving gouge is a stonecarver's reciprocating air hammer (center) that accepts a standard ½-in. shank. Right, ¾-in. #11 sweep has been cut down at the handle flange so a length of ½-in. steel rod could be welded on. The steep-sided #11 enters and leaves the wood easily, without becoming buried, but carvers' preferences vary. The large gouge at left has an added T-bar for better control. Top photo: the author demonstrates the use of the pneumatic gouge to an audience of sculptors.

(header) when the compressed air cools to its dew point. The water can corrode the receiver or the tools, and it may contaminate the work as the air escapes from the tool.

Small and medium-sized compressors carrying light loads can get by if the water is periodically drained by hand from the receiver. A regular check for moisture may be unnecessary if the tank is fitted with an automatic dump trap or automatic tank drain; these attachments usually cost from $50 to $100.

As air consumption increases, so does moisture. Accordingly, more complicated devices become necessary to control it. Extractors with filters very effectively remove condensed water, stray oil and airborne debris from the main line. Most extractors use either baffle plates or an absorbent filter to deflect or trap contaminants from the air stream into a holding chamber for removal. This type of extractor does not expel water or oil in the gaseous state, and the filter system requires periodic maintenance. Extractors cost from $30 to $200.

Woodworking production shops and school studios that consume large volumes of compressed air can eliminate water condensation with one or a combination of air dryer systems. An after-cooler connected between the compressor and the receiver will eliminate the bulk of the water, oil and residues.

The after-cooler uses a water-circulation system to eliminate two-thirds of the water from the air before it reaches the receiver. The remaining moisture is in a vapor state. The cost of an after-cooler for a 5-hp unit is about $300, but be sure to check city codes before installing one.

An after-cooler will satisfy the needs of most studio/shops. But, if the air system requires numerous traps and extractors, a refrigerated or chemical air dryer can reduce the cost of the traps plus eliminate their maintenance. A studio/shop would probably use a low-maintenance refrigerated dryer, which will remove 95% of the moisture. A 5-hp compressor with a 19-cfm capacity will need one costing about $1,200. This cost is considerable, yet industry uses refrigerated dryers as it is believed that the dryer will pay for itself in the long run through low maintenance.

The most effective dryer is the chemical dryer, which produces nontoxic air that is safe for use in the food industry. There are two types: deliquescent and desiccant. Deliquescent dryers cost about $500 for a 5-hp model, and desiccant driers cost about $1,600. Both require frequent maintenance plus the cost of regularly adding fresh chemicals.

Air lines It is important to use the proper size pipe or hose to deliver the air from the compressor to the tools. When compressed air must travel long distances, its pressure begins to drop. The chart below matches compressor size and pipe length with pipe diameter.

The simplest piping arrangement, of course, is a hose directly connecting the receiver to a single tool. Where the main line is permanent or stationary for a distance of more than 10 ft., the line is usually made of pipe. Copper is the first choice, though galvanized pipe is probably used most often. Black iron pipe is also acceptable. The main line should slope slightly toward the receiver or toward moisture traps in the line. Stationary piping facilitates connection of extractors and *T*-joints for take-off stations. The take-off station or tool station, is where a

Main Air Lines		
hp	Lengths	Pipe dia.
⅓ & ½	All	¼"
¾ & 1	All	½"
1½ & 2	All	¾"
3 & 5	Up to 200'	¾"
3 & 5	Over 200'	1"
7½ & 10	Up to 100'	¾"
7½ & 10	100' to 200'	1"
7½ & 10	Over 200'	1¼"
15 & 20	Up to 100'	1"
15 & 20	100' to 200'	1¼"
15 & 20	Over 200'	1½"
25	Up to 200'	1¼"
25	Over 200'	1½"

Manufacturers of Portable Air Tools

Aro Corp.
One Aro Center
Bryan, OH 43506
(routers, sanders, grinders, drills, hoses, reels, screwdrivers)

Chicago Pneumatic Tool Co.
Six East 44th Street
New York, NY 10017
(drills, grinders, sanders, saws, files)

Creative Engineering
216 Tosca Drive
Stoughton, MA 02072
(Tool-trax, Uni-crane, riveting tools, drills, screwdrivers, grinders, sanders)

Danair, Inc.
P.O. Drawer 3898
Visalia, CA 93277
(nail hammers)

Dynabrade Inc.
72 E. Niagara Street
Tonawanda, NY 14150
(small belt sanders, grinding sticks)

Ekstrom, Carlson & Co.
1400 Railroad Ave.
Rockford, IL 61110
(drum sanders)

Granite City Tool Co.
Box 368
St. Cloud, MN 56301
(carving hammers)

International Staple & Machine
1000 East Butler Road
Butler, PA 16001
(nailers, staplers, tackers)

Merit Abrasive Products, Inc.
201 West Manville
Compton, CA 90224
(sanders, die grinders)

National-Detroit, Inc.
1590 Northrock Court
P.O. Box 2285
Rockford, IL 61131
(orbital, straight-line sanders)

Nicholson File Co.
Box 728
Apex, NC 27502
(rotary burrs)

Nitto Kohki USA, Inc.
111 Charlotte Place
Englewood Cliffs, NJ 07632
(sanders, files, die grinders, chisels, drills)

Rockwell International
662 N. Lexington Ave.
Pittsburgh, PA 15219
(drills, grinders, orbital and straight-line sanders, saws, routers, laminate trimmers)

Rotor Tool Co.
26300 Lakeland Blvd.
Cleveland, OH 44132
(drills, die grinders, screwdrivers)

Sand-Rite Mfg. Co.
1611 N. Sheffield Ave.
Chicago, IL 60614
(drum sanders)

Sculpture Associates Ltd., Inc.
114 East 25th Street
New York, NY 10010
(woodcarving tools, hammers, grinders)

Severance Tool Industries, Inc.
3790 Orange Street
P.O. Box 1866
Saginaw, MI 48605
(rotary burrs, files)

Sioux Tools, Inc.
2901 Floyd Blvd.
Sioux City, IA 51102
(drills, grinders, laminate trimmers, routers, sanders, saws)

SME Corp.
P.O. Box 126
Fairfield, NJ 07006
(convex rotary planer heads)

Stanley Air Tools
700 Beta Drive
Cleveland, OH 44143
(drills, grinders, routers, screwdrivers)

Star Dental Mfg. Co., Inc.
Ford Bridge Road
Conshohocken, PA 19428
(dental lab handpieces)

Starlite Industries, Inc.
1111 Lancaster Ave.
Rosemont, PA 19010
(die grinders)

Stuhr Manufacturing Co.
5005 27th Ave.
Rockford, IL 61109
(sanders)

Superior Pneumatic & Mfg.
P.O. Box 9667
Cleveland, OH 44101
(drills, die grinders, sanders)

Thor Power Tool Co.
175 North State Street
Aurora, IL 60507
(drills, grinders, sanders)

Trow and Holden Co.
45 S. Main Street
Barre, VT 05641
(carving hammers)

Willson Division, E.S.B. Corp.
P.O. Box 622
Reading, PA 19603
(safety glasses, respirators)

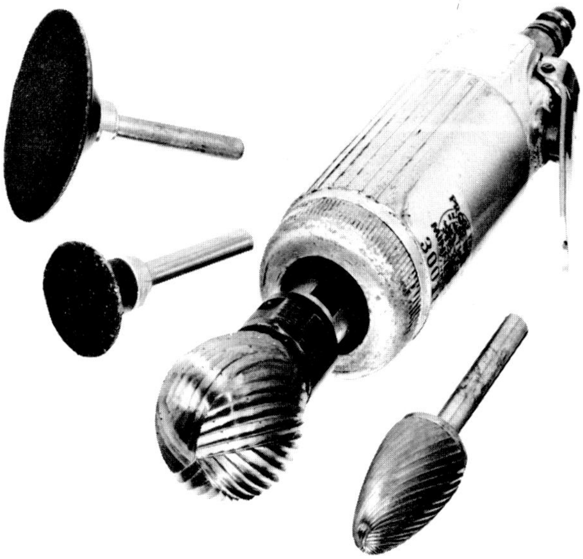

Bill Snyder Films, Inc.

The die grinder is extremely valuable for woodcarving and sculpture. This one weighs only a pound, yet the burr twists at 22,000 rpm, saving hours of gouge-tapping. The burr shown was specially designed by Severance Tool Industries for sculptor Wendell Castle. It is No. NNB ball mill, ¼-in. shank, 1¼-in. diameter, 5½ teeth per inch double cut. It costs $22 in high-speed steel, $143 in carbide; both can be resharpened. The tree-shaped burr, right, is a standard pattern. Merit Power-Lock flexible sanding pads, left, snap on and off the shaft, which remains chucked in the grinder.

Pneumatic Tools

Tool	Weight (lb.)	cfm	psi	hose dia. (in.)	free speed (rpm)	Approx. price (1978)
Carving hammer	1⅞ -3½	4 - 6	90 -100	⅜	5,200 -6,200	$220
Dental handpiece	3/16	2.5	36 -60	⅛	25,000	$250
Drills	1½ -3¼	4	90 -100	¼ - ⅜	330 - 5,200	$40 -$120
Grinders, die	¾ - 2⅝	14 - 18	90 -100	¼	20,000 -25,000	$70 -$140
Grinders, pencil	5/16	7	90 -100	⅛	50,000	$115
Grinders, vertical	10	15 - 20	90 - 100	½	6,000	$400
Laminate trimmer	2 - 3¼	22 - 54	90 - 100	¼	22,000 - 28,000	$150 - $210
Routers	3 - 8	22 - 54	90 - 100	¼ - ⅜	6,000 - 22,000	$270 - $370
Sanders, belt	15	22 - 54	90 - 100	⅜	1,120 - 1,900 ft./sec.	$550
Sanders, disc	4½ - 5	24	90 - 100	⅜	5,000	$120
Sanders, drum	¾ - 3½	14	90 - 100	¼	2,400 - 2,600	$200
Sanders, orbital	3⅜ - 6¼	5.3 - 15	75 - 90	¼ - ⅜	8,000 - 15,000	$70 - $120
Sanders, random orbital	4	15	90 - 100	¼ - ⅜	9,000 - 10,000	$64 - $135
Sanders, straight line	5½ - 30	8 - 15	75 - 90	¼ - ⅜	1,100 - 3,000	$70 - $780
Saws, circular	16 - 24½	25 - 70	90 - 100	½	3,000 - 6,000	$810 - $870
Saws, jig	5¾	22	90 - 100	¼	4,000	$230
Saws, panel	3½ - 3¾	22	90 - 100	¼	1,400	$325 - $410
Saws, reciprocating	5 - 8½	24	90 - 100	¼ - ⅜	1,500 - 1,600	$535 - $600

The rolling pin sander (right) has no electrical equivalent. It consists of an in-line pneumatic drill (the more common gun drill, above, can be substituted) fitted with an inflated drum and a ball-bearing handle. The drum conforms to convex shapes, although the sanding sleeves must have J-weight cloth backing for flexibility. The sander is made in several diameters from 1 in. to 3 in., and in lengths from 6 in. to 10 in. Pneumatic sanders are also made in the usual orbital, random orbital, disc, straight-line, belt and vibrating modes.

Veneer mills use the rotary planer, or power adze (right), for stripping bark. Sculptors find it especially good for wasting large amounts of green wood (above) and stacked glued forms. The power unit is a medium or heavy-duty vertical grinder, which produces almost 2 hp at 6,000 rpm, at a cost of 20 cfm of air at 90 psi. The three-knife planer head is 5 in. across. Straight cutters (Indiana Manufacturers Supply) and convex cutters (SME Corp.) are available. The depth of the cut is adjustable; the whole unit weighs about 10 lb. Blade guard, goggles and ear protectors are essential.

T-joint is placed in the main line to gain access to the compressed air. If the air system does not include an after cooler or air dryer, then some form of drain or extractor should be located at the take-off staion and at low points in the line.

The tool station may require accessories for special situations. Where a spraying operation may be affected by water or oil in the air, a water and oil coalescer (filter) must be used to remove oil aerosols, water droplets and suspended particles. To reduce air pressure, say, from 90 psi to 35 psi, a regulator, also called a diaphragm or transformer, is included in the take-off station. Regulators are also manufactured in combination with coalescers and extractors.

Tools that need small amounts of oil for lubrication and to prevent rust can be serviced with an automatic lubricator attached to the tool station or the air intake of the tool. Some manufacturers build automatic oilers into the tool, although the expense of an automatic lubricator can be bypassed by putting a drop or two of pneumatic oil into the tool's air intake every 15 or 20 minutes.

Flexible hoses are easily connected and detached with couplers, also called quick couplers. Couplers are attached to the work station, to the ends of hoses and extension hoses, and to the air tool. The female coupler and male fitting engage and disengage quickly by sliding the locking sleeve on the female coupler. The work station is always fitted with a female coupler; hoses and extension hoses have a female and

male fitting at their ends, and the air tool is always equipped with a male fitting.

Air hoses from the main line to the tools should not be any longer than necessary, to keep the pressure up. Some tools require hoses of specified inside diameters, which the manufacturer will provide, although general requirements are given in the chart on page 88. There are several types of hose: non-oil resistant, oil resistant and nylon Re-Trak. If oil can enter the line via a lubricator at the work station, oil-resistant hose must be used. Nylon Re-Trak, available in ¼-in. and ⅜-in. diameters, is formed in a spring-like coil and will wind itself up when left to its own devices.

A useful accessory in a busy shop would be an overhead track system that pivots in a full circle, to prevent a clutter of hose on the floor. Industry uses retractable cable balancers to support tools at work stations for long operations. Auto service stations usually store hose in a self-winding reel, very handy. If you are installing an air system, don't neglect a small blowgun, invaluable for cleaning up and blasting chips out of holes and awkward recesses. □

Further reading

The Compressed Air and Gas Institute (1230 Keith Building, Cleveland, Ohio 44125) publishes a handbook that I have found useful. The fifth edition should be available in 1985. In addition, Binks and many other manufacturers publish pamphlets on compressed air, pneumatic tools, hoses and fittings.

Designing for Machine Craft
Desmond Ryan's route to handsome boxes

by Roger Holmes

For nearly ten years Desmond Ryan has been making little wooden boxes—boxes for all sorts of things, from jewelry worth fortunes to sentimental trinkets. He makes boxes one at a time and in batches of ten or twenty, with traditional hand tools as well as with modern machinery. His favorite machine has become the overarm router that stands in the middle of his shop; Ryan has learned to use this router with the sensitivity usually associated with a handtool, and his designs capitalize on the machine's strong points. He's succeeded in blending craft with industrial design, handwork with machine work—he is toolmaker, jigmaker and old-fashioned bench craftsman all rolled into one.

Last fall I visited Ryan at his shop, in a 176-year-old paper mill in the town of Maidstone, 37 miles east of London. The mill sits in a tight wooded valley, and Ryan's shop, a long narrow room lit by a wall of windows, is on the second floor of a timber-clad building. It is a large shop for one man, but Ryan prefers to work alone. The extra space is for making furniture, a side of his work overshadowed by the success of his boxes. "Nobody actually needs boxes," he told me, "they aren't necessary like tables, chairs and cabinets. But it is surprising how many people indulge themselves."

Few craft woodworkers have exploited the router as thoroughly as Ryan has for his boxes. Almost every woodworker has a router; they are cheap, take up little space, and can perform a bewildering array of operations. The router can replace whole chests of molding planes, hollows, rounds, gouges and more. It works quickly and precisely—sometimes too easily. The unwavering accuracy of a routed surface doesn't complement

every design. Ryan therefore designs with the router in mind. He derives the basic shapes and joints of many of his boxes from it, and often a routed detail will tie a whole design together. The jewelry box shown at the top of page 93 is a good example. A coved rabbet frames the ends of the box when closed, and it connects with the routed handles on the four trays when they are set into the open box for display. "It is one object closed and a different object when open," explained Ryan. "I usually try to do this with boxes. I try to keep them simple on the outside, and when you open them, there is a more complex but visually harmonious interior."

One-off boxes need a lot of handwork. Ryan's batch-production boxes are almost entirely machine-made, and usually routed out of a solid block of wood: no assembly necessary. Some of his production ideas develop from one-off commissions, like the paint box (see page 93) and some of his game boards; others come while playing around with ideas and with the machine itself.

Batch production has different requirements for design, production and materials than one-offs. The designer must eliminate complicated, time-consuming constructions or details. These can be absorbed when done once, but are prohibitive when they must be repeated over and over. A logical succession of simple, quick and accurate operations is the key to successful production, and there isn't much margin for error. "You have got to have an absolute sure-fire way of controlling production operations," says

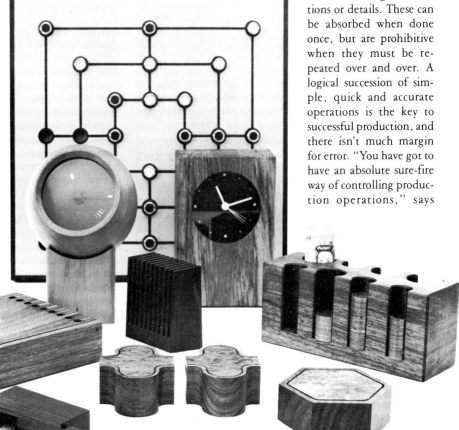

Some of the items that Ryan machines in small batches on his router, drill press, lathe and other machines. In the back is a board for the old English game of Nine-Man's Morris.

Photos, except where noted: Maggie Ellis

Ryan's drawing board and workbenches share the same room, where he often works well into the night. Small machines line the windows: a bandsaw, router, drill press, 5-in. jointer and disc sander. He hoards scraps of exotic woods in the 70 or so cardboard tubes on the left—raw material for boxes. Router jigs hang on the far wall. The other end of the shop is taken up by a 10-in. Wadkin table saw, a metal lathe and a massive, aged, 12-in. over-under thickness planer. Downstairs in a

musty room, Ryan keeps a three-platen veneer press, a couple of disassembled machines and his lumber store. Ryan's overarm router, left, is not a heavy-duty production machine, but a Watford 18,000-rpm router body bolted to an overarm stand. The throat is 24 in., and the table, moved up and down by foot, has four adjustable stops that can be preset for a sequence of cuts at different depths. Slip-on collars, placed over the pin, determine the size of the openings.

Ryan. "If you work to the sort of precision possible with the machine and you fit one piece into another, the consistency has got to be there."

Ryan chooses his materials as carefully as he constructs his jigs. "When I'm doing a production piece," he says, "I don't see individual pieces of wood. With the hexagonal boxes [page 95], for example, I wasn't trying to create interest in the wood. I used walnut or rosewood for their color against which I contrasted an interesting wood, amboyna, which is decorative in itself, but is a bit like wallpaper. One box lid was different from another, but it was really the color and texture I was after, not a specific piece of wood."

I wondered if he couldn't just as easily make his boxes from metal or plastic. "I suppose I use wood rather than metal because I like the warmth and feel of it. It also machines well, handles easily and can be worked with hand tools." The ideal wood? He laughed, "I suppose it would be something like a firm cheese that you could work and harden up afterwards."

Having worked on the design, made the first jigs and started a half dozen prototypes, Ryan is liable to abandon the project. "That happens quite a lot. Either I reject them because I am not happy with them visually, or I feel that the price is going to be too high to justify finishing them off. It is very costly."

A box that has made it past these obstacles must still prove itself. "I like to leave boxes lying around and observe people handling them," Ryan said. "The longer they keep one in their hand, perhaps turning it over absent-mindedly while talking, the more successful the box."

Ryan's pleasure in the boxes is designing them, figuring out the jigs, and wrestling with the machine, seeing what he can make it do. "The trouble," he confesses, "is really that I lose interest when I've made all the jigs and done the first one. My production pieces are never in that high a production, usually tens or twenties. I spend perhaps two or three weeks with a pro-

duction piece, take it to a certain stage and then it gets left and taken on to the next stage later. There is never enough time between commissions to finish them." They are not, therefore, great money makers. Friends, steady clients and exhibitions take most of them off his hands.

Recently, Ryan has spent more time making furniture, a change from boxes that he finds stimulating. "Boxes are an isolated thing and fit into whatever scheme of decoration people have," he says. "Furniture has got to fit in with what is already there." At first glance, his chunky furniture seems much different from his precise boxes. But the same functional economy and attention to detail is there. Other ideas carry over, too. He doesn't want the wood to compete with the form, in boxes or furniture, so he builds table tops, for instance, of thin strips of wood rather than wide, figured boards.

Ryan is interested in doing more with decorative effects, but he's wary of them. Game boards whose surfaces are necessarily decorative were an easy first step. "But I can't bring myself to use decoration much on furniture," he said. "I want to use a decorative surface without destroying the form. Perhaps I'm afraid of it and don't want to push too hard in case something strange comes out." He has firm beliefs about furniture, and if they seem old-fashioned, they are nevertheless sound. "You make furniture to be used. There are similarities with sculpture, painting, and so on, but I can't accept furniture that doesn't do what it should—be useful."

Ryan has been interested in furniture since he was a boy; after technical school, he studied furniture and industrial design at Beckenham Art College and at the Royal College of Art, where he received a masters degree in 1965.

All this college training—eight years studying design— may seem odd to Americans who are more likely to knock together a bench, buy a few tools and open for business, picking up design and woodworking skills as they go. The British

A museum in Munich, Germany, commissioned this rosewood box (19½ in. by 16½ in. by 9 in. when closed) to display as well as to store its changing collection of jewelry. Ryan wove the function of the box together with its appearance. The reveals on the end frames set off the panels against the seamless surface of the box. When the box is open, the upper of the two panels in each half can be removed, and the four trays positioned by brass pins. The curve echoes throughout the box: the coved rabbet bends around the mitered corners, the handles flow into the trays—even the hinges, lock plate and dead bolt are radiused.

The characters of production and of one-off work contrast in these two paint boxes made by Ryan. The one at right (unfinished) is his most complicated production piece, requiring several cutters, jigs, router-fence settings and about five hours to machine. It was designed to serve the basic needs of any watercolorist. The box below was commissioned by a professional painter to hold exactly what he needed for his tramps around the countryside. Though there is as much machine work in this as in the production box, it has more personality than the production box.

Photos of jewelry box and of paint box, left, by Ken Adams.

Ryan's dressing table, commissioned in 1975, is really three boxes on a stand, but boxes and stand have merged—the rails of the stand are also the sides of the boxes. The table is 42 in. long when closed, 13½-in. wide, 29 in. high and is finished with cellulose lacquer.

He is a self-taught woodworker and doesn't think of himself as a craftsman. He said, "I suppose designer-craftsman is the closest one can get to a classification. What fascinates me most is problem solving: linking the object's function to its appearance and juggling them to get the most exciting result with the least compromise."

Like many designer-craftsmen, most of Ryan's work is commissioned. "I think people like to buy something from the person who has made it," he said. "They are buying a bit of somebody's life, almost."

Today, at 41, Ryan is established and earns a living from his workshop. But it has been a long time coming. He subsidized his work for many years by part-time teaching, but he found that this proved to be a distraction that took the edge off his business drive. Each time he dropped a day's teaching his own work improved. Still, it wasn't until 1978 that he could afford to work wood full time.

I asked him about all the eager newcomers setting up workshops today, what were the prospects for them? He thought that a lot of them would fall by the wayside. "It's not just training you need, you have got to be right for it, it's more of a vocation. It's got to be a vocation to work for the money you get and the long hours you put in." He paused and continued, "Every job that I take on, I treat as if it is the one and only thing in my life, and I've got to do it to the utmost. This isn't necessary if you just want to make a living, but it is if you want to say anything. That is what I want to do—it is a means of expression, I suppose." Momentarily embarrassed by his own profundity, he fussed with his pipe and added with a smile, "though I don't know what it is I'm trying to say...."

Whatever it is, his clients get the message: "One of the nicest comments I've received was from a client who said, 'You know, Des, every time I come down in the morning those objects of yours give me pleasure and I see something new in them.' All the effort that I had put into things that seem so simple paid off." □

Roger Holmes is associate editor of Fine Woodworking *magazine.* *For more on pin routing, see pages 83 to 85.*

have always followed a more formal path. Until the 1960s, many makers of craft furniture endured an apprenticeship of five or even seven years, or else spent several years as a paying student in a workshop. During the last twenty years, however, students from art and design colleges have chosen to make, as well as to design, for their livings.

Ryan was one of the first of this generation. A year in industry followed college and convinced him that making was as important to him as designing. "Industry was too restrictive," he said. "Designing on paper at drawing boards is like composing music that is never played. I strongly believe that you should design as much in the workshop as on paper, by making mockups and prototypes as well as finished pieces."

The top of this huge pine table—11 ft. long, 3 ft. wide and over 2½ in. thick—rests on hefty trestles uncluttered by any additional underframing. The table has the commanding presence of the medieval tables Ryan admired as a student. But instead of the wide boards of the old tops, which he felt distracted from the overall form of the tables, Ryan glued up narrow strips, side by side and end to end, to break up the color and strong grain pattern of individual planks.

How Ryan makes hexagonal boxes

Ryan is a master at coaxing precise work out of his overarm router. His secret is accurate jigs. A jig may be just a piece of wood clamped to the router table or it may be a more complex construction that guides the cut by means of a template. Either way, careful preparation and set-up are essential.

Much of Ryan's work is pin-routed, clamped to a baseboard which is attached to a template. The template guides the cut by running against a pin set into the router table; the pin's centerline is the same as the cutter's above it. With a rise-and-fall table, this set-up is ideal for excavating solid blocks of wood to make boxes.

The little hexagonal box pictured here is made in batches of ten or twenty, and takes advantage of production economies even at that small scale. Ryan pin-routs the inside of the solid block, and routs the foot and the lid rabbet against a fence. He uses the disc sander like a milling machine to grind the outside surfaces of box and lid to size while keeping their edges sharp. The lid is about 1/64 in. undersize (for what Ryan calls a "rattling good fit"); it closes with a satisfying click. Here are some tips on making jigs like Ryan's.

Preliminary jigs: Use rough-and-ready jigs to test rough-and-ready designs. You can even nail or screw the prototype blank to the baseboard and make the template from wood—the jig will be used only once or twice. Work from the design to the jig and back again to eliminate small errors and inefficiencies—they make a big difference when repeated tens or hundreds of times.

Production jigs: After the bugs have been worked out and the final design has been decided, make production jigs. They need not be expensive or complicated, just sturdy and accurate—they must produce exactly the same cuts time after time. Jigs should be heavy enough to help counteract the router's torque and large enough to keep hands well away from the cutter, but they should not be unwieldly. Chipboard is ideal for baseboards. The template gets the most wear; good template materials are mild steel and Formica.

The template size: The size of the template is determined by the sizes of the router cutter and the pin. If the pin and cutter are the same size, the routed shape or opening will be exactly the size of the template. If the pin is smaller than the cutter, a routed opening will be larger and an outside shape smaller than the template by the difference in their respective diameters. For example: A 1/4-in. pin and a 1/2-in. cutter will produce an opening 1/4 in. larger than the template. Likewise, a pin larger than the cutter will produce a smaller opening.

Pin collars: Ryan routs different sized openings in the same piece, without changing cutters, pins or jigs, by slipping collars of various diameters over a single pin. The smallest collar produces the largest opening, and larger collars produce the smaller openings.

The cutter: Ryan uses high-speed steel router cutters. A carbide edge lasts longer, but a high-speed steel edge can be honed. Sharpening a fluted cutter minutely alters its diameter, so check this regularly and alter the jig to compensate. Ryan hones both face and bevel of the cutting edges with a triangular Arkansas slipstone. He sharpens after every four or five boxes for such hard stuff as rosewood, to produce surfaces that require only light sanding or scraping to finish.

The design of this rosewood and amboyna hexagonal box takes advantage of the overarm router's production strengths.

Different sized collars (above) can be slipped over the router's pin. By bearing against a template, they control the size of the rabbet or box opening as shown below.

Hexagonal box router set-up

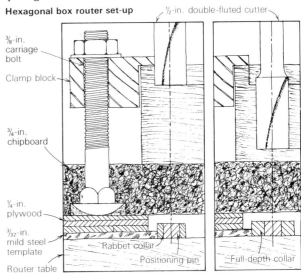

3/8-in. carriage bolt

Clamp block

1/2-in. double-fluted cutter

3/4-in. chipboard

1/4-in. plywood

3/32-in. mild steel template

Router table

Rabbet collar

Positioning pin

Full-depth collar

The jig

To make the router jig for his hexagonal box, Ryan started with the template. First he laid out the exact size of the template in the center of a piece of ¼-in. plywood. He positioned the 3/32-in. metal strips, each the width of a box side, and screwed them in place. Taking the strips off, he cut a slightly oversized hole in the plywood so the strips would project slightly beyond the opening. Next he screwed the strips back in place, tapping them into exact position. He ran epoxy glue around them to ensure against movement. Finally he flushed off the strips and screwed two additional ones at the two ends for stability (photo **A**).

To make the baseboard (**B**), Ryan positioned the clamping block and its two hanger bolts, transferring the template position to the baseboard top by measurement. The box blank must be held directly over the template, and the clamp bolts must clear the router, yet be close enough to exert direct pressure on the blank. Ryan bolted the hard maple clamping block in place, and routed out its center by guiding the template on the pin collar for the box's rabbet—the largest opening to be routed. Then he enlarged this hole to comfortably fit a blank, chopping to within ¼ in. of the clamp's top surface. The fit need not be tight—three chisel-pointed panel pins embedded in the baseboard keep the blank from twisting while it's being routed.

A

B

The box

Ryan starts a batch of boxes by bandsawing the blanks about 3/16 in. oversize, from selected rosewood or walnut blanks planed to final thickness. He drills the waste from the center of each blank, then clamps it to the jig. He places the first (smallest) collar on the router pin and routs the rabbet for the lid to its full depth in one cut (**C**). Using the second (largest) collar and three depth stops, he routs the inside of the box to its full depth (**D**). Safe depth depends on the wood, the cutter size and sharpness, and on the power of the machine. With the final collar, minutely smaller than the second, he takes a finishing cut of a couple of hundredths of an inch to remove tears and burns left from the heavier cuts. As before, he goes to full depth in three steps.

All router work should be moved into the cutter against the direction of rotation, otherwise the cutter self-feeds and grabs the work. Sometimes difficult grain requires feeding in the same direction as the router rotates—in tough spots like these, Ryan hogs the waste in small bites and finishes by careful back-cutting, making sure his clamps are tight and his hands well clear.

With the inside cuts completed, Ryan moves to the 12-in. disc sander to shape the outside (**E**).

The sanding jig is glued up from two pieces of ¼-in. plywood the exact size of the box rabbet, but one of them has radiused corners to fit the routed opening. Inserted into the box, the sharp-cornered piece forms the jig's template. It is pushed against a brass strip that is fixed to the edge of a board clamped on the sander's worktable. The distance between the strip and the disc determines the thickness of the box's walls.

Ryan sands around the box several times, taking care not to overheat the wood. When the boxes have all been sanded with 80-grit, he changes the disc to 120-grit and moves the board with the brass strip fractionally closer to the disc for a finishing pass.

C

D

E

Back at the router, Ryan clamps a fence to the table, sets a depth stop and routs a foot on the bottom of the box using a double-fluted cutter ground to a very small radius (F). This completes the machining.

Ryan hand-sands the outside faces with two grades of fine paper glued on opposite sides of a flat board. He draws the box across the paper, taking care not to lose the sharp edges, then sands small, crisp chamfers. He removes small ridges on the inside with tightly-rolled sandpaper.

F

The lid

To make the box lid, Ryan planes, thicknesses and bandsaws to size solid padouk blanks, aligning the points of the hexagon with the grain direction. He veneers the blanks top and bottom with amboyna, the richly figured burl wood of padouk. After veneering, the lids are rough-sanded on the disc (G) to remove glue and tape—a difficult and risky operation when hand-holding such a thin piece.

G

He shapes the lid on the disc sander the same way he shaped the box. A plywood jig (H) is cut the exact size of the lid; it should allow for slight shrinkage in the box. A rabbet in the jig forms the template and lets the jig clear the brass fence and just touch the sanding disc. Small radii worked on the points on the underside of the template fit the lid to the box rabbet. Four tiny pins set in the jig hold the lid in place during the machining—their holes are lost in the wild figure of the amboyna.

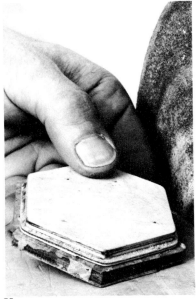

H

On the router, Ryan works a decorative rabbet around the top of the lid (I), using the rounded cutter that routed the box foot. As he routs, he works around each corner with a series of small cuts, keeping the edge of the lid hard against the fence. Any difficult grain is back-cut—very carefully.

I

Next he routs a stopped rabbet on two adjacent sides of the bottom of the lid (J). Pushing on this corner pivots the lid on the rabbet stops and pops it up for removal. Ryan uses the same set-up as before but moves the fence so the width of this rabbet will just exceed that of the ledge in the box. The depth remains the same. Pencil lines on the baseboard mark where to begin and end the cut. This rabbet starts 3/16 in. from one point of the hexagon and moves through an adjacent point, ending 3/16 in. from a third. It includes two sides that run across the grain direction of the veneered padouk so the thin division between the lid's upper and lower rabbets will be end grain and not weaker edge grain.

J

Ryan finish-sands the lid on the fine-paper boards and then he lightly chamfers its edges. Finally he wipes the box and lid with teak oil, keeping the oil clear of the bottom where the suede must be glued, then he stamps his name on the bottom.   —R.H.

Keeping Quality in Production Runs
The efficient use of space, waste and technology

by Dean Santner

Production, production craft, limited production, craft multiples—let's face it, none of these terms has a very good connotation for those of us involved in craft work. The assumption is that when more than one of a piece is made, the value of the original automatically diminishes, and each subsequent piece is just as bad as or worse than the one preceding it. Right? Well, to be honest, probably. Certainly we don't have to look too far to find the abuses of production technology; consider the tools we often have to use. Good design and quality construction are frequently sacrificed to satisfy the demands of large production runs and to suit the real or imagined budget and the uneducated tastes of the masses. Production has also become synonymous with making an inordinately high profit, which is distasteful and alien to many craftspeople.

But does production have to mean poor design and shoddy construction? European countries have shown otherwise. Quality production can be seen in the sensitive designs and careful construction of wood furniture in many Scandinavian shops. The technically ingenious and innovative designs of the modern Italian furniture manufacturers make quality work possible, not in spite of production techniques, but because of the access to a technology not easily available to one-of-a-kind applications. The product and not the process can and should be the principal concern of any production process. Unfortunately in our quest for original, museum-quality craft pieces, we believe that producing in quantity detracts from quality and that the craftsworker is demeaned in the process. I don't feel this attitude is justified, unless, of course, we are actually producing poor work. I'm not saying quantity production can or should replace the one-of-a-kind approach to craft. It can't and it shouldn't try. There is a need for both one-of-a-kind and quantity craft production, yet the worth of the latter has been largely unrealized.

Except for a brief period when I made one-of-a-kind furniture pieces, for the last ten years my shop has addressed itself almost exclusively to the design, development and production of original craft multiples of functional wood accessories. It's my experience that because of a number of advantages associated with production, a small, efficiently operated shop with good equipment and sensitive people who are sympathetic to the same quality and design concepts can produce work of exceptional character, worthy of craft recognition. I believe that this can be done while imparting personal dignity and pride of workmanship to those involved. And although I haven't been able to prove this point yet, I believe it can be done with a reasonable profit for everyone involved.

Santner's work is a model of efficiency—smaller shell box is produced with the waste left after bandsawing the drawer in the egg box (koa wood, 14 in. by 8 in. by 3¾ in.).

Our shop produces a limited variety of designs for boxes (like the ones shown above), cutting boards, hand mirrors, wine racks and conceptual-style toys. All items are designed for production in quantities ranging from several pieces over a period of years to hundreds within the same year, depending variously on the degree of technical complexity, public demand and the maximum amounts we choose to make in a given period. Whether in large quantities or small, we are responsible for all we produce, from conception to packaging.

People—The people who work with me are the main element in the work we are able to accomplish. Currently we are a highly skilled group of five full-time co-workers and a part-time independent accountant, all functioning as a team during working hours. Each person in the group is sensitive to fine craft and to the other workers. Responsibility for the smooth operation of specific areas of the business is divided among us all. Each person takes on as many operations and duties as his or her training and skill will allow.

Since boredom is the biggest threat to quality in a quantity run, it is important that each of us has the skill to trade duties with someone else to sustain interest at each stage of each piece. Still, as in any quality work, personal discipline is necessary. New people must make a commitment to the group and to our procedures. If they focus only on the repetitive nature of what we are doing, they miss what the shop represents and therefore don't do their best work, aren't particularly interesting to work with and don't last very long. We select new employees by a group vote, following a group discussion.

Work schedules are organized so each person in the shop has as much personal time as possible, and at present most

Photo this page: Steve Ortland; All others: Dean Santner

everyone has important outside interests in one-of-a-kind woodworking, fine art or in starting another business. The stability of our shop helps to sustain these diverse activities. We work a four-day week for the first nine months of the year and five or more days during the last three months. After-hours use of shop facilities is encouraged for individual work and is considered part of the pay. Our pay scale is considered high for a craft shop; however, everyone agrees that it's more than money that keeps us working as hard as we do.

Facilities—Except for the initial kiln-drying of lumber and the occasional use of a wide belt sander, all the production details of each design are done under our complete control within our shop. The shop space is a 2,900-sq. ft. building, 23 ft. wide and divided into a 66-ft. long machine room, a 17-ft. assembly room, a 20-ft. finishing and shipping room and an office. Lumber is stored in cantilevered racks at the front of the machine room near an overhead door. The shop and equipment were purchased with our designs in mind, and although twice as much space wouldn't be too much, careful organization of space and procedures has created an efficient, comfortable and safe working environment. Most of the machines are set along the wall, which allows more space for traffic. Only the jointer, planer and table saw are placed out from the wall, and these are angled to maximize infeed and outfeed space. The machine room can easily handle four of us working at one time. Up to six different designs are under production at once, so if a bottleneck develops, it can be alleviated simply by working on a different design in another area of the shop. All changes in equipment or structural elements of the building are tested first using a scale model. Planning went into such things as the use of natural light (there are six skylights, and more to come), point-source lighting where inspection is required, wall and underground power to machines, compressed-air outlets and an atmosphere-recycling dust-collection system. The shop is thoroughly cleaned every day for fire safety as well as for comfort and appearance. Small tools are not misplaced in piles of sawdust, and we can all concentrate on the work at hand.

Thus, concerns for efficiency, comfort and safety often prove interrelated. A dust-collection system that is atmosphere-recycling, for instance, helps maintain consistent temperature and humidity, which are controlled not only for comfort, but also for optimum stock storage, gluing and finishing. So with many machine accessories. After a bad accident on the table saw, we bought an automatic suspension-style feeder that can also be used on the jointer and shaper. The advantages are higher yield from our stock, cleaner joints, and faster, easier, and safer operation. And because it sits right over the blade or cutter, there's less noise.

Access to technology—Combining recent technological developments, particularly in carbide cutters and in abrasives, with the more established woodworking techniques has enabled us to produce our designs more efficiently without compromising their quality. In some cases, new technologies have inspired new designs or design improvements.

While it might be obvious why one would be interested in new technology, it's not so obvious how to obtain it or to decide whether it's worth using. First, you must know what's available and the technical language to order it. Writing to the largest manufacturers in the fields you are interested in

and asking for information packets is a good way to start. But often you must then be able to place an order in sufficient quantities to make it worthwhile for the manufacturer. Here is an important advantage of being a shop committed to the long-term production of a limited number of designs.

For example, three years ago we became aware of a new abrasive product, zirconia alumina, that is extremely aggressive, sharpens itself, has long life, and resists heat deterioration and burnishing. On further study we learned of a few drawbacks: It is limited to only three flexibilities, is offered only in a very heavyweight backing, and is much more expensive than the more commonly used aluminum oxide, garnet and silicon carbide. Then we learned that because it's not a stock item you must meet the industrial basic unit quantities. Because we are a production shop and could foresee using some kind of abrasive in quantity, we were able to try this product. We ordered one unit of 20 belts for our stroke sander (100 grit, open coat, Q flex, Y-weight cloth). The cost was about 40% more than for aluminum oxide, but the zirconia has lasted more than three times as long. Now we use zirconia on all our abrasive machines, except for finish sanding, because it's not available in finer grits. (Norton Co., Troy, N.Y. 12181 manufactures zirconia-based products.)

Another recent discovery has replaced steel wool in our finishing room. We dunk most of our products in Danish oil and allow them to dry on wire racks (reclaiming the dripping finish in a pan at the bottom if it's suitable for re-use) in 65° to 70° temperatures for 12 to 16 hours. We then rub two coats of polymerized tung oil into the surface, allowing 4 hours drying time between coats. After another 4 to 16 hours the heavy oil finish dries, leaving the grain raised and the surface bubbled and rough. Instead of hand rubbing with steel wool, we use a series of nylon discs (called Bear-Tex and produced by Norton), which are impregnated with fine silicon-carbide or aluminum-oxide chips. Mounted on a 3,200-RPM shaft, they scrub off the excess oil but are not aggressive enough to sand the wood. Next we apply a coat of carnauba wax and

Santner's shop is not large, but it's carefully laid out. Most of the machines are along the walls. Only the planer, table saw and jointer are in the center, each angled to the others to maximize infeed and outfeed space. Four people can easily work at once in the 66-ft. by 23-ft. machine room.

1. *Because the designs are already known, it is most efficient to mill the stock to blanks as soon as the lumber shipment has been checked for moisture content and drying stresses. The blanks can then be stacked in space-saving, fire-safe piles and left to reach equilibrium moisture content with the shop atmosphere. Here a 3-roll, 8-speed automatic feeder by Forest City, which can also be used on the jointer and shaper, helps to rip egg-box blanks safely, quickly and cleanly. The saw is a dual-arbor 16-in. Yates American with 5 HP per arbor. There's a 32-tooth carbide, glue-joint-ripping blade on one arbor and a 60-tooth crosscut blade on the other.*

2. *A Plexiglas template (Plexiglas allows defects to be seen and avoided) is used to mark band-saw cuts on the 8/4 drawer blanks. The cuts produce what will be the center carcase lamination, the drawer (the saw kerf will be glued back together and clamped with motorcycle inner tubes) and a central waste piece, which is used to make another design, the shell box. Drawer and carcase member are numbered and later rejoined to maintain continuity of figure.*

3. *The insides of the drawers are shaped to identical size with a shaper jig before rabbeting the lower edge for press-fitted drawer bottom. Handles screw down to clamp drawer blank in place. Heavy ⅜-in. steel base (laminated with Masonite to slide easily on shaper table) dampens vibration as precision-ground cutout is guided around fixed shaper collar. An adjustable angle-iron indexer for positioning the drawer blank also acts as a scatter shield. The segmented carbide cutter is quieter than standard cutters.*

allow it to harden for 12 to 36 hours. Then it is buffed at high speed with non-impregnated soft nylon (also made by Norton) leaving a lustrous but not glossy finish.

Over the years we have kept careful records of what new technology has worked for us or why it didn't and what might be changed to improve it. Abrasive manufacturers in particular are interested in this kind of feedback, and specialized sales representatives can be very helpful in suggesting and sometimes engineering products that suit your needs. The important thing is to do your homework first, acquire the basic knowledge of the product, and go back to the manufacturer with specific experiences and requirements.

Design and construction—Because our shop makes a commitment to each design, long-term refinement is possible. It is a continuous, slow, and carefully thought-out process, making the most of available resources in balance with the realities of being in business. Once again, superficially conflicting concerns, like quality and efficiency, turn out to be compatibly interrelated. For instance, we make our freeform

cutting boards in only six basic shapes that over the years have proven the most practical and the most aesthetically pleasing. These shapes have also been developed to make maximum use of stock: The free-form templates are paired to fill various standard rectangular blanks.

Commitment to a limited number of designs also makes possible the long-term refinement of construction techniques. Quality equipment, custom bits and special one-piece cutters (which are safer and faster to set up) can be purchased and amortized over an extended period of anticipated return. Specialized jigs, fixtures, clamps and tools can be devised not only to expedite the construction process, but also to improve working tolerances and quality and to increase safety. Waste and cutoffs can be used to maximum advantage by designing new items out of predictable leftovers.

The egg box, whose production is illustrated above, is one of our first production designs, and it still has strong appeal after 10 years. I was impressed with the simple beauty of Art Carpenter's bandsawn boxes and the shapes Wendell Castle gets out of laminated wood. Starting with a few prototypes,

4. Parts are selected according to figure, and 4/4 top and bottom are glued to 8/4 carcase center. Using aliphatic resin glue for joint elasticity, the gluing surfaces are sized (precoated for maximum fiber penetration) and stacked in specially made egg-box clamp. Pressure applied evenly through threaded rods achieves optimum 0.002-in. glueline.

5. Because there are fewer and easier machine setups, the rest of the production run is divided into smaller groups so more attention can be given each box. Drawers are fitted to their carcases and, after bandsawing the outline and rounding it over on the shaper, the top and bottom surfaces are crowned on the stroke sander. A padded, graphite-covered hand platen is used first, then a graphite-coated glove.

6. At the pneumatic sander, far left, the surface is smoothed, first with 50-grit at 12 lb. to 15 lb. of pressure, then with 120-grit at 6 lb. to 8 lb., and then with 240-grit at 4 lb. to 6 lb. The shape of the box, carefully chosen abrasive products and their backing, and the use of a tire pressure gauge make possible the radical increments in grit. Adjustable dust-collection intake and point-source lighting add to the comfort and accuracy of this operation. Left, sharp edges are sanded by hand before final sanding (to 500-grit) on Vonnegut flap sander.

the initial run was seven boxes of black willow. Since then the egg box has been made in eastern walnut, claro walnut, cherry, Tennessee cedar, butternut, African naga, California oak, elm, shedua and most recently Hawaiian koa. The design has undergone refinements that typify the interrelationship of design and construction improvements. The first drawers, for instance, were hogged out of solid wood. Not only was this time-consuming and wasteful, but the resulting drawer tended to warp and stick closed. We tried bandsawing out the whole center of the drawer and inserting a plywood bottom, which was faster, but the hardwood drawer sides would contract around the unyielding plywood bottom, cup and still stick closed. Shaving down the back of the drawer to clear the inside of the carcase only made the drawer too loose, on being pulled out, to remain in its track. The solution we have developed is to use ¼-in. thick sugar pine for the bottom. It is press-fitted and glued into a rabbet in the bottom of the hardwood drawer sides, and because it is solid wood and more yielding than the hardwood, it expands and contracts compatibly with the sides.

The waste from the insides of the drawers accumulated until we could hardly move through parts of the shop. Finally we conceived of the shell box (photo, page 98), made by resawing this waste, hollowing out the halves and hinging them back together. The corners of the rectangular blank from which the egg box is bandsawn were more pieces of waste until we designed a segmented toy snake, and now we use those too.

I can't honestly say that I'm proud of every single box we've made over the last ten years. But, having put the necessary time and effort into the egg box, we have been able to refine the design and technique to where only a small percentage is unusable. The screening for quality begins with the rough wood. For a variety of reasons, units or parts of units will fall out of production along the way. The final product is also inspected, and only about 50% of the finished output can be considered gallery quality. Those of unusual quality we prefer to sell directly and that way are assured that the customers know and appreciate what they are buying. □

Dean Santner Woodworking is located in Emeryville, Calif. Santner is available as a design and production consultant.

Woodshop Computers
They're best at figuring cutting lists

by Paul Bertorelli

The electronic technology that's creeping into every other facet of daily life has now pried open the door of the village woodshop. And though a microcomputer can't direct the spokeshaving of a chair spindle, these fascinating and versatile machines can do such useful jobs as calculating cutting lists and controlling small machines and tools.

In big furniture factories, main-frame computers can help designers visualize three-dimensional objects, and computer-controlled tools have been commonplace for at least the past decade. They've speeded production and freed workers from mind-numbing, repetitive jobs. This technology has bypassed the small shop, however, mostly because custom shops don't have enough "dumb" work to justify a sophisticated, expensive machine. But, as some cabinetmakers are finding out, there is still work for a small computer in the small shop.

Two companies are selling computer hardware and software (hardware is the computer itself, software the lists of instructions, or programs, that make it work) designed specifically for calculating materials lists and cutting lists, a job that consumes hours in custom shops. One, Cabinets Built by Computer Systems (CBCS) of Nutley, N.J., sells a basic software package that figures cut lists and costs, as well as other programs as separate options, at a price most shops can afford. A California firm, Cybix Intelligent Systems, sells a more elaborate system that uses rudimentary computer graphics to help the cabinetmaker design and draw his kitchens. Other companies (see Sources of Supply) sell hardware/software packages aimed more at retail businesses that sell and install ready-made modular cabinets.

John Castronova, a lifelong professional cabinetmaker, started CBCS about nine years ago. He wondered if the microcomputers then new on the market could be programmed to do the simple but ponderous addition and subtraction required to compile the bill of materials and the cutting list for a kitchenful of cabinets. Once he had taught himself how to program it, Castronova found that a microcomputer could calculate an error-free cutting list in about 30 minutes, a job that took a full day with pencil and scratch pad.

Castronova started out by selling his computer sizing service on a subscription basis but as the number of affordable mini-computers proliferated, he found a ready market for custom software. For $2,500, Castronova's customers get a computer disc (and an instruction manual) containing the electronic framework to calculate a cut list for each cabinet's carcase, drawer and door parts, plus a master list that totals up all the materials needed to do the job. For an additional charge, Castronova will write programs that figure cut lists for different styles of door construction or keep track of job costs, or a special program that computes cut lists for odd-shaped carcases. Each disc is tailored to suit a particular shop's construction methods. For example, if you build carcases out of ½-in. plywood joined at the corners with a ¼ by ¼ in. offset

tongue, that information is written onto the disc. To use the software, you plug the disc into any IBM compatible computer and the machine responds with a series of menus framed as questions. Essentially, the computer asks you the overall size of each cabinet you plan to build, how many doors and drawers it will have and the like. Knowing your construction methods, the computer is able to calculate the size of each component. At the end of this process, which takes a half-hour for a typical kitchen, the computer spits out a printout with the totals.

Proven Design Inc., a four-man cabinet shop in Roselle Park, N.J., has used the CBCS system for several years. Designer Paul Horvath says that the computer, combined with a big investment in specialized machinery, has about doubled his shop's output. "Before we had the computer," he explains, "I could outsell the shop. We had customers waiting six months for cabinets. At one point we had 12 men, and they weren't putting out enough work to pay their own expenses." Now, says Horvath, the computer cutting lists let his men concentrate on cutting parts accurately, not puzzling over drawings for sizes. They cut all the parts for a kitchen at once, instead of having to complete the carcases before moving on to doors and drawers. With strict adherence to the lists, all the parts come together at assembly, eliminating time-consuming cut-and-fit.

As handy as the cutting lists are, Horvath says that the real forte of the CBCS system is cost control. The computer ruthlessly accounts for the price of every scrap of plywood, every hinge and every screw needed for an entire kitchen. Instead of

Cybix Inc.

With its light-pen data entry and isometric drawing talents, the Cybix Intelligent Systems computer, an Apple II, helps you design cabinets by quizzing you on various design features. It then calculates cutting and materials lists, and prints out a complete drawing of the job.

guessing, Horvath updates the computer's program each time the price of an item goes up. This control has sharpened his estimates and changed the way he responds to competition. "Now we know what it costs us to make a cabinet. We go into the market with the correct price at the profit we want. It's not affected by what the guy down the street charges."

While Castronova's computer sizes the cabinet parts from a regular drawing, the Cybix Intelligent System actually helps design the cabinets and then draws them. Cybix sells the software for $5,750, leaving the customer to buy his own Apple II computer from a local dealer for $3,500 to $4,200. Like CBCS, Cybix writes a custom program to suit a shop's standards, and includes with it a graphics package that projects isometric cabinet drawings onto the computer screen.

To use the system, you type in basic dimensions. The video screen responds with a drawing of a plain box depicting the cabinet to be built. The computer then asks a series of multiple-choice questions about such features as the number of drawers, shelves and doors. By touching an electronic light-pen to the screen, you signal what you want. The machine fills in the details of the drawing as you go. When you're satisfied with the design, you punch a key that starts the sizing and costing work. That information is printed out along with an isometric drawing.

Ron Shattuck, Cybix's president, says it takes about 40 minutes to design a kitchen on his system and another hour or so for the computer to complete its calculations. Cybix's checklist design routine reduces errors, says Shattuck, because the operator talks to the computer with the light pen instead of through a keyboard. But the light pen won't replace the draftsman's pen, at least not yet. "When you ask the computer for a particular door style, one doesn't look any different from another on the screen or on the printout," says Shattuck. "Microcomputers aren't capable of that kind of resolution." Even if screens and printers could reproduce the detail, the operator might spend hours keying in the right commands, defeating the time-saving appeal of this technology.

The Cybix computer is a bargain version of the CAD-CAM (computer-assisted design and manufacturing) systems used in state-of-the-art industrial design. On a CAD-CAM screen, whose futuristic graphics make eye-popping car commercials, a designer can draw a three-dimensional object and then alter it in any way he wishes. It's possible, for instance, to project an image and then take a "real time" excursion that mimics walking through or around it. It's a trick you can't duplicate with a sketch pad, and it takes getting used to.

Woodworkers who've used CAD-CAM systems report that learning to design with a computer is a slow, frustrating experience—for all their sophistication, computers can do only exactly what they're told. Tom Lacagnina, a sculpture teacher at the New York State College of Ceramics, conceived the sculpture pictured above as a drawing, then used a Xerox 560 computer to calculate the hundreds of compound angles that form the piece's spherical surfaces. "I'm basically lazy," Lacagnina says. "I probably wouldn't have made the piece if I didn't have the computer to figure the angles."

Yet he was disappointed when he later had a technician punch the sculpture's outline into a CAD-CAM so he could fiddle with the shape. "I couldn't understand the way the computer would see the form . . . the whole process is very abstract. I found that I could think something, but it was really

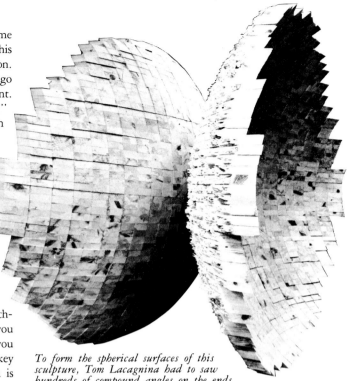

To form the spherical surfaces of this sculpture, Tom Lacagnina had to saw hundreds of compound angles on the ends of 2x4s. A Xerox 560 computer speeded the calculations. He later manipulated the shape on a CAD-CAM, which drew the sculpture in movable perspective. The surfaces were textured by breaking off the ends of the 2x4s on an arbor press.

hard to get the computer to do it." He compared drawing on the CAD-CAM to trying to cut curves on a tablesaw. "You can do it, but it's forcing the issue."

While CAD-CAM machines won't replace drawing tools and modeling clay just yet, the technology behind them is turning up in some mundane woodworking applications. Black & Decker has put a microprocessor—the electronic chip that forms the working guts of small computers—into a plunge router. It's programmed to measure and to display on a digital readout the cutting depth in 0.020-in. increments. A similar microprocessor in a B&D drill press is supposed to protect you against injury if you forget to clamp the work being drilled. By monitoring current and torque, the microprocessor shuts off the motor if the bit jams, keeping the work from being spun out of your hands.

Just how much further toolmakers can go with this technology depends mostly on how well it's accepted by craftsmen. Microcomputers are already so able that designers sit up nights thinking up new things for them to do. If manufacturers can resist tacking on flashing readouts as sales gimmickry, power tools might acquire useful little brains that will make them faster, safer and even more fun to use. □

Sources of Supply

Cabinets Built by Computer Systems, 291 Bloomfield Ave., Nutley, N.J. 07110; (201) 667-9065; (800) 526-6389. Cutting lists, materials lists, and costing hardware and software.

Computerized Cabinetry Inc., 1107 Lake Ave., Lakeworth, Fla. 33460. Design, cutting lists, and graphic hardware and software packages.

Computer Mart, 170 Main St., Nashua, N.H. 03060. Hardware and software for fitting pre-built cabinets.

Cybix Intelligent Systems Inc., 21601 Marilla Ave., Chatsworth, Calif. 91311. Design, cutting lists, materials lists, costing software.

Index